Eternal in the Heavens

Analyzing Theology Series

Eternal in the Heavens

Time, Heaven, and Resurrection

Jonathan C. R. Hill

CASCADE *Books* · Eugene, Oregon

ETERNAL IN THE HEAVENS
Time, Heaven, and Resurrection

Analyzing Theology Series

Cascade Books
An Imprint of Wipf and Stock Publishers
199 W. 8th Ave., Suite 3
Eugene, OR 97401

www.wipfandstock.com

PAPERBACK ISBN: 978-1-6667-9110-5
HARDCOVER ISBN: 978-1-6667-9111-2
EBOOK ISBN: 978-1-6667-9112-9

Cataloguing-in-Publication data:

Names: Hill, Jonathan C. R. [author].
Title: Eternal in the heavens : time, heaven, and resurrection / Jonathan C. R. Hill.
Description: Eugene, OR: Cascade Books, 2024 | Analyzing Theology Series | Includes bibliographical references and index.
Identifiers: ISBN 978-1-6667-9110-5 (paperback) | ISBN 978-1-6667-9111-2 (hardcover) | ISBN 978-1-6667-9112-9 (ebook)
Subjects: LCSH: Heaven. | Time—Philosophy. | Immortality. | Resurrection. | Philosophy and religion. | Future life—Christianity. | Philosophical theology.
Classification: BL540 H55 2024 (print) | BL540 (ebook)

To Tonya and Edwin, without whom heaven would certainly be boring.

But the skull was laughing again; this time making a thoughtful, almost kindly noise. "Remember what I told you about time," it said. "When I was alive, I believed—as you do—that time was at least as real and solid as myself, and probably more so. I said 'one o'clock' as though I could see it, and 'Monday' as though I could find it on the map; and I let myself be hurried along from minute to minute, day to day, year to year, as though I were actually moving from one place to another. Like everyone else, I lived in a house bricked up with seconds and minutes, weekends and New Year's Days, and I never went outside until I died, because there was no other door. Now I know that I could have walked through the walls."

—Peter S. Beagle, *The Last Unicorn*, 236.

Contents

Analyzing Theology

The 1980s witnessed a sea change in the academic, philosophical study of Christian doctrines on the heels of a renewal in philosophy of religion initiated by such prominent figures as Alvin Plantinga, Marilyn McCord Adams, William P. Alston, Eleonore Stump, and Nicholas Wolterstorff. At the turn of the second millennium, interest in the analysis of Christian doctrine only grew more profound as analytic philosophers and systematic theologians began to interact in more substantive ways. These interactions eventuated in the rise of analytic theology, an explicitly constructive theological program equipped with the tools and methods of analytic philosophy.

Despite its significant promise for driving theology forward in both the academy and the church, much of analytic theology remains outside the grasp of nonspecialists. One of the fundamental goals of this series is to broaden analytic theology's audience and influence.

Analyzing Theology is a series of books in Christian theology that showcases cutting-edge work in analytic and systematic theology. Monographs in the series are aimed at: (i) introducing cutting-edge analytic and systematic theology, (ii) providing a platform for original contributions in analytic and systematic theology, and (iii) connecting questions of theoretical significance to theology with the practices of actual theological communities.

Analytic theology is an emerging methodology that draws from the tools and methods of contemporary analytic philosophy to serve the ends of constructive systematic theology. Those methods make use of contemporary logical and conceptual analysis, emphasize the virtues of clarity and concision (as employed within the analytic philosophical tradition), and typically include a commitment to the objectivity of truth, goodness, justice, and rationality.

The monographs in the series span a range of Christian traditions and encompass a range of subject matter. This includes discussions of the method of analytic theology, exploring its engagements with other theological disciplines (such as biblical studies), as well as exemplifying this method by addressing underexplored theological topics from an analytic perspective.

Series Editors:

Joshua Cockayne, honorary lecturer in analytic and exegetical theology in the School of Divinity, University of St Andrews; city centre mission lead, Diocese of Leeds

Jonathan C. Rutledge, researcher at the Logos Institute for Analytic and Exegetical Theology, University of St Andrews; research fellow at the Center for Philosophy of Religion, University of Notre Dame

Christa L. McKirland, former researcher at the Logos Institute for Analytic and Exegetical Theology, University of St Andrews; lecturer in systematic theology at Carey Baptist College; executive director of Logia International

Editorial Board:

Amy Peeler, associate professor of New Testament at Wheaton College

Patrick Smith, associate research professor of theological ethics and bioethics; senior fellow, Kenan Institute for Ethics, Duke University

Eleonore Stump, Robert J. Henle, SJ, Professor of Philosophy, Saint Louis University

Helen de Cruz, professor of philosophy; Danforth Chair in the Humanities, Department of Philosophy, Saint Louis University

Alan Torrance, professor emeritus of systematic theology, University of St Andrews

Mark Wynn, Nolloth Professor of the Philosophy of the Christian Religion, Oxford University

Linda Zagzebski, George Lynn Cross Research Professor, Kingfisher College Chair of the Philosophy of Religion and Ethics, University of Oklahoma

Acknowledgments

I have been thinking about heaven for many years, though perhaps not quite in a way that Jeremy Taylor would approve. This book incorporates some material from presentations that I have made during that time at the Lampeter Philosophy Colloquium, University of Wales Trinity St David; the Logos Institute for Analytical and Exegetical Theology, University of St Andrews; and the Helsinki Analytic Theology Workshop, University of Helsinki. I would like to thank the organizers of all of these events for their kind invitations, and the participants for their questions and comments, which have helped to hone the arguments and ideas in these chapters. In addition, my colleagues at the University of Exeter, and the undergraduate and postgraduate students I have taught there about the philosophy of heaven, have also given me endless opportunities to test and rethink these ideas. I am grateful to them all, with of course the proviso that any flaws that remain are all my own.

Abbreviations

AAS	*Amerikastudien/American Studies*
ACPQ	*American Catholic Philosophical Quarterly*
AH	*Al-Hikmat*
AJPh	*Australasian Journal of Philosophy*
AJPs	*The American Journal of Psychology*
Ana	*Analysis*
APQ	*American Philosophical Quarterly*
Aps	*American Psychologist*
Bib	*Biblica*
BS	*Bibliotheca Sacra*
CDPS	*Current Directions in Psychological Science*
CJP	*Canadian Journal of Philosophy*
Cog	*Cognition*
CTJ	*Calvin Theological Journal*
CTQ	*Concordia Theological Quarterly*
Dia	*Dialectica*
EJPR	*European Journal for Philosophy of Religion*
ER	*The Ecumenical Review*
Erk	*Erkenntis*
FP	*Faith and Philosophy*
HJAS	*Harvard Journal of Asiatic Studies*
HPL	*History and Philosophy of Logic*
HPQ	*History of Philosophy Quarterly*
HJ	*The Heythrop Journal*
HTR	*The Harvard Theological Review*
IJHSS	*The International Journal of Humanities and Social Sciences*

IJPR	*International Journal for Philosophy of Religion*
Imm	*Immanuel*
JAAR	*Journal of the American Academy of Religion*
JAT	*The Journal of Analytic Theology*
JBL	*Journal of Biblical Literature*
JMB	*The Journal of Mind and Behavior*
JP	*The Journal of Philosophy*
JPE	*Journal of Political Economy*
JPL	*Journal of Philosophy of Life*
JPSP	*Journal of Personality and Social Psychology*
JR	*The Journal of Religion*
JRA	*Journal of Religion in Africa*
JRE	*The Journal of Religious Ethics*
JSJPHR	*Journal for the Study of Judaism in the Persian, Hellenistic, and Roman Period*
JSOT	*Journal for the Study of the Old Testament*
JTS	*The Journal of Theological Studies*
LA	*Logique et Analyse*
ML	*Mythlore*
Mon	*The Monist*
MQ	*Mystics Quarterly*
MT	*Modern Theology*
NB	*New Blackfriars*
Neo	*Neotestamentica*
NN	*Nature Neuroscience*
NS	*The New Scholasticism*
NT	*Novum Testamentum*
PA	*Philosophia Africana*
PAS	*Proceedings of the Aristotelian Society*
Phil	*Philosophy*
Phron	*Phronesis*
PP	*Philosophical Perspectives*
PPR	*Philosophy and Phenomenological Research*
PQ	*Philosophical Quarterly*
PR	*Philosophical Review*
PhS	*Philosophical Studies*
PsS	*Psychological Science*
QAJP	*Quest: An African Journal of Philosophy*
RFNS	*Rivista di Filosofia Neo-Scolastica*
RM	*The Review of Metaphysics*
RR	*Renaissance and Reformation*

RS	Religious Studies
SHPMP	Studies in History and Philosophy of Modern Physics
SM	Studia Monastica
ST	Summa Theologica
STP	Social Theory and Practice
TCS	Trends in Cognitive Science
Them	Themelios
TMB	Theoretical Medical Bioethics
Trad	Traditio
Tran	Transformation
USQR	Union Seminary Quarterly Review
Viv	Vivarium

Introduction

"What do you two talk about?"
"Today we were talking about heaven."
"But you don't believe in heaven!"
"No, but I know a lot about it."
Yolande laughed. "There speaks the true academic."

    —DAVID LODGE, *Paradise News*[1]

T here have been changes afoot in the world of philosophy of religion. Once, those few analytic philosophers who took religion seriously at all focused their attention on big, broad topics such as the existence of God. They analyzed the arguments for God's existence and responses to the problem of evil. They still do that today, of course, but there is a new wave of interest in doctrines unique to particular religions, primarily Christianity. Rather than dissect arguments for or against their truth, philosophers have become interested in whether—and how—these doctrines can be articulated coherently.

Doctrines such as those concerning the Trinity, the incarnation, and the atonement have been analyzed in exhaustive detail. And a number of philosophers are arguing with growing confidence that, contrary to what generations of both analytic philosophers and liberal theologians have taught, theologically conservative forms of these doctrines can be articulated quite coherently. There are now books and journals dedicated to the sub-discipline of analytic theology, which uses the methods of analytic philosophy in articulating and assessing different understandings of theological doctrines. It is a sub-discipline that straddles philosophy and theology, with proponents drawing on modern ideas in both fields as well as historical

---

1. Lodge, *Paradise News*, 276.

materials, particularly from medieval scholastic philosophy. For some writers, analytic theology is not merely an academic enterprise: it is a spiritual path in its own right.[2]

Heaven is the latest doctrine to be dismantled and then reassembled by the analytic theologians. Traditionally, philosophers of religion were interested in the bare notion of life after death, and whether it might be possible. Today, they are more interested in what it would be *like*, particularly given Christian teachings about the rewards God has in store for the blessed. Suppose there really were an afterlife of eternal perfect happiness. What would it be like to live there? Is such a thing even conceptually possible? Would there be free will in heaven? Could people sin there? What sort of knowledge would they have that we lack here on earth? Would they take care of each other, or of those they have left behind? What if they got bored?

And with this increased attention has come something of a new orthodoxy. Most analytic theologians who have written on the subject of heaven have argued not merely that the doctrine is coherent, but that one particular version of it is the most plausible. On this conception, dubbed the "dynamic" conception of heaven by some of its proponents,[3] heaven is a place of change and development. The blessed can look forward not to an eternity of passive contemplation but to never-ending progression, both intellectual and moral. They will be constantly learning and doing new things, increasing in virtue, yet always satisfied, and never tiring.

According to the proponents of this way of thinking about heaven, it solves many of the problems associated with the doctrine, such as those of boredom and moral inertness. It does justice to the idea that a perfect existence is one of activity, creativity, and freedom of the will. It allows for the biblical picture of heaven as a city whose inhabitants interact with each other and with God. Perhaps most fundamentally, it gives us a *human* heaven, one that has at least some points of contact with our earthly lives. What we value most in this life will be ours in the next life too, but to a vastly greater degree.[4]

My purpose in this book is to challenge this conception. I will argue that dynamic views of heaven do not offer the benefits their proponents advertise. I present instead a quite different conception of heaven as *atemporal*. The notion that heaven exists outside time altogether has a long heritage, going back to Augustine of Hippo, but has rarely been set out or defended

2. See, for example, Wood, "Analytic Theology."

3. Silverman, "Conceiving Heaven," calls it this, and I follow his terminology—at least for now: for more on this see ch. 6.

4. Swinburne, "Life of Heaven," takes this desideratum as a key argument in favor of a dynamic understanding of heaven.

at length, and is unfashionable today.[5] On the version of this model that I develop, the blessed do not enjoy an existence of infinite duration in heaven. There can be no change in heaven, or any development of the kind that is central to the dynamic conception. On this conception, the activity of the blessed is focused on God. They enjoy not a life of moral striving or self-improvement but the "beatific vision" described by medieval philosophers: perfect comprehension in the intellectual light of God. This, I contend, is a way of thinking about heaven that is not only coherent but can resolve a number of problems.

The doctrine of heaven

A standard way of beginning a book or paper in analytic theology is to quote some creed or conciliar declaration—preferably patristic—setting out the doctrine under consideration, before analyzing that statement to yield a precise formulation of the doctrine. This is not easy to do with heaven. The Nicene Creed merely states:

> [Jesus Christ] went up into the heavens and is seated at the Father's right hand; he is coming again with glory to judge the living and the dead; his kingdom will have no end. . . . We look forward to a resurrection of the dead and life in the age to come.[6]

"Heaven," or οὐρανός, here simply refers to the location of God. It is where Christ descends from when he becomes incarnate, and where he returns to when he is glorified. There is no indication that it is somewhere for humans to go to. Humans, instead, are raised from the dead at a future point in time, after which they are judged and then live under the unending rule of Christ. Nothing more is said about what that life is to be like, not even whether it will be good, bad, or indifferent. That is, perhaps, unsurprising. The purpose of the creed was to give explicit direction on contested doctrinal points. The

5. My project in this book can, in a way, be thought of as an exercise in historically inspired philosophical speculation. Suppose we take Augustine's claim that salvation involves being "freed from time" (*Tractates*, 31.5, p. 34) as a basic premise. What would be the truth conditions for such a claim? What commitments, both philosophical and theological, would a person have to make if they believed it? If nothing else, it seems to me that the importance of Augustine in the history of Christian theology makes it worth asking such questions, even if my way of answering them takes us well beyond anything Augustine himself said.

6. Tanner, *Decrees*, I 24. This is from the confession of faith attributed to the First Council of Constantinople in 381, which is the form usually referred to today as "the Nicene Creed." The actual symbol of Nicaea makes no mention of the future resurrection or the age to come. See Tanner, *Decrees*, I 5.

line about Christ's kingdom having no end was there because Marcellus of Ancyra had denied it;[7] the line about the resurrection of the dead was there because Origen had (supposedly) denied that. That was about the extent of patristic controversy on the subject, and so the councils of the period simply had nothing more to say about it.

The New Testament gives more, but mostly in the form of either vivid imagery or brief hints. The two main passages are 1 Corinthians 15 and Revelation 21–22. In the former, Paul insists upon the importance of the doctrine of the resurrection of the body, stressing that the hope of the resurrection is central to the faith. He has little time for those who ask what the resurrection life will be like, merely emphasizing its difference from the earthly life. The book of Revelation, by contrast, ends with a colorful depiction of the future life of the blessed in the new Jerusalem, described in terms of precious jewels, gold, crystalline rivers, and trees of life. Presumably we are not meant to take this imagery literally, but what then should we take from it?

The bulk of Christian tradition from the late patristic period onwards divides the afterlife into two phases.[8] First, upon death, the individual is subject to what Helen Foxhall Forbes nicely dubs a "triage system,"[9] but which Catholic theology gives the more somber name of "the particular judgement."[10] In 1336, Benedict XII outlined what happens:

> According to the general disposition of God, the souls of all the saints . . . and other faithful who died after receiving Christ's holy Baptism . . . already before they take up their bodies again and before the general judgement, have been, are and will be with Christ in heaven, in the heavenly kingdom and paradise, joined to the company of the holy angels. Since the passion and death of the Lord Jesus Christ, these souls have seen and see the divine essence with an intuitive vision and even face to face, without the mediation of any creature by way of object of vision; rather the divine essence immediately manifests itself to them, plainly, clearly, and openly. . . .[11]

Many Protestants share this belief. The Westminster Confession gives a more succinct account of what happens immediately after death:

7. On Marcellus and his influence on the creed, see Logan, "Marcellus of Ancyra"; Lienhard, *Contra Marcellum*; Parvis, "Joseph Lienhard."

8. For more on the background to the concept of an intermediate post-mortem state, see Turner, *Resurrection*, 27–42.

9. Forbes, "Theology of the Afterlife," 154.

10. *Catechism*, 1022, p. 233.

11. *Benedictus Deus*, in Dupuis, *Christian Faith*, 943.

> [T]he souls of the righteous being then made perfect in holiness are received into the highest heavens where they behold the face of God in light and glory, waiting for the full redemption of their bodies.[12]

The term "heaven" properly refers to this state.[13] The Catholic Catechism describes it like this:

> By his death and Resurrection, Jesus Christ has "opened" heaven to us. The life of the blessed consists in the full and perfect possession of the fruits of the redemption accomplished by Christ. He makes partners in his heavenly glorification those who have believed in him and remained faithful to his will. Heaven is the blessed community of all who are perfectly incorporated into Christ.[14]

But this state is temporary. At the last day, God will reunite all these souls with their bodies and judge them. The Westminster Confession continues:

> [T]hen shall the righteous go into everlasting life and receive that fulness of joy and refreshing which shall come from the presence of the Lord. . . .[15]

This is the second phase of life after death for the blessed. The Catholic Catechism states:

> *For man*, this consummation will be the final realization of the unity of the human race, which God willed from creation and of which the pilgrim Church has been "in the nature of sacrament." Those who are united with Christ will form the community of the redeemed, "the holy city" of God, "the Bride, the wife of the Lamb." She will not be wounded any longer by sin, stains, self-love, that destroy or wound the earthly community. The beatific vision, in which God opens himself in an inexhaustible way to the elect, will be the ever-flowing well-spring of happiness, peace, and mutual communion.[16]

---

12. Westminster Confession ch. 32.1, in Bray, *Documents*, 461.

13. For simplicity's sake, I am here ignoring purgatory, which the Westminster Confession rejects (ch. 32.1, in Bray, *Documents*, 461). In Catholic theology only the saints go immediately to God's presence upon death. The rest of the righteous must be purified in purgatory first, before going to God's presence. See *Catechism*, 1030–2, p. 235.

14. *Catechism*, 1026, p. 234.

15. Westminster Confession, ch. 33.2, in Bray, *Documents*, 461.

16. *Catechism*, 1045, p. 239 (italics original).

This is the "new heaven and the new earth" of the book of Revelation. Ideally, this should not be called "heaven." It is less confusing to refer to it as "the resurrection life," or something similar. However, Christian preaching and belief at the popular level has confused these distinct ideas. The idea of the resurrection life has receded, and the idea of the intermediate "heavenly" state has advanced, so that in popular piety "heaven" refers to a permanent state, with "resurrection" sometimes becoming little more than a metaphor. N. T. Wright, who has written at length on this subject, complains:

> Most Christians today, I fear, never think about this from one year to the next. They remain satisfied with what is at best a truncated and distorted version of the great biblical hope. Indeed, the popular picture is reinforced again and again in hymns, prayers, monuments, and even quite serious works of theology and history. It is simply assumed that the word heaven is the appropriate term for the ultimate destination, the final home, and that the language of resurrection, and of the new earth as well as the new heavens, must somehow be fitted into that.[17]

For Wright, the hope of the resurrection life is the main eschatological message of the Bible, and the emphasis on a disembodied heavenly state is largely a hangover from Platonism (for Wright, always a negative influence) and medieval imagery. The result is that even most Christians do not know what Christianity is supposed to teach on this subject. Wright's remedy is to focus on the resurrection life and forget about the "heaven" of popular piety as much as possible.

Many theologians and philosophers alike seem to have taken Wright's advice even before he offered it. Some of the early Reformers, notably Martin Luther and William Tyndale, promoted the notion of "soul sleep," the idea that between death and resurrection, the soul exists (if at all) in only an unconscious state, and that the "heaven" of Catholic theology therefore does not exist. This remained a common, though minority, doctrine among Protestants for centuries. And the idea that there is no period at all between death and resurrection has re-emerged over the last few decades in some

---

17. Wright, *Surprised by Hope*, 19. Wright argues (pp. 36, 41) that the two-stage eschatology is not the result of combining Jewish and Greek ideas. Rather, the notion of an intermediary stage before resurrection was always part of the Jewish belief in resurrection. (On this, see also Benedict XVI, *Jesus of Nazareth*, 215.) So Wright seeks not to eliminate belief in the intermediary stage but to redirect theological focus away from it. Murray Harris (*Raised Immortal*, 133–42) has also argued for the biblical provenance of the doctrine of the intermediate state, though he stresses the paucity of information about it. John Cooper (*Body*) mounts an extensive defense of the intermediate state as taught by the Bible, arguing that since the intermediate state presupposes dualism, so does the Bible.

academic theological circles. The 1970s and 80s, for example, saw a move-ment known as "immediate resurrection" in German Catholic theology, according to which a person is resurrected immediately upon death in a way that involves being taken out of time altogether.[18] A parallel movement in philosophy of religion has been inspired by John Hick's and Peter Van Inwagen's related ideas that God might remove people's bodies upon their death (to be raised somewhere else) and replace them with replicas.[19] Dean Zimmerman and Kevin Corcoran have both developed the idea into one of fission, according to which when a person dies, their atoms divide, allowing for a resurrected version of themselves to exist in some parallel space even while their corpse remains on earth.[20] In discussions of these and related ideas, life after death is a matter solely of resurrection, and any concept of an intermediary, disembodied, state between death and resurrection is tacitly dropped.[21] More recently, Joshua Mugg has criticized the traditional argu-ments in favor of an intermediate state,[22] while James Turner has argued that the very notion of an intermediate state is inconsistent with the belief that the resurrection of the body is an essential element of heaven.[23]

I am going to follow this trend in some ways. The passages mentioned earlier, in 1 Corinthians and Revelation, look forward to a bodily hope, and say nothing about any intermediate state where the soul exists in God's pres-ence, temporarily disembodied. In this book, then, I will assume a unitary eschatology—that is, one where the blessed enjoy a single, permanent post-mortem state. For simplicity's sake, I will call that "heaven," though "the res-urrection life" or something similar would be more accurate (and I will call the life we enjoy before death, and the universe in which we live it, "earth"). I will not follow the Catholic Catechism in assigning some passages (e.g., Luke 16:19–31; 23:43) to an initial, temporary, disembodied state and oth-ers (e.g., Revelation 21–22) to a subsequent, permanent, embodied state.[24]

18. Theologians proposing this include Gisbert Greshake and Jacob Kremer, *Resur-rectio Mortuorum*, who argue for an immediate resurrection of the dead without any intermediate state. On this, see also Pannenberg, *Systematic Theology*, 577–80. Joseph Ratzinger, *Eschatology*, criticizes this view at length.

19. Hick, *Death*, and Van Inwagen, "Possibility."

20. Zimmerman, "Compatibility," and Corcoran, *Rethinking*.

21. On this, and for a more positive appraisal of the doctrine of an intermediate state, see Guillon, "Heaven before Resurrection."

22. Mugg, "Can I Survive?," esp. 88–90.

23. Turner, *Resurrection*, 20–73. For more on this argument, see chapter 5.

24. Not a great deal hangs on this. As I shall argue in the conclusion, the main idea that I am arguing for in this book—the coherence of an atemporal conception of heaven—is independent of some of the subsidiary claims I shall argue for. One could accept the main point about atemporal heaven without necessarily having to agree with others, such as the elimination of the intermediate state.

All of this raises the thorny question of what weight a philosopher should place on biblical exegesis, a question that is really concerned with what philosophy of religion—or, more precisely, analytic theology—is trying to do. Elsewhere, for example, N. T. Wright comments:

> Theologians routinely invoke scriptural authority; scriptures require exegesis; and exegesis (of any text) is a branch of history. Without history, exegesis collapses into eisegesis, or mere fantasy-projection. . . . Biblical exegesis, more specifically, is a branch of ancient history, that specific branch which aims to discover what a particular biblical text first meant to writer and readers. Theology will wish to say more, but ought not to say less. And, with that "more," we bring historical exegesis into engagement with systematic, analytic and philosophical theology. We exegetes often wish those disciplines took historical exegesis more seriously. Any Christian theology worthy of the name cannot do without it, and ought not to try.[25]

But Robin Le Poidevin takes a different view:

> [S]uppose someone were writing a book about the metaphysical possibility of time travel (they probably are). It would be quite out of place to object that all this a priori argument is worthless unless based on a well-attested case of actual time travel. To the indignant cry "where is your evidence?", the author of that metaphysical essay would surely reply that *possibility* need not imply *actuality*, and the question of possibility is worth pursuing in its own right.[26]

These two very different outlooks reflect different understandings of what the task of analytic theology is. For Wright, it is essentially *constructive*. The job of the (analytic) theologian is to establish and articulate the faith of the church, a faith that is built primarily upon the witness of scripture. What, after all, is the point of arguing that some theological or philosophical claim is entailed by a given text if one has misunderstood that text? For Le Poidevin, the task is essentially *analytic*. The job of the analytic

---

25. Wright, "Meanings," 1. Wright is a little unfair, as there are certainly analytic theologians who engage seriously with textual scholarship in developing their analysis. To give just one example, James Turner (*Resurrection*; and Mugg and Turner, "Bodily Resurrection") does this particularly well.

26. Le Poidevin, *And Was Made Man*, xiii (italics original). J. L. Tomkinson, "Sempiternity," 178, articulates the considerably less friendly view that "the alleged data of supernatural revelation can have no philosophical weight." I take this to be incompatible with the approach of analytic *theology*, which must at least respect the doctrinal authority of whatever tradition it is working with, even if it doesn't engage with it.

theologian is not to establish the historical or biblical basis for the doctrine under consideration, or even necessarily to engage with that basis at all: it is merely to establish the *possibility* (or otherwise) of the doctrine. Where the analytic theologian does engage with history, it is not with biblical history so much as with theological history: the analytic theologian is interested in *what people actually believe* and whether that belief is coherent. Whether that belief is true to the Bible, and whether an alternative belief might be more so, is not a question that analytic theology can tackle.

I am sympathetic to both of these views. Wright is correct to point out a need for systematic theology to be engaged with historical biblical scholarship, but Le Poidevin is also right to point out that *analytic* theologians are often not really doing constructive theology at all. In the case of this book, there is a constructive element to my approach, as I am, to some extent, creatively constructing a particular conception of heaven, and I want to show that it is a *good* one. So there will be points where I relate it to biblical texts, as well as other authors in the Christian tradition, and seek to show that it is faithful to their concerns. At such points I will engage with historical scholarship as Wright advocates. But this is primarily a work of *philosophy*, and the degree to which I can move away from that focus is constrained by both space and the limitations of my own expertise. For the most part, my aim is to show that the conception of heaven I am interested in is philosophically coherent (and that rival views are perhaps less so), a question on which historical scholarship has less to say. So my methodology is primarily analytic, like Le Poidevin's. The questions with which this book is mostly concerned, above all the relation of heaven to time, are not questions that any biblical author addressed. Even the notion that *God* is atemporal—never mind heaven—is not a biblical one, for the concept of atemporality is not found in the Bible and was first applied to God in later centuries. That is not to say that this doctrine is "unbiblical" in the sense of being contrary to biblical teaching—rather, the Bible is neutral on such matters.[27]

This also raises questions about which sources of theology to privilege. Should we take the Bible alone as the standard of orthodoxy (and if so, which canon)? The decrees of the Seven Ecumenical Councils? The Catechism of

27. The statement that to God "a thousand years . . . are like yesterday" (Ps 90:4 NRSV; cf. 2 Pet 3:8) does not teach atemporality—quite the contrary, since if to God a thousand years are *like* a day then God experiences the thousand years in a temporal way, though an unusual one. In fact, of course, the verse is not intended to make a metaphysically precise claim about the divine nature at all. In the psalm, it is meant to draw a contrast between the ephemeral nature of human life and the permanence of God, as part of a "lament over mortality" (Hossfeld and Zenger, *Psalms* 2, 422). In 2 Peter, it is part of an explanation for why the parousia has not yet happened, and it also has an ethical role in exhorting moral behavior as a response to the shortness of human life (Mbuvi, *Jude and 2 Peter*, 144).

the Catholic Church? Are some doctrinal constraints more important than others, should we find ourselves having to choose between them? My own background is Anglican. Perhaps inevitably, then, I instinctively take the standard of orthodoxy to be anything that is believed by Catholics, Orthodox, *and* Protestants, which amounts in my mind to a rather vaguely defined amalgamation of the first four Ecumenical Councils (and, to a lesser degree, the other three), the Apostles' Creed, and the more familiar parts of the New Testament. In this book, I will try to take the Bible and the Seven Ecumenical Councils to be the primary constraints on orthodoxy, but I will also refer to other sources, such as papal encyclicals or the works of influential theologians, where relevant.

As a rough start, I suggest that a doctrine of heaven should include the following elements:

(1) Heaven should be *the happiest state possible* for human beings. It is consistent with this that it might not be *perfectly* happy; there might be unpleasant aspects to heaven. (Perhaps they are required for its overall perfection; perhaps a happy state without anything unpleasant is incoherent.) But there should be no possible hope that is better than heaven, and it should be vastly happier than our current state. According to Revelation, God "will wipe every tear from their eyes," and "mourning and crying and pain will be no more."[28]

(2) Heaven should be *focused on God*, or, as Revelation has it, "the Lord God will be their light."[29] This is closely linked to (1). Boethius claimed that true happiness lies only in God,[30] or, as Thomas Aquinas put it, in the vision of the divine essence.[31] God, as the first cause of everything, is also its final cause, the goal of everything.

(3) Heaven should involve *the whole person*. Traditionally this is expressed in terms of bodily resurrection. In 1 Corinthians 15, Paul links the future resurrection of Christians closely to the resurrection of Christ; he argues that if there is no future resurrection then Christ was not resurrected, in which case the faith falls apart. For Paul, both resurrections are bodily, although he makes it clear that this does not mean physicality as we know it. The notion of a bodily resurrection was accordingly central to patristic and medieval eschatology, reflected in 1215 at the Fourth Lateran Council's decree that "all will

28. Rev 21:4 NRSV.
29. Rev 22:5 NRSV.
30. *The Consolation of Philosophy* III.10, in Boethius, *Consolation*, 86–92.
31. Aquinas, *ST* IIa q. 3 a. 8, vol. 6, p. 50.

rise with their own bodies, which they now wear."[32] Embodiedness, then, is essential to an orthodox concept of heaven.

(4) Heaven should be, in a sense, *already present on earth*. Although the heavenly state is very different from the earthly one, it is possible to experience a taste of it on earth. Paul wrote that "[e]ven though our outer nature is wasting away, our inner nature is being renewed day by day" (2 Cor 4:16 NRSV). Although there is an abrupt change when a person dies and moves from earth to heaven, the transformation has already begun in their earthly life. In particular, the church on earth offers a foretaste of the heavenly life.

(5) Heaven should be *eternal*. This must mean that, like God, heaven is either atemporal or of infinite duration. Either way, it has no temporal end.

Methodology

My aim is not to show that the conception of heaven I shall develop is *true*. It is the more modest one of showing that it (and the doctrine of heaven more broadly) is *plausible*. Analytic theology typically involves weighing competing "models" of the doctrine in question, and trying to determine which is most plausible (the meaning of which I consider below). A "model" is, roughly, a detailed account of the truth-conditions of the doctrine—the things that would have to be the case for the doctrine to be true. Because most doctrines are, historically, defined rather loosely or briefly, there is scope for different models for each one. For example, the doctrine of incarnation states that God became human, and that Jesus of Nazareth is fully divine and fully human. But there are different models that articulate this in different ways.[33] For example, compositionalist models suggest that the divine Son became human by uniting to himself a human body and soul,[34] while proponents of some materialist models hold that the divine Son became human by being transformed *into* a human body and soul.[35] Analytic theologians compare these models by various criteria and argue for the superiority of one over the others. To do so is not necessarily to try to show that that model is true, or even that the doctrine it models is true. Rather, it

---

32. In Tanner, *Decrees*, I 230.

33. For a summary, see Hill, introduction to *Metaphysics of the Incarnation*.

34. See, e.g., Leftow, "Timeless God," and Crisp, "Compositional Christology."

35. Merricks, "Word Made Flesh."

is to show that this is the best way of thinking of that doctrine. If the model can be shown to be plausible, it follows that the doctrine itself is plausible.

So analytic theology can have an apologetic purpose. For example, if a given model of the incarnation is successful in providing coherent truth conditions for the doctrine of incarnation as traditionally believed, then the charge that the doctrine of incarnation is incoherent has been answered. However, there can be purposes to analytic theology beyond the apologetic, and even beyond the confessional. The study of different models of religious doctrines has philosophical interest in its own right, as we can think of them as thought experiments that help us to examine our own intuitions about key philosophical topics. Consider again the compositionalist model of incarnation and its claim that God the Son became human by being united to a human body and soul. That is a claim about the conditions under which something can rightly be considered human. It is also a claim about what it is for something to *become* something, and a claim about the relation that may hold between a person and her body. The degree to which we find compositionalism plausible will tell us something about how firmly committed we are, or are willing to be, to those philosophical claims that underlie it, and that is of interest quite apart from its theological ramifications.

I take *plausibility* to have three components.

First, *coherence*. A plausible doctrine must at least be possible: it *could* be true, at least in some possible world. That means it must be internally consistent. It is even better if it is consistent with other known facts about the world, in which case it may be that it is true in the actual world.

Second, *orthodoxy*. From a Christian perspective, there is little value in showing that some doctrine is coherent if it contradicts key Christian beliefs. A plausible doctrine must conform to some standard of Christian faith. As I have indicated, though, this can be a difficult criterion to apply, given that there is no universally agreed standard.

Finally, *advantages*. A plausible model of a given doctrine needs to have some reason to prefer it over its rivals. In particular, it needs to offer good solutions to the criticisms leveled against the doctrine in question. For example, a traditional criticism of the doctrine of incarnation is that it is impossible for one person to be both divine and human, as the essential properties of divinity are inconsistent with those of humanity. The proponents of compositionalism argue that their model can answer this objection—by assigning the divine properties to Christ's divine nature and his human properties to his human nature, and conceiving of these two natures as distinct property-bearers—in a way that rival models, such as physicalism, cannot.[36] If this claim can be upheld then it is reasonable to say that, other things being equal, compositionalism is more advantageous than its rivals. And of course, a plausible model should not be open to serious objections that its rivals do not face.

So in the case of this book, I am articulating and examining one model of the doctrine of heaven. I defend it against possible objections and argue that it is, overall, more *coherent*, *orthodox*, and *advantageous* than alternative models of heaven. If I am successful in showing this conception of heaven to be plausible, I am defending the Christian doctrine of heaven (and, more broadly, Christianity in general) as coherent. If I am successful in showing my model to be more plausible than its rivals, but unsuccessful in showing it to be very plausible overall, the conclusion may be that the doctrine of heaven is untenable, since its most plausible formulation is still pretty implausible. And if I am unsuccessful even in showing my model to be more plausible than rival models, I may at least show what philosophical and theological assumptions underlie these different models and our reactions to them.

To go about this, I will examine the doctrine of heaven from the point of view of an analytic philosopher. Precisely what that involves, methodologically, is disputed. Typically, analytic philosophers lay particular claim to logic, rigor, and precision, as if writers in other disciplines lack those qualities. Michael Rea has given, to my mind, a helpful summary of the *style* that characterizes analytic philosophy as distinct from both continental philosophy and theology:

> P1. Write as if philosophical positions and conclusions can be adequately formulated in sentences that can be formalized and logically manipulated.
>
> P2. Prioritize precision, clarity, and logical coherence.
>
> P3. Avoid substantive (non-decorative) use of metaphor and other tropes whose semantic content outstrips their propositional content.
>
> P4. Work as much as possible with well-understood primitive concepts, and concepts that can be analyzed in terms of those.
>
> P5. Treat conceptual analysis (insofar as it is possible) as a source of evidence.[37]

---

36. For example, Stump, *Aquinas*, 412–15.

37. Rea, introduction to *Analytic Theology*, 5–6.

To this, I would add that analytic philosophers work with a commonly agreed set of topics and positions, and jargon to describe those topics and positions. For example, many people—philosophers and otherwise—debate the meaning and existence of free will. But only analytic philosophers do so using the terms "compatibilism" and "incompatibilism" to refer to particular positions on the nature of free will. One analytic philosopher can say to another, "I am an incompatibilist," and expect to be understood. And when analytic philosophers write about free will, they will do so in reference to an established body of literature within the analytic philosophical tradition that defines these terms and discusses their advantages and disadvantages.

One of the key features of analytic *theology* is that it discusses theological topics in relation to this same body of material. Analytic theologians use terms such as "compatibilism" and "incompatibilism," or "perdurantism" and "endurantism," or "internalism" and "externalism," and all the rest of the jargon drawn from analytic philosophy, and their bibliographies are full of analytic philosophical literature on the positions denoted by those terms. In other words, analytic theology is done within the conceptual framework provided by analytic philosophy, which means it presumes familiarity with that framework on the part of the reader.

This is my approach. As an analytic philosopher, I am interested in how a theological subject such as the concept of heaven can be related to the concerns of analytic philosophers, such as issues of personal identity, the nature of time, the nature of embodiment, and so on, and I discuss them in terms drawn from analytic philosophy. I try to articulate the concept of heaven and related concepts as precisely and literally as I can, to make apparent the relation between different claims and ideas. In this way I hope to build a case that the atemporal conception of heaven is plausible in the way outlined above, and that even those who are not convinced that it is preferable to other models of heaven should take it seriously. At the very least, the superiority of dynamic models should not be assumed to be as self-evident as some proponents have suggested.

My aims overlap, to some degree, with those of Christopher Brown, whose recent *Eternal Life and Human Happiness in Heaven* is an important antidote to the prevalence of the "dynamic" view of heaven. His aim is to undermine arguments for that view, as well as arguments against the desirability of heaven at all, through philosophical exegesis of Thomas Aquinas. Like Brown, I think that the Christian tradition has sufficient resources to counter the "dynamic" view, and in this work I engage with Aquinas and with other classical theologians. But my approach is more conceptual than exegetical, and I shall make some suggestions that Aquinas would not have endorsed.

Plan of the book

The first three chapters lay the foundation for the development of the atemporal model of heaven. In the first chapter I consider whether heaven is somewhere we would want to go at all. I argue that although much attention has been paid to arguments that heaven would be *unpleasant*—most notably because it would inevitably be boring—there is a potentially more worrying category of arguments according to which heaven would be undesirable *even if* it were supremely pleasant. I look at these arguments and conclude that most of them are not very strong. The strongest ones, however, presuppose that heaven is temporal. This means that if we can conceive of heaven as atemporal, we will have a good answer to these arguments.

This leads to the question of temporality and atemporality, which is the subject of chapter 2. Here I consider what it would mean for something to be atemporal, and whether only abstract things (such as numbers) can be atemporal. In so doing I set out the different ways of conceiving of time itself, and argue that if one assumes divine atemporality (as I do) one is committed to a particular conception of time and of identity over time. I finish with a discussion of whether a *person* could be atemporal, arguing that there is no good reason to think not.

Chapter 3 builds on this to consider whether a temporal person could *become* atemporal. The very notion seems incoherent, but I argue that it is possible to make sense of it. An atemporal state cannot *temporally* succeed a temporal state, but it can succeed it in other ways.

Having laid out this groundwork, I turn in chapter 4 to setting out a model of an atemporal heaven. I argue that such a conception avoids what I call the "bottleneck problem" of temporal heaven. It also allows one to make sense of the resurrection of the body, such that the resurrected body is *numerically the same* as the body that died.

Chapter 5 considers the activities of the blessed in heaven. The first half of the chapter considers the "dynamic" conception of heaven and the notion that the blessed are eternally advancing in virtue and understanding. I argue that such a notion is inconsistent with fundamental Christian commitments, particularly about the person of Jesus. In the second half I focus on the concept of the beatific vision, arguing that such a concept is coherent and consistent with an emphasis on the resurrection of the body.

Chapter 6 continues this discussion by considering the nature of heavenly transformation. I look at the doctrine of *theosis* or divinization, and argue that it can be based on a version of the beatific vision where the blessed share in God's understanding and love of all things. I consider how this transformation can involve the earthly self as well as the heavenly self, and finish by discussing how it can be extended to the entirety of creation, not just human individuals.

In the conclusion, I summarize the main points and consider how the picture of heaven presented in the body of the book can be modified. I also say a few words about the language used to describe heaven, and the degree to which it can be taken non-literally.

Heaven and values

I stated earlier that part of the interest of analytic theology, from the viewpoint of a philosopher, comes from treating the doctrines under discussion as thought experiments that shed light on our intuitions on broader philosophical matters. The doctrine of heaven seems to me especially interesting in this regard, as we can use it as a grand thought experiment about *happiness*, or, more broadly, *value*. What makes us happy, or what do we think makes us happy? What do we value, or what should we value? The concept of heaven is, among other things, the concept of life that is valuable in the most unqualified way possible. What a person thinks heaven would be like—whether or not she thinks it actually exists—tells us a lot about what that person values and the kind of life she would like to lead. Indeed, one could learn much about the values of a particular society by looking at their dominant concept of heaven, if they have one.[38]

In this book I argue that the atemporal conception of heaven avoids problems that plague alternative models, so it is to be preferred to them on rational grounds of consistency and coherence, as well as conforming to theological constraints. But I am biased: this conception of heaven also reflects what I personally would value in the best life, and that is not really something I can argue for. It is not necessarily what I think that heaven *would* be like, supposing that heaven exists at all. Rather, it is what I would *like* heaven to be like. One of the reasons I wanted to write this book was simply that I found the alternative models of heaven presented in contemporary literature so unappealing. Whether or not the "dynamic heaven" solves the problem of boredom, or resolves the tension between free will and sinlessness, or any of the other puzzles that philosophers of religion write about, I wouldn't particularly want to go there. Perhaps that merely reflects my own lack of spiritual enlightenment, in which case I should probably worry less about what heaven is like and more about whether I am destined

38. McDannell and Lang, *Heaven*, offer something along these lines as part of their pioneering study of the history of thought about heaven.

to end up there.[39] But either way, it is impossible to approach a subject like this with Vulcan-like detachment. One's assessment of a concept of heaven will inevitably come down ultimately to taste. The only way to construct a concept of heaven that avoids this subjectivity is to develop a complete philosophy of human nature detailed and well-supported enough to show that one's concept of heaven really would satisfy everyone's deepest needs, whether or not they realize it now. Attempts at such a philosophy exist: Thomas Aquinas' *Summa Theologiae*, for example, could be characterized without great distortion as one enormous argument for why the beatific vision is the best final end for human beings. But I do not think it is possible to develop an argument of this kind that will convince those who are not already predisposed to prefer the vision of heaven on offer. I am certainly not going to attempt one in this book.

That means that, underneath all of the rational arguments and appeals to biblical authority, in both this book and other writers' works on the same subject, there is an inescapable, brute subjectivity. Either you share the values that underpin this (or any other) vision of heaven or you do not, and it is hard to see how to change your mind about that beyond presenting those values in as clear and unqualified a way as possible and seeing how you react. If the resulting picture seems repugnant, then treat it as a reductio ad absurdum of the values that underlie it, and consider what it tells us about what you *do* value.

There is one other point to make about the practice of philosophizing about heaven. John Smith has argued that one of the reasons philosophy of religion is valuable is that it keeps philosophers focused on "those questions that stand at the boundary of human existence." Without this nudge, he contends, philosophers tend to focus instead on "critical pursuits aimed more at clarifying the meaning of concepts already on the ground than at offering constructive answers to perplexing philosophical issues."[40] In other words, without religion to remind philosophers of the big, important questions, they would spend all their time arguing about minutiae of language and logic lacking in any existential significance. I would add to Smith's argument the observation that a potential danger of analytic theology is that it reverses this process and imports the philosophical minutiae back into religion. When philosophers do not simply consider questions raised by religion but try to do theology using philosophical methods, the result can

39. Katherin Rogers, "Anselmian Meditations," 36, makes a similar suggestion in response to Brian Ribeiro's argument that he would not want to undergo the changes required to make him fit for heaven. I think it is a little more charitable to restrict such speculation to myself, even when being facetious.

40. Smith, "Philosophy and Religion," 105.

be that they overlook the really important *point* of the doctrine under consideration and focus too much on technical matters that are of little interest to non-philosophers. Simon Hewitt has articulated this point acutely in a review of one of the recent volumes on the subject of heaven:

> The questions [asked in this volume] are philosophers' questions—for instance "will there be scepticism in heaven?", not I imagine a question anybody has ever asked a rabbi on their deathbed. Philosophers' questions need not be fruitless and once asked must be dispatched, either through being answered or through being deflated. Once this has been done, however, we might be left with the Wittgenstein of the *Tractatus* suspecting that the things that really matter have yet to be touched upon. This is certainly true when the subject under consideration is the afterlife. After we've cleared up the epistemology and metaphysics of the blessed, and supplied identity conditions for resurrected bodies, there remain not only the issue of how heaven relates to the earthly pursuit of justice, but also the deep human themes of grief, loss, continuing bonds, unfulfilled hopes, shattered dreams, the fear of death, prayers to saints, and vigils for the dead. Thoughts and concerns about these and other topics arise naturally out of the lived experience of death in a religious context. No philosophy which does not engage with them can fully claim the title of a philosophy *of religion*.[41]

This is a difficult demand to meet, but I think Hewitt is right to point out its importance. In this book, I will be considering "philosophers' questions" of the kind Hewitt mentions. But I do not want to neglect the other questions either. Heaven is not simply a philosophical thought experiment, or a theological datum, or a biblical story. It is something that people believe in because it seems important and it helps to answer important questions about how they should live their lives. So in this book—particularly in chapter 6—we will be considering the relevance of the picture of heaven we develop to real life. I will argue that one of the advantages of the atemporal conception of heaven is that it maintains a focus on life on earth. Even though, on this model, the blessed are cognitively transformed by the vision of God, it is a transformation of their whole lives, not simply something that affects them after death and leaves life on earth untouched. That means that this model offers the prospect of re-evaluating our own lives, including the worst parts of them, that may go some way towards addressing the "deep human themes" that Hewitt identifies.

41. Hewitt, review of *Paradise Understood*, 445.

1

The Desirability of Immortality

The singer Nick Cave maintains a blog, *The Red Hand Files*, in which he answers questions from fans on a vast range of topics. One fan asked him: "If you could live forever (and remain healthy in body and mind) would you do it?" Another asked him: "Where do we find meaning in life?" Cave replied to both at the same time:

> Elise, you asked if I would live forever if I could, well, the answer must be no. I wouldn't because, as far as I can see, the meaning of life is nested within the set terms of our own mortality. "Forever" is both incomprehensible and utterly meaningless. I don't believe we live just for the sake of it; rather we live our lives within the poetry of our own demise, within our own time, and our own limitations, and for that very reason alone we do so meaningfully. We work, we love, we care for each other, and we suffer together, knowing that one day we will die. The children in the schoolyard run headlong toward adulthood and their own disappearance, and we adults are the living breathing reminders of that. The man who waves at me as he walks his dog up the lane will die, as will the people filing into the church at the ringing of the bell, and the shop assistant hurrying to work, and the parking inspector, and the street sweeper, all will die in time—oh, and the squirrel (ah, there he is), he too will die (ouch), and the flowers, the swaying trees, and the earth itself. It is toward this temporal inconvenience—our finitude—that we move, with only a few precious moments to add value to this world. What can we do in this time that we are given, that is running through our fingers, even now? How can we lighten our mutual predicament that is drawing ever closer? Assaf, there lies

the meaning in life—it is in the expansion of ourselves, in our benevolence, to fully occupy our allotted time.[1]

In rejecting the desirability of immortality, Cave draws on an ancient tradition that goes back at least to the Epicureans. In his great account of Epicurean philosophy *De Rerum Natura*, the Latin poet Lucretius presented a series of arguments for why death—conceived of as annihilation—is not something to fear. For Lucretius, it can only be rational to fear a state in which we suffer; but if we do not exist, we do not suffer; therefore, it is not rational to fear nonexistence. He also presents what is known as the "symmetry argument": we do not recoil from the fact that there was once a past time when we did not exist; it would therefore be irrational to fear a future time in which we will not exist.[2] But Lucretius was content to try to cure his readers of their fear of death. He did not seek to teach them to *welcome* the fact that they will die. The idea that death is not merely not an evil, but a good thing, without which life would have no meaning, is much more modern.

We can distinguish, then, between two claims:

(1) We should not fear annihilation.

(2) We should not wish for eternal existence.

Although clearly related, these are not equivalent. It could, for example, be the case that we should fear annihilation *and* that we should not wish for eternal existence, because both annihilation and eternal existence would be dreadful. (If that is so then the outlook is bleak whether there is life after death or not!) In this chapter, I will leave (1) to one side, as it is not directly relevant to my purposes in this book, and focus on (2). Should we actively prefer there not to be an eternal life after death?

There are arguments both in favor of the desirability of an eternal life after death and against it,[3] but most of the contemporary discussion has

1. https://www.theredhandfiles.com/if-you-could-live-forever-would-you/ (accessed June 30, 2022).

2. Lucretius, *De Rerum Natura*, III.830–42, pp. 252–53; III.972–77, pp. 264–65. There is a substantial and continuing literature on these arguments, particularly the "symmetry" argument. These include: Mitsis, "Epicurus"; Warren, "Lucretius"; Kaufman, "Late Birth, Early Death." For defences of versions of the symmetry argument, see Rosenbaum, "Symmetry Argument"; Feldman, "Brueckner and Fischer"; Finnochiaro and Sullivan, "Yet Another 'Epicurean' Argument." For critiques of the symmetry argument, see Williams, "Makropulos Case"; Nagel, *Mortal Questions*, 1–10; Parfit, *Reasons and Persons*, 149–86, esp. 174–75; McMahan, "Death"; Brueckner and Fischer, "Why Is Death Bad?"; Kagan, *Death*, 205–33.

3. Yujin Nagasawa, "Pro-Immortalism," considers both, though rather than assessing

tended to focus on the arguments against its desirability, primarily the boredom argument. In this chapter I will also focus on arguments of this kind (though not the boredom argument, for reasons given below). Part of my rationale for this is that it seems to me—at least on the basis of introspection—that the desirability of life after death (if it *is* desirable) is a basic desire. It is part and parcel of the natural desire to live with which all animals have been equipped by evolution. As such, it is a value that, as I indicated in the introduction, cannot really be rationally defended: one either shares that value or one does not. The arguments *against* the desirability of immortality therefore seem much more interesting to me, as they suggest—if successful—that this natural desire is, in some way, wrong-headed.

Arguments against heaven

We can divide the arguments against the desirability of an eternal afterlife into three broad categories, of increasing seriousness, which I shall call categories A, B, and C.

Category A

Category A need not detain us for long. These are arguments that appeal to the unattractive nature of certain portrayals of life after death. On this view, heaven simply sounds unappealing: we might think, for example, that an eternity spent singing hymns or sitting on clouds is not something we would wish to experience. The obvious reply to such arguments is that they reflect a poverty of imagination. Any conception of heaven that portrays it as involving activities or situations we find unappealing is, *ipso facto*, an inadequate conception. Heaven will, on the contrary, be the greatest experience one could imagine—or, indeed, something better than we could ever

---

each one on its merits, he argues that *in general* no argument (either way) is successful in establishing the overall desirability of immortality/mortality. Part of the reason for this is that such arguments can, at best, show that there is some negative (or positive) element of immortality (or mortality); but they cannot show that this element would not be overridden by a contrary one. For example, even if it is true that an immortal life would become boring, that does not mean it could not have other, positive features that would make it desirable on balance (pp. 125–27). However, it is important to note that the doctrine of heaven requires more than that immortal existence is, on balance, positive. As I indicated in the introduction, any serious doctrine of heaven requires the claim that heaven is the best possible state for human beings, and that it is vastly happier than our existence on earth. So while it may well be true that an immortal existence that is full of boredom could nonetheless be desirable overall, it is hard to see how such a state would be heaven.

imagine. I think this is a reasonable response to arguments of this kind, and indeed we do not find arguments of this kind seriously presented very often.[4]

Category B

Arguments of Category B are sometimes confused with Category A, but they are quite different and much more important. These purport to show that, no matter how glorious heaven might be, it *must inevitably* become intolerable. In other words, while arguments of the first kind criticize *particular* accounts of heaven on the grounds of intolerability, arguments of the second kind aim to show that *any* concept of heaven must be intolerable—and that, consequently, the concept of an eternal and perfectly happy afterlife is actually an incoherent concept. So these arguments, if successful, show that heaven is impossible, no matter how one conceives of it.

Category B arguments typically revolve around the charge that an eternal existence must inevitably become boring, and there is now a substantial philosophical literature on this idea. Contemporary discussion began with Bernard Williams' influential 1973 paper, in which he argued that life can only be meaningful for as long as one has "categorical desires," which are desires for goals one values so much that one wishes to continue living in order to accomplish them. Williams introduced the concept in the first half of his paper as a rebuttal to the Epicurean argument that death is never a harm, since if one dies with categorical desires still unfulfilled, this would be a harm.[5] In the second half of the paper, he subtly (and, I think,[6] invalidly) shifts from the claim that death is harmful as long as one retains unfulfilled categorical desires to the claim that *not* dying is harmful if one *lacks* any unfulfilled categorical desires, which is why an infinitely prolonged existence would, in his view, inevitably become boring.

I will not discuss this argument, or the various responses to it, in depth here, as I have written about it elsewhere. My view is that the boredom argument is potentially more worrying to Christian theology than is commonly thought, because the standard theological answer to it—that heaven could never be boring because God is infinite and therefore infinitely engaging—is

---

4. A typical example is George Bernard Shaw's play-within-a-play *Don Juan in Hell*, where we learn that heaven is the kind of place where people pretend to enjoy themselves because they feel they ought, while anyone with any sense leaves and goes to hell instead. See Shaw, *Collected Plays*, 631–89.

5. Williams, "Makropulos Case," 86–88.

6. See Hill, "Defence of Inactivity," for more discussion of this.

inadequate. This is because if divine infinity is understood quantitatively (e.g., God is *infinitely powerful, infinitely loving,* and so on), it gives no reason at all to think that God is infinitely interesting. The set of all whole numbers is infinitely large, and I could spend an infinite amount of time counting them, but that would not be interesting. Conversely, if God's infinity is understood qualitatively, as a kind of property that God has *simpliciter,* rather than as a feature of God's properties, the concept is obscure and the argument becomes no more than an appeal to divine mystery.[7] Despite this, I do think that the boredom argument can be overcome—not by appealing to the nature of God, but by considering the nature of boredom. In my view, it is false to suppose (as many proponents of the boredom argument seem to do) that boredom is our default psychological state, to which we revert in the absence of any positive stimulation to keep us entertained. Rather, boredom has a specific set of causes, and there is no reason to suppose that those causes must be present in heaven or indeed in any infinitely prolonged existence.[8]

Category C

Arguments in both Category A and Category B purport to show that heaven would be undesirable because it would be intolerable. They base their rejection of heaven upon its supposed unpleasantness for the people who would be in heaven. But arguments of Category C do not do this. They do not seek to show that heaven would be unpleasant to experience—indeed, all of them are compatible with the notion that heaven would be supremely pleasant. Rather, arguments in this category seek to show that we do not—or should not—desire immortality for reasons *other* than how enjoyable it would be to experience. Consider again the quotation from Nick Cave above. Nowhere in that passage does Cave argue, or even assert, that an eternal existence would be unpleasant or even less than perfectly enjoyable. But he nevertheless rejects it.

For this reason, arguments of Category C seem to me to be, at least potentially, more serious and radical than those in Category B. If it really could be the case that heaven could be as rapturously wonderful as its believers hold, *and yet* still we should not want it, that represents a severe challenge to religious belief. It would mean that the efforts of defenders of heaven to respond to arguments in the second category by insisting upon the enjoyability of heaven would be beside the point. If all else fails, a believer in

---

7. I argue this in more detail in Hill, "Boredom."

8. And I argue for this in Hill, "Defence of Inactivity."

heaven can respond to arguments of Category B by insisting that, no matter how dull or otherwise unattractive heaven might appear to us now, God has the ability to change us so that we would find it infinitely enjoyable. Such a reply is not very satisfying, as it is effectively simply an *assertion* that heaven would be attractive rather than an *explanation* why, but it is at least a coherent one. But such a reply will not do against arguments of the third category.

Despite this, arguments of Category C have not, as far as I can tell, been much discussed by analytic philosophers of religion. This is, perhaps, a consequence of the much-discussed divide between analytic and continental philosophy, for as we shall see, most of the arguments in this category are associated with continental philosophers.

A couple of points need to be made before we examine some of these arguments. The first is that "eternal," in the context of "eternal life," is ambiguous. It could mean "everlasting," in the sense of a time without end; or it could mean atemporal, in the sense of being "outside time" altogether. What these two very different conceptions of eternity have in common is that, either way, the eternal thing has no end in time. Some of the arguments we shall consider are much more forceful if one takes heaven to be everlasting, but less so if it is atemporal. This is a point we shall return to at the end of the chapter.

Second, these arguments are often framed—as with the passage from Nick Cave—in terms not of the prospect of heaven but of an everlasting existence in this world. Some arguments against the desirability of an everlasting earthly existence are clearly not relevant in the context of heaven. An example is Jonathan Swift's fictional account of the Struldbrugs, people who are born naturally immortal.[9] While Gulliver initially envies them, he is quickly disabused of this attitude when he is informed that everyone else in their society regards them with pity and horror. This is because although they live forever they do not enjoy eternal youth, and are therefore horrifically decrepit. Clearly such problems would not apply to an everlasting existence in heaven. In the case of some other objections to the desirability of everlasting existence, it is harder to judge whether heaven would be immune to them, as we shall see.

Let us, then, consider some of these arguments of Category C. We can divide them into two main groups. The first (and most common) group, which I will call Category C1, are arguments that appeal to *value* of some kind. The second group, Category C2, are arguments that appeal to concerns about the *experience* of immortality.

---

9. Swift, *Gulliver's Travels*, III.10, pp. 309–21.

Heaven and value

The passage from Nick Cave with which we began states, though does not argue for, the view that our finitude is what gives value to our actions. The philosopher most associated with views of this kind is Martin Heidegger. In *Being and Time*, Heidegger includes a section on "Dasein's possibility of Being-a-whole, and Being-towards-death," which itself constitutes the first part of the lengthy Division II on "Dasein and Temporality." It is clear that, for Heidegger, time—and the finite nature of our experience of it—is fundamental to human existence. Indeed, the fact of one's future death, understood as "Being-no-longer-in-the-world,"[10] colors one's experience of life. Death is not simply something in the future; it is a feature of present experience:

> [J]ust as Dasein *is* already its "not-yet," and is its "not-yet" constantly as long as it is, it *is* already its end too. The "ending" which we have in view when we speak of death, does not signify Dasein's Being-at-an-end, but a *Being-towards-the-end* of this entity. Death is a way to be, which Dasein takes over as soon as it is.[11]

For Heidegger, both authentic and inauthentic Being-towards-death are possible, and his concern in the final pages of this section is to distinguish between them. However, at no point in his discussion does Heidegger consider how things would have been different if there were no death, or if we could be certain of further existence beyond it. His concern is with the meaning of death as a fact of life, not with alternative hypothetical scenarios. He writes, for example, that "holding death for true . . . demands Dasein itself in the full authenticity of its existence."[12] But this is not because authentic existence would be impossible without death. Rather, it is because, *given* the fact of death, authentic existence requires recognition of it. Death colors life, but Heidegger never suggests that this is an inherently good thing, or that life would have been worse off without death. There is certainly nothing in his writing resembling an argument for such a position.

Some commentators make rather stronger statements than Heidegger himself does. James Demske, for example, writes:

---

10. Heidegger, *Being and Time*, 281.

11. Heidegger, *Being and Time*, 289 (italics original).

12. Heidegger, *Being and Time*, 309–10.

> Death is even seen to be the possibility which gives all one's other possibilities their goal and final meaning, since they all flow into it, converge upon it, and find in it their completion.[13]

Although Demske does not say so explicitly, one can read this as implying that, without death, the other possibilities in life would lack a "goal and final meaning." But no explanation is given for why this should be. What does it mean to say that other possibilities in life "flow into" and "converge upon" death? If I am faced with a choice—say between pursuing a career in one field as opposed to another—then certainly, no matter which one I choose, the life it will lead to will end with my death. But it does not follow from this that I make my choice with the *goal* of its ending with my death. Neither does it follow that, were I to be immortal, my choice of one career rather than the other would have no meaning or purpose.

Moreover, the whole context of Heidegger's discussion of death is in relation to our life in this world. To say that death is inevitable, for Heidegger, is to say that our existence in this world will necessarily come to an end. It need not mean that our existence will necessarily end altogether, and he explicitly remains neutral about whether there may be a life after death. Nothing Heidegger says about death, then, is meant to have any bearing on the possibility or desirability of an infinite afterlife.[14]

So Heidegger does not make a case against the desirability of heaven. The concept of heaven lies outside Heidegger's concerns, which revolve exclusively around life in the here-and-now. He is interested in analyzing how we understand and react to the fact of death, not in comparing this reality to hypothetical immortality.

But can we nevertheless construct an argument against the desirability of infinite future existence on the basis of the idea that it undervalues our present existence? I think that there is a common intuition that if there were an infinite future life, its sheer extent would dominate our existence to such an extent that everything in our past, no matter how apparently significant, would be utterly swamped by it.

Here is my best attempt to express this as an argument:

13. Demske, *Being*, 38.
14. Heidegger, *Being and Time*, 292.

The out-valuing argument

(1) In an infinitely prolonged existence, the future is infinitely longer than the past.

(2) The longer something persists, the more value it has.

(3) Therefore, if an infinite future lies ahead of me, then what I have done up until now is of negligible value compared to what is to come.

(4) Therefore, if an infinite future lies ahead of me, then what I have done up until now is of negligible value.[15]

Premise (1) is true, at least on the assumption that the past is finite. From a Christian point of view, at least, this is uncontroversially true if we accept the second council of Constantinople's condemnation of belief in the pre-existence of souls. The crucial premise is (2). This rests on a principle that I shall call *value is proportional to duration*, or VPD:

VPD: Other things being equal, the longer something persists, the more value it has.

Given VPD, it does indeed seem that my infinite future existence must be infinitely more valuable than my past, finite existence. But is VPD true? I do not see any reason to think that it is. A four-hour film is not, other things being equal, necessarily better than a two-hour one. Indeed, on some aesthetic systems things may be considered more beautiful the shorter they are. The Japanese term *mono no aware* famously refers—among other things—to a sort of melancholy appreciation of the transience of beautiful things, the idea being in part that it is their very transience that enhances their beauty.[16] The classic example—so common it is a cliché—is cherry blossom, which is no more intrinsically beautiful than other kinds of blossom but is valued more highly precisely because it lasts for such a short time. Perhaps more importantly, deeper value of a non-aesthetic kind also seems to have little to do with duration. Consider a case where two people have a loving marriage

---

15. Christopher Brown articulates an argument rather like this against the suggestion that the blessed can advance morally in heaven. He calls it the "Eternity of Choices" argument (or EOC). See Brown, *Eternal Life*, 50–51. However, his argument is specifically concerned with the relative merit of charitable habits in life and in heaven: if one could go on improving in heaven, then one's charitable habits in life would be entirely insignificant by comparison; but they cannot be insignificant, because they determine whether one goes to heaven at all.

16. On this, see Yoda, "Fractured Dialogues"; Meli, "Motoori Norinaga's Hermeneutic."

that is tragically cut short after a couple of years when one of them dies. Is that marriage less valuable—less significant to the surviving partner—than an equally loving one that lasts for half a century? Not necessarily. There are many factors that could affect the significance of the marriage from the perspective of the partners. The duration of the marriage could be one of those factors, but it need not be. The surviving partner might move on emotionally and think of the short-lived marriage as having mostly only past significance, but she might equally find that it continues to shape her perception of life even decades later.

Similarly, it may be true that the things I have done and the experiences I have undergone in my life to date are of negligible duration compared to an infinite future existence, but it does not follow from that that they are of negligible value. On the contrary, a very short event or experience in my life might have tremendous significance to me.

Considerations of this kind indicate a problem with any claim about how much "value" something has. Value is relative: what has value to me may not have value to you.[17] Premise 2, and the VPD principle on which it rests, talk about "value" as if it were some objective property, but this is sloppy thinking. If we recast them into terms of value *to a particular person*, their falsity is more apparent:

> VPD`: Other things being equal, the longer something persists, the more value it has to the person who experiences it.

And evidently this is not true. So premise (2) is false. In addition to this, the slide from (3) to (4) is not warranted. Even if it is true that my past actions and experiences are of negligible value *compared to what is to come*, it does not follow from this that they are of negligible value absolutely. If I give a hundred dollars to help the homeless, that may help someone significantly, even if it is negligible compared to a billion dollars donated by a wealthy philanthropist. Similarly, if I give a hundred dollars today, that is significant to the person I give it to, even if I go on to give a hundred dollars every day for an infinitely extended future. I conclude, then, that this argument is

17. To say that something has value to a particular person could mean (a) that that person considers it to have value to them, or (b) that the value of something to a given person depends in part upon that person's particular circumstances. In the case of (a), this would suggest that value is subjective, being entirely a matter of what the individual thinks is valuable, while (b) is consistent with the notion that a thing can be valuable to a person even if that person thinks it is not valuable. (I am grateful to Robin Parry for pointing out this distinction.) The question which of these is the correct view of value is too vast to go into here, but for our purposes, it is enough to note that the VPD` principle suggested above is false given either of these understandings of the relativity of value.

unsuccessful: the existence of an infinite future life would *not* render past actions virtually valueless.

There is something of a paradox here, though. Although the argument we are examining is unsuccessful, it is supposed to support the view that it would be better if there were no heaven. In making this case, it depends upon VPD, the principle that things are *more* valuable if they last for longer. And yet one might think that, if one were to accept this principle, this should imply that it would be better if heaven *did* exist:

(1) If heaven exists, then my existence is infinitely longer than it would be if heaven didn't exist.

(2) The longer something persists, the more value it has.

(3) Therefore, if heaven exists, my existence is infinitely more valuable than it would be if heaven didn't exist.

Conversely, consider the *mono no aware* view mentioned above. We could base a principle on this that we can call *value is inversely proportional to duration*, or VIPD:

VIPD: Other things being equal, the longer something persists, the less value it has.

VIPD is, clearly, the opposite to VPD. The fourteenth-century writer Yoshida Kenkō, often considered an early proponent of this view, writes:

If man were never to fade away like the dews of Adashino, never to vanish like the smoke over Toribeyama, but lingered on forever in the world, how things would lose their power to move us! The most precious thing in life is its uncertainty. . . . We cannot live forever in this world; why should we wait for ugliness to overtake us? The longer man lives, the more shame he endures. To die, at the latest, before one reaches forty, is the least unattractive.[18]

While one might hesitate to agree with the whole of that passage, it is clear that if one accepts VIPD, an infinite heavenly existence would surely be undesirable.

In other words, both VPD *and* VIPD can be used to support *both* the view that heaven is desirable *and* the view that heaven is undesirable. I have argued that even if one accepts VPD, one cannot validly conclude from it that our earthly actions are of negligible value considered absolutely, so it does not provide a good basis for rejecting the desirability of heaven. What

18. Kenkō, *Tsurezuregusa* 7, in Keene, *Essays*, 7–8.

about the Kenkō argument against the desirability of heaven on the basis of VIPD? That might look like this:

(1) If heaven exists, then my existence is infinitely longer than it would be if heaven didn't exist.

(2) The longer something persists, the less value it has.

(3) Therefore, if heaven exists, my existence is infinitely less valuable than it would be if heaven didn't exist.

This parallels the argument given above for the desirability of heaven on the basis of VPD. What are we to make of these two arguments? I have suggested that there is no good reason to hold VPD. Similar objections can be made to VIPD. While it is true that a tragically curtailed marriage may be just as significant to the surviving partner as one that lasts a lifetime, it is equally true that a lifelong marriage may also be just as significant as a short one. This suggests that the value or significance of an event is not necessarily dependent upon its duration. Sometimes a shorter event seems more significant than a longer one (and its shortness may be a factor in this), and sometimes a longer event seems more significant than a shorter one (and, again, its length may be a factor in that), and sometimes the duration may make no difference at all.

If this is so, then all of the arguments considered in this section—whether for or against the desirability of heaven—are unsuccessful.

The possibility of reversal

Here is an alternative way of appealing to value in order to show that heaven is undesirable, which avoids appealing to VPD or anything like it:[19]

The possibility of reversal argument

(1) In an infinitely prolonged existence, anything I do now would be more likely to be reversed or outweighed by my future actions than if my existence were finite in duration.

(2) The more probable it is that an action could be reversed or outweighed by my future actions, the less value it has.

---

19. To my knowledge, nobody has ever advanced this argument, but it seems to me at least an initially plausible one.

(3) Therefore, if my existence will be infinitely prolonged, my actions
   have less value than they would if it will not be infinitely prolonged.

Consider premise (1) first. It is important to distinguish this premise from a
principle that Timothy Pawl and Kevin Timpe articulate:

> [F]or any period of time t_1 such that it is before t_2, the opportu-
> nity to improve one's character in t_2 minimizes the importance
> of improving one's character in t_1.[20]

As Pawl and Timpe rightly argue, this principle is false. However, my premise (1) is different in that it envisages an *infinitely prolonged* time t_2. It is easy
to see that my actions in t_1 might continue to be significant even after my
actions in a later, finite t_2; but does it make a difference if t_2 is of infinite duration? I am not sure. Clearly there are some actions that cannot be reversed
no matter how long I live. If I kill somebody, I can never bring them back
to life even given an infinite existence. What if I spend the rest of eternity
doing good deeds to try to compensate for the murder? One might think
that an *infinite* amount of good deeds should outweigh any finite evil, but
perhaps murder is infinitely grave and can never be outweighed in such a
way. Nevertheless, it is plausible to suppose that *many*—perhaps most—of
our actions are such that, given enough time, they could be reversed or
outweighed.

Still, premise (1) only holds if I spend the infinite amount of time
doing things that might outweigh my previous actions. If I spend eternity
utterly inert, my past actions are no more likely to be outweighed than they
would have been if I had been annihilated after doing them. This argument,
then, is a more serious challenge to conceptions of heaven in which the
blessed are eternally active than it is to those where they are not.

Is (2) true? Once again, it founders on the difficulty of assigning
"value" to things as if value were an objective property. An act I perform
today may have tremendous value to me, or to other people involved, even
if I perform another act tomorrow that outweighs it. Putting this to one side
though, suppose we grant that an act that *actually is* later outweighed has
less value as a result of the outweighing. Does it follow from this that an act
that *only might be* later outweighed has less value, even if the probability of
its being outweighed is relatively high?

Consider the following scenario: Mr. Scrooge reluctantly agrees to
grant his employees a day off for Christmas. Scrooge is notoriously ungen-
erous, so the probability of his later forcing his employees to do extra work
to make up for the day off is very high. Mr. Fezziwig, by contrast, happily

20. Pawl and Timpe, "Paradise," 105.

grants his employees a day off. The probability of his later demanding extra work is low, because he is consistently generous. In the event, neither employer imposes extra work later on. Which employees value their day off more? At the time, surely Fezziwig's employees do, because they are confident they will not have to pay for it later on, whereas Scrooge's employees have the probability of extra work in the future hanging over them, spoiling their enjoyment. This is the case even if that extra work never materializes. In retrospect, however, Scrooge's employees may look back on their unexpected day off and value it more highly precisely because, contrary to their expectations, they did not have to do the extra work.

What this thought experiment suggests is that we do value people's actions less if we think there is a good chance they will later perform some other action to outweigh them. But a high probability of outweighing can cause us to value them *more* highly later on if the outweighing does not take place. However, if we assume that an infinite lifespan means that the possibility of outweighing always remains live, then we could never be certain that it is not going to happen. If Scrooge's employees are doomed to work for him for an infinite amount of time, they could never be confident that he will not demand extra work to make up for that day off.

It would seem, then, that this argument does have some weight. If one accepts a view of heaven in which the blessed remain active for an infinitely prolonged period, and if one also assumes that they retain the ability to perform acts that outweigh their earlier ones, then we probably would value the actions of the blessed less than we would if their future existence were finite.

The significant choice

Jeff Noonan gives a rather different argument against the desirability of immortality based on weighty actions:

> In a finite life people set goals to become this or that sort of person, and they must make these choices, because finite life-time does not permit the exploration and realization of an unlimited number of possibilities. . . . Were death somehow overcome, then people would no longer need to struggle to exist, and if they no longer needed to struggle to exist, they would no longer need to make evaluative choices between different possibilities. Such lives would be insipid, devoid of meaning because they would be devoid of the limitations that force mortals to reflect upon different possibilities for action: which course is better,

which is worse, which is good, which is bad, which is right, which is wrong.[21]

We can formalize this argument like this:

The significant choice argument

(1) To be meaningful, a choice must be between incompatible possibilities, such that to choose one is to reject the other permanently.

(2) In an infinitely prolonged existence, no choice would have this property.

(3) Therefore, in an infinitely prolonged existence, there could be no meaningful choices.

I am not sure that (1) is true, but let us grant it for the sake of argument. Is (2) true? Certainly, many choices that in a finite existence are between incompatible possibilities would not have this property in an infinite existence. If I choose to devote myself to an academic career, I am in so doing cutting off the possibility of various other careers that I might have followed instead. But if I were immortal, such avenues would always remain open to me.

However, this is not the case with all choices, because some are one-time-only. If I choose a particular song for the first dance at my wedding, once the wedding is over I cannot change it. I might get married again, perhaps, but it would always be the case that I chose *this* song for *this* wedding, even if I live for ever. Indeed, there is a sense in which this is true of *all* choices. If, given unlimited time, I become first an academic and later an Olympic athlete, it is true that my becoming an academic did not preclude my becoming an athlete later, but it is also true that my becoming an academic first *did* preclude my becoming an athlete first. So it seems that (2) is false. And this is even more so if we consider acts of great moral weight. If I choose to murder someone, I have made an irrevocable choice to be a murderer, and nothing I ever do, even given infinite time, will undo that (even supposing that I can perform actions that will outweigh it).

But one might protest that Noonan's argument is not merely about the irrevocability of meaningful choices. It is about the moral seriousness that comes from having limitations. This suggests a quite different sort of argument:

21. Noonan, "Life-Value," 19–20.

The serious reflection argument

(1) Only through facing limitations such as limited resources and time can people reflect seriously on the moral weight of different possible courses of action.

(2) In heaven, there would be fewer limitations.

(3) Therefore, in heaven, people would have less capacity to reflect seriously on the moral weight of different possible courses of action.[22]

Let us assume for the sake of argument that (3) would be a serious problem—that a conception of heaven in which people lack the capacity to reflect seriously on moral matters is an inadequate one. I also take it that (2) is true, no matter what one's view of heaven. What of (1)? I do not really see any reason to think that it is true. Indeed, sometimes the reverse seems more plausible. If I make only just enough money to survive, I face serious choices about how to spend my money, but they are serious in a prudential sense rather than a moral one. I do not have to think seriously about which charity to support or how best to devote my spare time to helping others, because I do not have any money or time to spare. Whereas if I am a billionaire, and I wish to use my money to do good, I face very serious choices about how best to spend it, because there are so many possibilities.

From a theological viewpoint, an obvious counter-example to (1) is God, who is supposed to have perfect understanding of moral matters but without suffering any limits of resources. More generally, if (1) is true, it is surely only contingently true. Even if, in fact, having limited resources and time causes people to reflect more seriously about their moral choices, this need not be a necessary feature of humanity. It could be that in heaven God shares with us the perfect divine understanding of moral matters. I conclude, then, that arguments of this kind against the coherence of the concept of heaven are not successful.

The experience of immortality

These, then, are the arguments against the desirability of heaven of Category C1, that appeal to value. Category C2 consists of arguments that appeal to what the experience of being in heaven would be like. It is important to note

---

22. Noonan does not articulate this argument in the context of *heaven*, only of infinitely prolonged existence, but it seems to me that it is most effective as an argument against heaven since a heavenly existence is more obviously lacking in limitations than an earthly immortal one.

again that these arguments do not seek to show that being in heaven would be *unpleasant*—arguments of that kind belong to Category B. Rather, these arguments appeal to other supposed features of immortal existence.

Motive

Hans Jonas offers a very brief argument for the desirability of mortality:

> As to each of us, the knowledge that we are here but briefly and a non-negotiable limit is set to our expected time may even be necessary as the incentive to number our days and make them count.[23]

Jonas' suggestion is that our very mortality is what motivates us to do anything. The implication is that if we were immortal, we would have no motivation to do anything. We can express this argument like this:

The motive argument

(1) I can be motivated to do something only if there is a limited period of time in which I can do it.

(2) In an infinitely prolonged existence, there is unlimited time to do anything.

(3) Therefore, in an infinitely prolonged existence, I cannot be motivated to do anything.

We may start by pointing out that (1) is imperfectly expressed. Surely what is relevant to my motivation is not whether there is *actually* a limited time in which I could act, but whether I *believe* there to be a limited time. After all, perhaps I really will live for ever, but I do not believe that I will, and this motivates me to act. Similar objections can be made against a number of other arguments we shall consider in this chapter. However, I shall assume, at least for now, that objections of this kind are not relevant in the context of discussions about heaven. Presumably, if I am in heaven I know that I am in heaven, and I know that my time is not limited.

So, given this, why would we accept premise (1)? It seems to me to rest upon what we might call the *procrastination principle* (PP):

> PP: If I can postpone performing an action, I will do so.

23. Jonas, *Mortality*, 98. Yugin Nagasawa, "Pro-Immortalism," 121, also cites Leon Kass and Viktor Frankl as proponents of this view.

If PP is true, then it does indeed seem that, given an infinite amount of time, I won't do anything. I can always put it off until tomorrow, and there will always be another tomorrow. But however much my own slothful nature tempts me to endorse PP, it clearly is not true, at least not universally. After all, right now I *could* postpone writing this paragraph until tomorrow (the deadline for this book is still a good way off), but I am not doing so.

But one might say: I am not putting it off, because although I could put it off until tomorrow, I know that the supply of tomorrows is not unlimited. I do have to get it done by a future time that is not *very* remote. That gives me a motivation to do it that I would not have if I had unlimited time.

However, this is to overlook the role of *desire* in action. We do many of the things that we do because we *want* to do them. If my favorite band releases a new album, I listen to it right away because I *want* to—not because I am anxious that if I fail to listen to it now I will miss the opportunity or run out of time. I would still want to listen to it now even if I knew I had infinite time in which to do so. Indeed, if (1) were true, we might expect people to become more motivated to achieve things as they grow older, as their available time shrinks, and they become an "old man in a hurry," as Randolph Churchill branded Gladstone. But this does not seem to be generally the case. Consider, for example, how many great artists and musicians have created most of their significant work in their twenties—not a time of life when most people are brooding about the limited time available to them. The trope of the creative genius who dies young is of course a very common one, and sometimes it is accompanied by the idea that it is their very genius that contributes to their premature death—as we see in the mythology surrounding figures as diverse as Thomas Chatterton, Vincent Van Gogh, and Robert Johnson. But it is less plausible to suppose that their premature death somehow *caused* their genius. Are we really to imagine that, say, Buddy Holly wrote and recorded so much by the age of twenty-two *because* he was going to die at that age? Neither he nor any other great artist worked hard in their youth out of fear that their time was limited—they did it because their art was simply what they did. I see no reason to suppose that an immortal Holly would have achieved less by that age. To a twenty-two-year-old, the prospect of death is as remote as if they really were immortal.

Brooke Alan Trisel suggests otherwise. He offers the following thought experiment: imagine a world in which everyone has differing life spans (as in reality), but in which everyone knows, with absolute and unchangeable certainty, when they will die. He writes:

> I suspect that our lives, on average, would be more meaningful under these conditions. How would having a definite expiration

date add meaning to our lives? Deadlines often motivate people to take action to achieve their goals. By knowing when we will die, it would provide a type of deadline that would motivate people to accomplish their goals. . . . By having a limited amount of time to live, one must prioritize what one wants to do in one's life and one cannot afford to procrastinate.[24]

Trisel supports this by appealing to evidence from psychological studies that indicate that awareness of mortality can change people's goals in a positive way.[25] However, the literature is more ambiguous than this suggests. There is indeed evidence that awareness of mortality can influence people to focus more on "intrinsic" values than "extrinsic" ones, but this goes alongside more negative effects as well. In particular, death anxiety is a well-known phenomenon that can greatly reduce a person's wellbeing. Studies show that when people are made more aware of their mortality, they react by seeking to enhance their feeling of self-worth, often in negative ways such as by showing greater affinity with people who share their worldview and greater hostility towards those who do not. There is thus reason to see mortality awareness as a partial cause of prejudice. In one experiment, for example, US judges were found to issue harsher bail conditions after being asked to contemplate their own mortality.[26] Little wonder, then, that Robert Firestone concludes on the basis of this experiential evidence:

We attempt to gain control over death through a process of progressive self-denial; that is, we deprive ourselves of experiences that would enhance our lives and give them value. We strive for immortality through our creative powers, attempting to live on through our children or sacrificing ourselves to a cause. We seek to please a higher power with the hope of attaining some form of life after death. We give up on the most meaningful aspects of our lives to have less to lose.[27]

This suggests that Trisel's thought experiment is a horrific one. If everyone had the date of their own future death permanently before them, we would expect to see not widespread striving for positive virtue and meaning but

24. Trisel, "Does Death," 65.

25. He also gives the example of Randy Pausch, whose terminal illness led him to deliver a deeply inspiring lecture. We might add the example of the musician Rainer Ptacek, who was spurred to greater creativity by *his* terminal illness. But while examples of this kind are inspiring, they are not good evidence for the claim that awareness of mortality is *generally* positive in its effects.

26. Solomon et al., "Pride and Prejudice," 201–2.

27. Firestone, *Challenging*, 188. Firestone's rhetoric here is very reminiscent of that of Lucretius in *De Rerum Natura* III, lines 31–93, pp. 190–95.

greater vindictiveness and intolerance towards those perceived as different. I certainly cannot imagine that I would find the knowledge of my expiry date empowering. On the contrary, it would seem enervating, a permanent reminder that time is running out.[28]

What about premise (2)? This looks reasonable at first glance. But it is not necessarily true. Even within our finite lives, there are some opportunities that are open to us only for a shorter span of time. There was a time when I could have seen David Bowie play live, but that is sadly no longer possible. Well, of course, if everyone lived for ever, the possibility would remain open. But death is not the only cause of the passing of possibilities. If Bowie had lived, but lost interest in performing and turned to new activities, the possibility of seeing him play live would still have passed. And even if he had continued to perform, the possibility of seeing him play *his final Ziggy Stardust concert of 3 July 1973* would have passed, no matter how long we all lived. Perhaps, given infinite time, that event might be repeated, perhaps infinite times—but even if the replication were perfect, none of those repeat performances would *be* the original iconic event. The opportunity to attend that would still have passed for ever.

So even given infinite time, opportunities might come and go, if for no other reason than the fact that the other people we share eternity with might change their interests. (2) is therefore false.

The argument from motive, then, is unsuccessful. Neither of its premises is true. Consequently, there is no reason to suppose that, given an infinite existence, we could have no incentive to act. We may also observe that even if the argument were correct, that would not in itself make immortality undesirable. Why *should* I want to be motivated to do anything? Is an eternity of inactivity, brought about by lack of motivation, inherently worse than one of activity? I see no reason to think that it is.

Immortality and memory

Jorge Luis Borges' story "The Immortal" suggests a possible line of argument against the desirability of immortality. In the story, a Roman military commander seeks the fabled City of the Immortals, only to find it deserted and surrounded by pitiful "Troglodytes" who, though human, live like irrational animals, spending their time lying in squalor. When one of them, nicknamed Argos, shows some dim awareness of the story of the *Odyssey*, the following exchange occurs:

28. Trisel himself notes that mortality awareness can have enervating effects, even alongside more positive motivating ones. See Trisel, "Does Death," 69–70.

I asked Argos how much of the *Odyssey* he knew. He found using Greek difficult; I had to repeat the question.

Very little, he replied. *Less than the meagerest rhapsode. It has been eleven hundred years since last I wrote it.*[29]

In Borges' typical style, he takes this startling twist and adds another, even more startling one. It emerges that Argos is not actually Homer: *the narrator himself* is Homer, but he has lived so long he has almost entirely forgotten being Homer and projected his own story onto another person. As he remarks, "As the end approaches, there are no longer any images from memory—there are only words."[30] The story ends with an unnamed editor pointing out a number of phrases in the story that echo a wide range of other works by authors as diverse as Pliny, de Quincey, Descartes, and Shaw. The implication is that the narrator has absorbed so many words from his reading and interactions with others over his impossibly long life that he has lost the ability to say anything new: everything he writes is a patchwork of the words of others.

In the course of one story, then, Borges sketches two horrific possible outcomes for the Immortals. In the first, the weight of years causes the Immortals to forget their own pasts, to degenerate to the state of beasts who care nothing for anything. The suggestion here is that the human mind can only store a finite amount of information. Once its limit is reached, memories of the past must inevitably degrade, until the person one used to be is irretrievably lost. In the second outcome, by contrast, the suggestion is that the mind's capacity is infinite. But this scenario is even more frightening than the first, as the amount of information absorbed over an immortal lifetime swamps the person's own memories to such an extent that they lose all sense of self. Either way, according to Borges, an immortal lifespan would lead to a devastating loss of identity.

We can express this argument like this:

The memory argument

(1) In an immortal lifespan, a person either has an unlimited capacity to remember events and information, or they do not.

(2) If they do not have such a capacity, then either (a) they cannot learn anything new, or (b) they will inevitably forget their former life.

29. Borges, *The Aleph*, 12.
30. Borges, *The Aleph*, 18.

(3) If they do have such a capacity, then inevitably the accumulation of new memories and information will swamp those of their former life to the point of indistinguishability.

(4) A person who loses the ability to learn or remember anything new suffers a serious loss.

(5) A person who forgets their former life suffers a serious loss.

(6) A person who cannot distinguish their own experiences from those of others suffers a serious loss.

(7) Therefore, any immortal person would suffer a serious loss.

I take it that (1), (4), (5), and (6) are true, or at least highly plausible. The argument therefore hinges on (2) and (3). Are these true?

(2) seems very plausible to me. I have separated it into two possibilities since, presumably, an immortal person with a limited memory could retain their original memories if they simply lost the ability to acquire any new ones. But clearly such a state would not be consistent with that of heavenly blessedness. What would be the point of being in heaven if one could not remember from one moment to the next what one was experiencing?[31] And wouldn't such a state be a degradation from our existence on earth, rather than an enhancement? Either way, then, if the blessed in heaven have only finite memories, they will suffer serious losses.

(3) is thus the most crucial premise. If a person is going to live for an infinite period without any limitation on their ability to remember, that person must have a memory with an unlimited capacity. It need never contain an actually infinite amount of information, because no matter how much time they spend in heaven, the amount of elapsed time will always be finite, since it had a definite beginning. But despite this, there can never be a limit to how much additional information can be added to this store. But how can this be true of a finite creature?

There are possible ways around this. One is to appeal to *theosis*, the notion that, in heaven, human beings are divinized and (in some way) take

---

31. One way around this might be as follows: the immortal person retains all their prior memories and also has a kind of additional working memory, which is finite, and which stores their heavenly memories. As new heavenly memories are acquired, the oldest ones are lost. So, perhaps, when in heaven I might remember everything I did in life, and also what I did in heaven over the past (say) fifty years. As my time in heaven progresses, my memories of earth remain clear, but my memories of heaven are constantly updated. This would allow me to retain memories of heaven from moment to moment. However, it feels very unsatisfactory to me. I would still be forgetting vast amounts of my own former (heavenly) experiences, which would constitute a serious loss, even if I continued to enjoy new ones.

on divine properties. We shall look at this in more detail in chapter 6, but as we shall see, a plausible account of *theosis* does not involve the supposition that human beings cease being finite. Another approach, which in a way is more radical, is to reject the assumption that a capacity for infinite memory requires that one possess storage of infinite capacity as part of oneself. God, after all, remembers absolutely everything with perfect clarity. What if, in heaven, the blessed remember past events not by accessing their *own* memories, but by accessing God's directly? They might remember "with" God's memories rather than their own—just as, by streaming the output of a powerful PC located somewhere else, I can play games on my own laptop that it lacks the power to run itself.[32]

As we shall see in chapters 5 and 6, I am quite sympathetic to the notion that the blessed could have access to God's knowledge, so perhaps they could retain functional knowledge of their own past experiences, even if these are infinite in extent, by tapping into God's knowledge of them. However, there are some problems with such a picture. One is that a memory is not simply knowledge that something happened in the past. I know, for example, what the first word I ever spoke was, because my parents have told me, but I do not remember actually saying it. Even if I could watch a video of myself saying it, this would not be the same thing as remembering it. And I think crucially, even if I could somehow tap into another person's memory of the event—if the encoding of the memory in my mother's brain could somehow be copied into my brain, so I could access it just as she does—the memory would not be from my own viewpoint. I would not remember it "as" something that I did. I would remember it "as" something another person did, with the peculiar feature that that other person is me. Similarly, if the blessed can access God's knowledge of their past lives, this would not really be the same, phenomenologically speaking, as remembering it. Knowledge of the past is not the same thing as memory of the past. Perhaps God's "knowledge" is not simply factual knowledge but includes conscious experience of everything that ever happens. If God is temporal

---

32. This suggestion is structurally similar to Nicolas Malebranche's famous claim that "we see all things in God" (*Search*, 230). For Malebranche, all thinking and perceiving must be done via "ideas," which are conceived as logical or even mathematical concepts that order our perceptions. For example, if my visual field contains a blob of color, I can perceive it *as* a cube only if my mind has access to the geometrical concept of a cube. For various reasons, Malebranche thinks it impossible that concepts of this kind exist in creaturely minds, and concludes that all perception and cognition requires the constant use of concepts in God's mind. On Malebranche's theory in general, see Schmaltz, "Malebranche on Ideas." On the logicist conception of ideas, see Jolley, *Light of the Soul*, esp. pp. 86–88. On the suggestion currently under consideration, the blessed would be using not concepts in God's mind but God's knowledge.

then God would have perfect memories of these experiences. If God is atemporal then we could perhaps talk of God's having memories$_{at}$, where a "memory$_{at}$" is phenomenologically like a memory but atemporal, in that it does not represent a *past* event.[33] Perhaps the blessed could somehow access such a divine memory and "experience" it for themselves. But even then, it would be phenomenologically distinct from their own memories, because it would not be experienced from their own viewpoint.

What if we suppose that God's infinite understanding includes the experience of every event from every point of view? So God does not simply know, as an intellectual fact, what the circumstances are of every event. And God does not simply perceive every event from a uniquely divine perspective. Rather, God *also* perceives every event from every possible perspective within it. In that case, if in heaven I have access to the divine understanding, I could perhaps access God's memories of all the events in my life, *from my own perspective*. And this would be phenomenologically similar to ordinary remembering—except, no doubt, with perfect clarity and accuracy of recall.

Such a conception will require quite a radical conception of divine omniscience, such that God does not merely know everything but experiences everything, which we might dub *omniexperience*.[34] It is questionable whether such a view is coherent. It is at least plausible to suppose that to experience (say) my current activity of typing this sentence, one must actually *be* me—and that this is a logical necessity, such that the notion that somebody could have this experience from my point of view without actually being me is an incoherent one.

Putting this worry to one side, if God is omniexperient then clearly there is an extremely close relation between God and the created world, which seems theologically satisfying. Such a conception of God might be appealing to those who conceive of God as suffering alongside creation, a view that has dominated modern theology.[35] It is easy to see the attractiveness of the idea that God literally shares the experiences of the poor, the

33. In what follows I will talk simply of divine "memories," for simplicity's sake, but on the understanding that this language could be translated into that of "memories$_{at}$" without loss of meaning.

34. The concept of omniexperience is similar to, though not quite the same as, the concept of omnisubjectivity, which Linda Zagzebski has defended in "Omnisubjectivity." Omniexperience requires omnisubjectivity, but not vice versa, at least on my understanding. Omnisubjectivity means thoroughly grasping every first-person perspective, but it seems to me coherent to suppose that God could do that without *actually experiencing* them all.

35. For summaries of the development and dominance of this view of God in the twentieth century, see Bauckham, "Suffering God," and Keating and White, "Divine Impassibility."

marginalized, and the suffering. However, an omniexperient God would equally share the experiences of the rich, the powerful, and the inflictors of suffering, which is less palatable. Indeed, such a God would experience the commission of every sin in history. A defender of omniexperience might say that although God shares the experience of (say) a murderer, God does not share the guilt of the murderer; God does not *make* the same choices as the murderer, merely *experiences* them in a passive way. I am not sure that this would be a coherent distinction. Remember that the purpose of floating this conception of God is to furnish God with memories that the blessed can appropriate as true memories from their own viewpoint. Suppose, once in heaven, I wish to remember an incident from my life in which I sinned. I access God's memory of the event. If this is to function meaningfully as if it were my own memory, it needs to include the experience of willing the sin and performing it. That is, I need to remember *actively committing the sin*. If I do not, then I am not really remembering it as *my own* act. God's memory, then, would have to include this feature, which means that God's experience of it at the actual time I did it would have to include sharing in this element of the event. It is hard to see how God could genuinely experience this without being complicit in the sin. But anything that distances God from the commission of the sin makes God's "memory" of the event inadequate as the basis of my heavenly remembering of it.

Fortunately, there is a way around this problem. So far I have been assuming that memory works as if it were a simple recording of the event, a view of memory that goes back at least to Plato's analogy of the wax tablet.[36] On this view, our memories are "impressions" of our experiences, and when we remember something, we summon up those impressions. This is a commonsense way of conceiving of memory. But there is an alternative conception of memory, associated with the work of psychologist Frederic Bartlett, who conducted a series of experiments in the early twentieth century suggesting that memories do not merely atrophy over time but are imaginatively reinvented. He concluded that memories are inherently dynamic phenomena:

> Remembering is not the re-excitation of innumerable fixed, lifeless and fragmentary traces. It is an imaginative reconstruction, or construction, built out of the relation of our attitude towards a whole active mass of organised past reactions or experience. . . .[37]

36. *Theaetetus* 191a–196c, in Plato, *Complete Works*, 211–17.

37. Bartlett, *Remembering*. On Bartlett's theory and its reception in contemporary psychology, see Wagoner, *Constructive Mind*.

This "constructive" view of memory suggests that the memories we think of as recordings of the past are not really retrieved from some storehouse in our brains but are imaginatively created at the moment we "recall" them. Memories exhibit stability—my memories of Monday are much the same on both Tuesday and Wednesday—but this is not because these memories persist in the storehouse of my mind from one day to the next. When I remember the events of Monday, I construct them in my mind anew each time, but I do so under the same "schema," a term Bartlett used to refer to a dynamic model of the self,[38] and which can be thought of rather like a set of algorithms that generate memories. The persistence of the schema is what gives the illusion of the persistence of the memories that are constructed on its basis. However, the schema itself does change gradually over time. Because our schemata themselves are dynamic and constantly changing, so too are the memories they produce. As a result, my memory of the same event might be quite different at different times—not because it has degraded, like old film, but because *I* have changed and therefore construct the memory differently.[39]

If memory is constructive, as many psychologists today think, then it becomes easier to imagine how the blessed might rely on the divine understanding for their memories. Suppose I remember some past event in my life. On the constructive view, the phenomenological features of this memory are not retrieved from my mental storehouse but are actually constructed by my mind at the moment of remembering. If one of these phenomenological features is the experience of the event *as my own*, and myself as actively doing whatever I did during the event, then this feature could be constructed by my mind on the basis of information that does not contain such a feature. For example, I may know that I was in a certain place at a certain time, as well as many other facts about the event. I then "remember" it from the point of view of myself at that place and time. This "memory" is really a present construction on the basis of that information.[40] The feature of my memory that presents it from my own point of view is constructed at the moment of remembering, and is not present in the information that my mind uses to construct the memory. If this is so, all I need from God's understanding in order to construct a memory is information about the

38. Bartlett, *Remembering*, 199–200.

39. On this, and for a modern defense of this view of memory in general, see Schacter, "Adaptive Constructive Processes."

40. This is why false memory is indistinguishable, phenomenologically speaking, from true memory: the memories that the mind creates on the basis of mistaken information really are exactly the same in kind as those created on the basis of accurate information. Whether true or false, they are all constructed.

event. My mind will supply the phenomenological features of the event, including the experience of its occurring from my own point of view, from that information. There is no need for God's own "memories" to include my point of view, and consequently no need to suppose that God is omniexperient at all.[41]

However, there is a second, and more serious, problem with this notion of using the divine understanding as the material for the memories of the blessed. Suppose, in heaven, I want to remember a particular celestial event that occurred several million years earlier. Assuming the constructive account of memory just outlined, I access (perfect) information about this event from God's knowledge and "remember" it perfectly as a result. But how did I know which knowledge to access? How did I even know that such an event occurred, before I used my access to the divine mind in order to remember it? In order for this process to function, each person in heaven must have *constant* awareness of *all* of the information in the divine mind— or at least all of it relevant to their own histories—otherwise they would never be able to access any of it.[42] So now we have a picture of each person in heaven being constantly and perfectly aware of all divine knowledge of their own lives. Such a picture seems to me to be even more problematic than the original suggestion that they retain such information themselves. The notion that I might have an infinite storehouse of memory into which I can dip whenever I please is difficult enough. The notion that I might have this infinite spread of information about myself permanently before my consciousness is harder still. My capacity to process and understand information would have to be infinite.

So the very notion of a human person in heaven being able to remember the events of an infinitely prolonged life is deeply problematic. Suppose, though, that we set this problem aside and assume that it would, somehow, be possible.[43] Would the accumulation of memories eventually

41. An alternative idea, which is neutral regarding the constructive theory of memory, is to suppose not that God provides the blessed with God's own memories, or with the tools to construct their own, but rather that God provides them with "storage space" for their own memories. In effect, God could act like cloud storage with infinite capacity, into which the blessed could "write" their own memories without end. (I am grateful to Robin Parry for this suggestion.) I think such an idea is coherent, but it is still susceptible to the problem of how the blessed could access particular items within this unlimited expanse of storage.

42. Given the similarities between the view currently being considered and Malebranche's doctrine of "vision in God" (see note 32 above), it is unsurprising to find that he argued much the same thing. See Malebranche, *Search*, 227.

43. One way of doing so might be like this: it would indeed be impossible for a human consciousness to maintain awareness of an infinity of past events, but even if heaven is infinite in duration, any individual's *past* is still finite. If I have spent a million

be so great that our minds would become confused and lose the ability to distinguish between our own experiences and those of others, as Borges suggests? Plausibly, yes. This is because the qualitative feature of a memory that marks it out as "mine" is among the features that can degrade over time. I remember what I did yesterday as actions that *I did*. But when it comes to memories of events decades ago, I may easily misremember someone else's actions as mine, or my actions as someone else's. On the constructive view of memory, this is presumably because the schema by which I reconstruct these memories has changed so much. I am, in a sense, no longer the "I" who did that action, and so when I reconstruct the memory of doing it I misattribute it to someone else (or misappropriate their actions as mine). Given infinite memories, it is easy to see how this would become a systemic problem, because a finite schema could never reconstruct an infinite number of memories accurately. We could recall an infinite number of memories only at the cost of making each memory infinitely vague.

Conclusion

We have surveyed a number of arguments that purport to show that we should not value an immortal existence in heaven, *even if* heaven is supremely pleasurable. It is time to draw some conclusions.

Arguments in Category C1 depend on some notion of "value," which is notoriously slippery. In framing them, we have assumed that "value" is a property that things—particularly actions—have in some sense that is not observer-dependent. That is a dubious assumption. However, we can reframe the arguments to refer to value *to me* (or to some relevant person or persons) without losing much of their force.

But as I indicated in the introduction to the book, arguing about value is something of a futile task, because it is very hard to show that anyone *should* (or should not) value something except by appealing to something else that they value, and if the other person does not share your values, there is little to say to convince them otherwise. To the extent that these arguments have force, it is because, as a matter of fact, we *do* hold the values to which they appeal. It is unsurprising, then, that most of these arguments are usually expressed not as arguments at all but as assertions, though often

---

years in heaven, an infinity of time stretches ahead of me, but still only a million years lie behind me—and this remains true, *mutatis mutandis*, no matter how long I remain in heaven. However, the notion that I might have a million years' worth of memories at my fingertips—or a billion, or a quintillion—seems to me almost as inconceivable as the notion that I might have an infinite number. If there is any limit to the amount of memory I can access, then given infinite time, that limit will be met eventually.

eloquently expressed ones. I have tried to articulate them in the form of arguments, to make them more susceptible to analytic discussion, but we have repeatedly seen that they ultimately rest upon assumptions about values. Of these arguments, the one I have called the "possibility of reversal argument" seems the strongest. Given an infinite future existence, my actions right now seem less significant, since there is always the chance that I might do something in the future that reverses or at least outweighs them.

Arguments in Category C2 do not appeal to value, and therefore seem to be based on stronger ground. However, only the argument from epistemology seems compelling to me. An ever-growing history of memory and experience seems incompatible with our nature as limited creatures: how could we store, let alone access, a repository of memory that grows without end?

I conclude, then, that the "possibility of reversal argument" and the "memory argument" are the two strongest Category C arguments against the desirability of heaven. Although I have put them into different subcategories, they share a key feature: they target a *temporally extended* future life. In the case of the "possibility of reversal argument," the reason that my actions now seem insignificant is that *I might counteract them in the future*. If heaven is eternal in the sense of being atemporal, then there is no future in which this might happen. Similarly, the "memory argument" focuses on worries about an *indefinitely growing* body of memory. But, again, if heaven is atemporal, then I do not spend eternity acquiring new memories, because I do not undergo new experiences.

If the strongest arguments against the desirability of heaven are effective only against temporal conceptions of heaven, then we have a motive to see if we can develop an atemporal conception, one that will be immune to these arguments. This is our task over the next five chapters. In the course of our discussion, I shall argue that not only is such a conception coherent, but it has other attractive features, quite apart from its resistance to the criticisms we have seen in this chapter.

2

Time and Atemporality

W hen philosophers consider atemporal objects, they usually have abstract entities in mind. The most common examples are mathematical objects such as numbers, or geometrical figures: if Pythagoras' theorem, for example, is *about* anything, it is not about the imperfect triangles one might draw on paper, but about a set of ideal objects that exist neither in space nor in time. But abstracta of this kind, and the familiar debates over whether they exist at all, are not our concern in this book. We are interested not in universals but in particulars. Could there be an individual object— something akin to *this pen*—that exists atemporally?

According to classical theism, there is at least one such object, namely God. However, according to that same tradition, God is not really an object like others. God is, rather, being itself, the cause and ground of all existence. God is not to be numbered among the furniture of the universe.[1] So while the God of classical theism is not an abstract object, that God is also not exactly a particular object either. So the question whether non-abstract atemporal objects are possible remains unclear, even for a classical theist.

Time, ontology, and persistence

To begin our discussion of time and atemporality, we need to sketch out the conceptual terrain and stake a claim to some of the territory. Much of this is likely to cover familiar metaphysical ground, but there are some key points along the way that will become important later on.

---

1. See, for example, Sokolowski, *God*, 32–33, and Burrell, "Creation," 206–8.

Let us start by dividing ontologies of time, very broadly, into tenseless and tensed accounts.[2] The difference between them can best be understood in terms of John McTaggart's well-known distinction between what he called the "A-series" and the "B-series," which are rival ways of describing the relations between different events on a timeline.[3] In the "A-series," one particular moment on the timeline is privileged as the "present," and all events are related to that moment: they are past, present, or future. The "B-series," by contrast, privileges no particular moment. Events on the "B-series" can be temporally related *to each other*: one event may be earlier than another, later than another, and simultaneous with still another, but it cannot be called "past," "present," or "future," because there is no point on the timeline that is uniquely the "present."

Tenseless accounts are those that take the "B-series" to be ontologically prior to the "A-series." Defenders of tenseless accounts do not simply reject the "A-series," since we are within time ourselves and therefore do have a temporal point of view.[4] From my point of view, some events are past, some are present, and some are future. But for the tenseless theorist, these features are parasitic upon events' temporal relations to each other. A spatial comparison may be helpful: from my point of view, there is one place that is *here*, and other places are near or distant to varying degrees. But that does not mean there is anything special about "here," or that "here" has any reality that "there" lacks. Similarly, there is a time that is "now" from my point of view, but there is nothing special about it. From my point of view, the Colossus of Rhodes no longer exists, and the 100th president of the United States (assuming there will be one) does not yet exist. But that does not mean they are less real than things that exist right now. To put it another way, they all always exist in a tenseless sense, whether or not they exist at a given moment.

2. I take this terminology from Bourne, *Future*. I find it more helpful than the terminology of "eternalism" and "presentism," which in my view are somewhat misleading, partly because they do not exhaust all the possibilities, and partly because "eternalists" do not really think that objects exist *eternally*, at least for some definitions of "eternal." However, no categorization of theories of time is straightforward, since there are always some theories that do not fit the scheme, as will become apparent.

3. McTaggart, "Unreality of Time."

4. On this, see Bourne, *Future*, 4–5. For this reason, "tenseless" is something of a misnomer, as proponents of this view still believe that tensed language is meaningful. Theodore Sider characterizes their view more accurately as "reductionism" about tensed language: they hold that while tensed language is meaningful, propositions expressed in tensed terms can be restated, without loss of meaning, using only untensed terms. See Sider, *Four-Dimensionalism*, 13–15.

For some tenseless theorists, the "A-series" still has some ontological weight. On these theories, there is one particular moment on the "B-series" which *is* the "present." Precisely which moment is the present varies from one hyper-moment to the next,[5] a feature sometimes called the "moving spotlight" theory of the passage of time.[6] For more extreme tenseless theorists, the "A-series" has no ontological weight at all, and the passage of time is consequently hard to account for (or may even turn out to be merely an illusion).

A tensed account, as we might expect, holds that the "A-series" is ontologically prior to the "B-series."[7] On this view, there is a difference between past, present, and future events that goes beyond just my particular point of view. Precisely what that difference is varies between different kinds of tensed accounts. The most common such account is presentism, which is the view that only present things exist.[8] The past has gone, and the future has not yet come, so things that exist only in the past or future do not exist at all. On this view there is no "B-series" at all, because the only events that exist are all simultaneous with each other. A less extreme tensed account holds that past and present things exist, but future ones do not. This is often known as the "growing block" theory, since if one imagines the series of temporal slices that make up the whole of history as a three-dimensional block, the block is constantly acquiring new slices at one face as time progresses.[9] Indeed, on this view the passage of time may simply *be* the addition of new slices to the block's leading edge.[10] A less common alternative to the "growing block" is the "shrinking block," which holds the opposite view: present and future things exist, but past ones do not, so the list of existing

---

5. Brad Skow, "Why Does Time Pass?," 224, argues for the characterization of this view in terms of hypertime, for reasons that seem to me to be compelling.

6. Schlesinger, "How Time Flies," 502; Sider, *Four-Dimensionalism*, 17–18.

7. For some philosophers, a theory counts as "tensed" if it involves the claim that the "A-series" is real *at all*, without requiring it to be ontologically prior to the "B-series." Michael Tooley, *Time*, defends a "growing block" theory that is "tensed" in this sense. On the categorization scheme I am using this would be something of a hybrid theory, as it holds the "B-series" to be ontologically prior but considers the present moment to have objective significance.

8. This is typically how presentism is understood, but for some philosophers, presentism does *not* require commitment to the "A-series." See Rasmussen, "Presentists." For simplicity's sake I shall ignore this and stick to the categorization of theories of time described here, but it illustrates just how complex the conceptual landscape of this topic can be.

9. As with much visualization of time, this involves imagining each *three*-dimensional temporal slice as a *two*-dimensional one, which may confuse as much as it enlightens.

10. Olson, "Passage of Time," 445; see also Briggs and Forbes, "Growing-Block," 927.

objects shrinks as time passes.[11] Finally, a tensed theory that holds that past, present, and future all have equal existence is effectively the same thing as the "moving spotlight" theory.

Alongside these two broad categories of theories of the nature of time, there are two broad categories of theories about the identity of objects over time. First, endurantism, or three-dimensionalism, is the view that each object exists fully at any given moment, and identity across time is a matter of that object's moving from one moment to the next. Second, perdurantism, or four-dimensionalism, is the view that what seems to be a whole object at any given moment is actually just one slice out of the history of that object, which fills the temporal span of its lifetime. Perdurantism may in turn be divided into two: worm theory, which conceives of the whole object throughout its history as a genuine unity with temporal parts; and stage theory, which conceives of each of the temporal slices as a distinct entity, making the whole history of the object really a succession of distinct individuals.[12]

There is an important difference between endurantism and perdurantism. An object endures over a given interval if it is wholly present at each moment in that interval, that is, if its identity in that interval is not (partly) determined by anything outside that interval.[13] And it perdures over a given interval if it exists at each moment in that interval but is *not* wholly present at each of those moments. So a perduring individual's identity at any given moment is determined, in part, by conditions at other times. Whether or not a person P2 at time $t2$ is identical with a person P1 at time $t1$ is determined partly by the properties of P2 and partly by the properties of P1. But this is not the case for an enduring individual. If P1 endures through time to become P2, the question "What makes P2 the same person as P1?" is no more pressing than if P1 had moved through space. For this reason, Michael Della Rocca has argued persuasively that endurantism is based on the notion of "primitive persistence": that is, persistence over time is a basic notion that cannot be broken down or explained in terms of anything else.[14] But this is not the case with perdurantism. It *could* be that what makes P1

---

11. Casati and Torrengo, "Shrinking Future."

12. Some philosophers (e.g., Lowe, "Endurantism Versus Perdurantism," 713) deny that stage theory is a kind of perdurantism at all, because if stage theory is true then *I* (for example) do not persist through time at all: I am, rather, a fleeting stage in a succession of non-persisting momentary entities. Alternatively, one may view both worm theory and stage theory as differing only in the terminology used: what the worm theorist calls a "temporal part" the stage theorist calls a "stage," and what the worm theorist calls a "four-dimensional entity" the stage theorist calls a "succession of entities."

13. Hofweber and Velleman, "How to Endure," 56–57.

14. Della Rocca, "Primitive Persistence." See also Mullins, "Personal Identity," 102.

and P2 temporal parts of one and the same individual is basic and cannot be explained in terms of anything else. But it is also possible that it is not basic, and their roles as different temporal parts of the same individual can be explained in terms of some other properties or relations—just as the fact that two objects constitute *spatial* parts of the same individual can also be explained in terms of other properties and relations. As we shall see, for example, a common explanation involves appealing to causation: if P1 and P2 are temporal parts of the same individual this is so in virtue of a certain kind of causal story that can be told about them.

How do the different theories of identity relate to the different on-tologies of time? In theory, all kinds of identity theory can be (and have been) combined with all kinds of ontological theory.[15] In practice, how-ever, people who hold tensed theories of time are usually endurantists, and those who hold tenseless ones tend to be perdurantists.[16] It would seem, for example, to be very difficult to combine perdurantism with any tensed theory that denies the existence of both past and future events.[17] If I am a four-dimensional entity with past and future parts, it seems that at least some of those parts must exist, otherwise four-dimensionalism collapses into three-dimensionalism.[18] But a less drastic tensed theory, according to which at least some non-present events exist, could allow an individual to be composed of different temporal parts at different hyper-moments. Per-haps, if the growing block theory is true, at this moment I consist of a series of temporal parts dating from the moment of my birth to right now; and hyper-after a hyper-moment has passed I consist of that same series of tem-poral parts with an additional one; and so on.

Edward Lowe has argued that a tenseless ontology of time is incom-patible with endurantism.[19] This is because the endurantist holds that one

15. Lowe, "Endurantism Versus Perdurantism," 715.

16. Miller, "Metaphysical Equivalence," 95.

17. Berit Brogaard, "Presentist Four-Dimensionalism," argues otherwise, suggesting a view on which I am composed of temporal parts, but at any given moment I have only one temporal part. But while such a view is, I think, coherent, it is close enough to three-dimensionalism to make no difference for our purposes.

18. Kristie Miller, "Metaphysical Equivalence," 96, points out that endurantism seems incompatible with presentism for structurally similar reasons: how can an object at time $t1$ be identical with an object at some other time if no other times exist? If this is correct then presentism is incoherent whether one is an endurantist *or* a perdurantist.

19. Lowe, "Endurantism Versus Perdurantism." Lowe does not present the argument in these terms. He speaks, rather, of the view that time is a "dimension," which as he defines it is equivalent to what I am calling a tenseless view of time. He argues that if one accepts this view of time then endurantism and both varieties of four-dimension-alism are exactly the same thing, differing only in terminology. Miller, "Metaphysical

and the same object exists at different points along the timeline; but if all of these points are real then this object is effectively extended along the timeline—which is four-dimensionalism. This argument seems to me to be decisive. If one is going to accept a tenseless ontology of time, one must be a four-dimensionalist of some kind.[20]

To sum up, then: we have tensed and tenseless ontologies of time, and endurantist and perdurantist accounts of identity over time. On endurantism, identity over time is basic, but on at least some kinds of perdurantism, it can be explained in terms of other properties or relations. And, finally, endurantism is incompatible with a tenseless ontology. All of these claims are contestable, but I think most metaphysicians would find them at least highly plausible.

Subjective and objective atemporality

With all of this under our belts, we can start to think about how God might relate to time. Virtually all theists agree that God is eternal, but as is well known, they do not agree on what this means. Typically, philosophers of religion distinguish between the view that God is *sempiternal*, or everlasting, and the view that God is *atemporal*. On the first view, God fills time, so that there is neither beginning nor end to God's existence. On the second view, God is outside time altogether, so that although "God exists," uttered at any time, is true, "God exists now" is never true.

The question of which of these is the best way to think of divine eternity is a much discussed one.[21] Rather than argue for one position over the other, though, I will assume from the outset that divine eternity should be thought of as atemporality. My reason is simple: in the following chapters I will be arguing for the coherence and plausibility of heaven as an atemporal state. I assume that heavenly atemporality is only a viable view in the context of divine atemporality. Anyone who rejects divine atemporality will have little

---

Equivalence," gives a similar argument for the more wide-sweeping (and controversial) position that three-dimensionalism and four-dimensionalism are *always* metaphysically equivalent, no matter what ontology of time is used.

20. Trenton Merricks, "Persistence," meanwhile, argues for the equivalent position that endurantism entails presentism.

21. To name just two of the most influential philosophers on this question, Richard Swinburne, *Christian God*, 72–95, defends a sempiternal concept of God, while Brian Leftow, *Time and Eternity*, 267–82, defends an atemporal one. Other important discussions of the topic include, among many others: Kenny, *God*; Stump and Kretzmann, "Eternity"; Tomkinson, "Sempiternity"; Yates, *Timelessness*; Rogers, *Perfect Being Theology*, 54–70; Epsen, "Eternity Is a Present"; Mullins, *End*.

time for heavenly atemporality. If heaven is atemporal, and heaven is the best possible state for humans, then either atemporality is inherently preferable to temporality or it makes possible some other good that is impossible given temporality. Either way, if humans can enjoy this good, it seems that God must also enjoy it (or something even better). If heaven is atemporal, then, God must be too.

However, I suggest that atemporality is not as easily defined as one might think. There are two quite distinct kinds of definitions in the literature. I will call these the "subjective" and "objective" definitions, and distinguish accordingly between "subjective atemporalism" and "objective atemporalism."[22]

"Subjective atemporalism" is suggested by the famous definition of Boethius, which most treatments of divine eternity cite at some point. Boethius gave a number of versions of his definition, leading to some disagreement about precisely what he meant by it,[23] but here is one version:

> What may properly be called eternal . . . has knowledge of the whole of life, can see the future, and has lost nothing of the past. It is an eternal present and has an understanding of the entire flow of time.[24]

Nicholas Everitt points out that, taken at face value, Boethius' definition is incoherent: if one can talk of "past" and "future" with respect to the eternal thing at all, then by definition past events and future events cannot be simultaneous with the present. To say they can is to do violence to the meanings of "past," "present," and "future."[25] But on a more charitable reading, Boethius is trying to describe what it is *like* to be eternal. For the eternal being, all events are equally "present," no matter when they may happen actually to occur. Compare ordinary experience: memories of the past, and anticipations of the future, are fundamentally unlike experiences of the present. This is not a matter of accuracy: even if I recall a past event perfectly, or anticipate a future one perfectly; and even if my experience of

22. This distinction is similar in some respects to the distinction that Charles Gutenson makes between what he calls "Augustinian timelessness" and "eternalism" ("Time," 118–20). However, Gutenson presents these as rival, mutually exclusive accounts of God's relation to time: the former portrays God as outside time, and the latter portrays God as universally present in time. He also attributes the former to Augustine and the latter to Plotinus. My categories of subjective and objective atemporality, by contrast, are consistent with each other, in the sense that both could be true of God.

23. On this, see Stump and Kretzmann, "Eternity"; Leftow, *Time and Eternity*, 112–22.

24. *Consolation of Philosophy*, V.6, in Boethius, *Consolation*, 169.

25. Everitt, *Non-existence*, 275.

what is happening now is vague and obscure (perhaps because I have just woken up, or am drugged), they are still fundamentally different sorts of experience. For the eternal being, by contrast, they all have the quality of what for us are present experiences. Let us call this rather elusive quality "qualitative presentness."

Not only that, but according to this definition, the eternal being experiences them all at once. It is not like the eternal being can summon a memory of a particular past event and experience it again as if it were happening now. Rather, the eternal being exists in a permanent state of experiencing *all* events. Within the eternal being's consciousness, there is no particular slice of experience that is distinct from the rest in terms of its concerning "now."

There is a sense in which we could all be considered subjectively eternal in this sense, if, as some thinkers maintain, what we experience as "the present" at any given moment is not really an instant of time with no duration, but extends slightly into the past and slightly into the future. On this view, we experience this temporally extended period *as if* it were only a single instant.[26] So we should specify that true subjective eternity covers a much greater duration—perhaps the whole of time.

So we can define subjective atemporality like this:

> SA: the state of (a) experiencing every moment, from the beginning of time to the end of time, with (b) qualitative presentness, such that (c) in this experience, no particular event or set of events is experienced as "now" in a way distinct from all the other events experienced.

This, I think, captures what classical Platonic philosophers such as Boethius were trying to articulate. Compare, for example, Plotinus:

> [I]t is never other and is not a thinking or life that goes from one thing to another but is always the selfsame without extension or interval; seeing all this one sees eternity in seeing a life that abides in the same, and always has the all present to it, not now this, and then again that, but all things at once, and not now some things, and then again others, but a partless completion, as if they were all together in a point, and had not yet begun to go out and flow into lines. . . .[27]

---

26. This idea is known as the "specious present." The concept arguably goes back to Thomas Reid (Levanon, "Thomas Reid"), but the term was coined by Edmund Clay and popularized by William James (Andersen, "Specious Present"). For more on this, and discussion of the controversy surrounding the concept, see Grush, "Brain Time"; Kelly, "Puzzle"; Power, "Metaphysics."

27. Plotinus, *Enneads*, III.7.3, pp. 303–5.

What of "objective atemporality"? Platonic philosophers also hint at this. After the above passage, Plotinus goes on to say:

> Necessarily there will be no "was" about it, for what is there that was for it and has passed away? Nor any "will be," for what will be for it? So there remains for it only to be in its being just what it is. That, then, which was not, and will not be, but *is* only, which has being which is static by not changing to the "will be," nor ever having changed, this is eternity.[28]

Here, the emphasis is on not the subjective experience of the eternal thing but its relations to other objects. The eternal thing has no past and no future. Plotinus talks about it in terms of a sort of eternal present—this passage rules out applying language of the past and the future to the eternal thing, but not language of the present. Indeed, Plotinus' concern here seems to be with emphasizing that eternity is *unchanging*. We might say the same of Aquinas' claim that "eternity has no succession, being simultaneously whole."[29] The idea here is that nothing happens in God's life, in the sense of there being any events in God's life that are temporally ordered. But this would be consistent with God's having temporal relations with other things.

Elsewhere, though, Aquinas gives a more modern-sounding account of atemporality, when he states that God is "wholly outside the order of time."[30] Modern philosophers typically focus on this idea, taking it to mean that all temporal language about God is mistaken. Brian Leftow gives a typical account of atemporality:

> If God is timeless, God exists, but exists at no time. Thus God bears no temporal relation to any temporal relatum—God does not exist or act earlier than, later than, or at the same time as any such thing. If God is timeless, such truths as "God exists" are timeless truths: though they are true, they are not true at any time.[31]

So we can articulate "objective atemporality" very succinctly like this:

OA: the state of having no temporal relations.

It should be clear that subjective and objective atemporality, as I have defined them here, are very different things. But typically in the literature, we find these two definitions run together to the point of confusion. Boethius

---

28. Plotinus, *Enneads*, III.7.3, pp. 305.
29. Aquinas, *ST*, I q. 10 a. 1, vol. 1, p. 98.
30. Aquinas, *On Interpretation*, 14.20, p. 118.
31. Leftow, *Time and Eternity*, 20.

is often cited, but in the context of a discussion of objective atemporality (despite the fact that neither Boethius nor any other classical author really articulates objective atemporality as clearly and unambiguously as Leftow does). This is perhaps a result of the analogies that are sometimes used for atemporality. Consider Aquinas' famous analogy of the man in a high tower looking down on a procession passing below.[32] It is *because* the man is not part of the procession (i.e., he does not see some parts of it as ahead of him and some as behind him) that he can see the whole procession equally clearly. Similarly, we may think, it is *because* God is not part of the temporal order of things that God perceives all of time in a single intuition of equal qualitative presentness. Subjective atemporality is parasitic upon objective temporality.

But in fact this does not follow. Assuming that objective and subjective atemporality are both possible states, it would be possible for something to exist in one but not the other. For example, a being could experience subjective atemporality without being objectively atemporal. Such a being would have temporal relations: it would exist at a particular time, and might have time-bound properties such as being in a certain location at a certain time. But it would be consistent with this that, at every moment of its existence, it might experience all events throughout time with qualitative presentness.[33]

Conversely, one might imagine a being that has objective atemporality without subjective atemporality. An obvious example would be the abstracta normally considered as candidates for atemporality: the number 7, if it exists, is not conscious of anything, let alone of the whole of time. But even if we imagine an objectively atemporal conscious being—assuming that consciousness at all is consistent with objective atemporality—that being need not be conscious of the whole of time. It could, perhaps, be conscious of a particular moment in time. That would be consistent with its not actually existing *at* that moment in time: it is just atemporally conscious of that moment, without experiencing it directly—rather as I can remember a past event without actually experiencing it at the moment of recall. Or, to change the analogy, if I am reading a novel, I may be consciously aware only of the events in the scene I am currently reading, though I am not "in" the timeline of the novel at all.

How does all of this relate to the different philosophical theories about time and persistence? It is easy to see that a tenseless theory of time, combined with divine simplicity, entails divine objective atemporality. If God is

32. Aquinas, *On Interpretation*, 14.19, p. 117.

33. The alien "heptapods" from Ted Chiang's *Story of Your Life* (first published in 1998) are an example of this: although existing within the normal bounds of spacetime, they are aware of all moments at once. See Chiang, *Stories*, 109–72.

perfectly simple, then God cannot have proper parts, including temporal parts. It would follow that God exists either for only one moment in time (clearly unacceptable) or outside time altogether. But the same reasoning does not apply to a tensed theory of time. God could be perfectly simple whilst enduring throughout time.

Suppose we *start* with divine atemporality. Can we draw conclusions about the nature of time from that? The claim that God is objectively atemporal is neutral towards ontologies of time. The supposition that God exists outside the temporal order tells us, by itself, nothing about the nature of that order.[34]

I shall argue, though, for two key claims. The first is that divine objective atemporality, combined with other commitments that most Christians would want to make, entails divine subjective atemporality. The second is that divine subjective atemporality entails a tenseless ontology of time, and with it four-dimensionalism.

First, let us define the property of *divine accessibility*:

DA: a moment (or event) is *divinely accessible* if and only if it is true, at that moment, that God is (timelessly or otherwise) aware of it.

Here is my argument:

(1) If God is objectively atemporal, then either God is subjectively atemporal or there are some moments that are not divinely accessible.

(2) If God is subjectively atemporal, then all moments in time exist.

(3) If all moments in time exist, then a tenseless ontology of time is true.

(4) God is objectively atemporal.

(5) All moments are divinely accessible.

(6) Therefore, a tenseless ontology of time is true.

Premise (3) is entailed by the definition of tenseless ontologies of time. As explained earlier, I am taking (4) as a basic premise. And I am assuming (5) as something virtually all Christians would want to endorse, even if they have a non-classical concept of God. For example, suppose that God is temporal, and moreover that God lacks infallible knowledge of the future

---

34. William Lane Craig also derives a tenseless ontology of time from divine (objective) atemporality, but by a different route: he argues that if a tensed ontology were correct, then God would necessarily become temporal upon creating the universe. See Craig, "Tensed," 246–48. However, his argument rests, among other things, upon the supposition that Aquinas' account of relations between God and created things is unfeasible, which I do not think he establishes. See below, ch. 3, n. 20.

(as suggested by open theism). If this is so, then today—Wednesday—it is the case that God is aware of the events of Wednesday, but God is not aware of the events of Thursday. When Thursday comes along, however, God becomes aware of Thursday's events, just as we do. So it is true on Thursday that God is aware of Thursday's events. And so on for every other time. As long as it is true *at time t* that God is aware of time *t*, time *t* counts as being divinely accessible, even if it is not true *at other times* that God is aware of time *t*. And clearly any Christian would want to suppose that this is true of all times. Otherwise, there would be some times when God is not aware of what is going on. Prayers uttered at such times would go not merely unanswered but unheard.

Premise (1) requires a little more unpacking. If God is objectively *temporal*, it could be the case that all times are divinely accessible even if God is not subjectively *atemporal*, for the reasons just given. This is because the awareness of a temporal God can change—such a God could be aware of all the events in one moment, and then aware of all the events in the next moment, and so on. But this is not so if God is objectively atemporal. The awareness of an objectively atemporal God cannot change. So if all moments are divinely accessible, and God is objectively atemporal, then God must be atemporally aware of them all together—and that is subjective atemporality.

There is a possible objection to this argument. Suppose that God is objectively atemporal, but not objectively ahypertemporal. That is, God is not located within time, but God *is* located within hypertime. It could then be the case that, from one hyper-moment to the next, God's attention shifts from one moment to the next. Indeed, if one were to combine such a view with the "moving spotlight" theory of temporal progression, one might say that the "spotlight" simply *is* God's attention. One might then have an explanation for why the passage of time is constant and unidirectional: because God is orderly in all things, and so the divine gaze sweeps across history in an orderly fashion.

As far as I know, nobody has ever defended such a view, and it is not hard to see why. Whatever reasons one may have for rejecting the idea that God is temporal apply equally to the idea that God is hypertemporal. The two major reasons, I think, are (a) time is part of the created order, and God transcends creation; and (b) God is immutable, and this entails objective atemporality. Both of these apply equally to hypertime. If there is hypertime, then it is not God and therefore it is part of the created order; and a God who changes from hyper-moment to hyper-moment is just as mutable as one who changes from moment to moment. So although a conception of God as bound by hypertime but not by time is coherent, it is difficult to motivate. I conclude that my premise (1) holds.

What of premise (2)? If a subjectively atemporal being exists, that being experiences all moments of time with qualitative presentness. That seems to require that those moments exist in order to be experienced. It is, of course, possible to have an experience with qualitative presentness even if the object of that experience does not exist, such as during a vivid dream. However, if God's experience of all moments of time is like that, it would not be true *awareness* of time. There would be no guarantee that God's experience is veridical—just as if I were to have a strong hallucinatory premonition of a future event. Assuming that I do not possess actual precognition, any resemblance between my hallucination and future events would be coincidental. Clearly, God's experience of all moments in time cannot be like that, because God cannot make errors.

One might try to resist this by constructing a theory of awareness that does not require the objects of awareness to exist. Such a theory might take inspiration from the fact that nonexistent entities can be the objects of meaningful speech and thought. However, it seems to me much harder to suppose that I can be *aware* of a nonexistent thing than to suppose that I can *know* propositions about a nonexistent thing. Consider two of the most prominent theories of discourse about nonexistent objects: the theory that such objects are *possible objects*, and the theory that they are *abstract objects*.[35] While I might be able to think and speak about possible objects and abstract objects, I do not see how I could be *aware* of either, because awareness requires the presence (in some sense) of the object of awareness. The object must be at least a part-cause of my awareness of it. But merely possible or abstract objects cannot do this.

An alternative possibility is that God does not passively experience history, but actively creates it. On this view, God experiences all moments of time with qualitative presentness, but God's experience is not *derived* from what happens in time, as our experiences are. On the contrary, history plays out as it does *because* God experiences it like this. In other words, the normal causative relation between event and experiencer is reversed. I see the tree fall because the tree falls; the tree falls because God perceives it to fall.[36] It could therefore be that God is aware of what will happen at every point in history without all of those events needing to exist (yet).

35. For fictionalism, see Lewis, "Truth in Fiction." For different versions of abstractism, see Kripke, "Vacuous Names"; Van Inwagen, "Creatures of Fiction"; Parsons, *Non-existent Objects*; Orlando, "Fictional Names." For an alternative approach, see Barker, "Expressivism."

36. I should stress that, despite the similar language, this is not Berkeleyan idealism. I am not suggesting that the tree or its falling *consist* of God's (or anyone else's) perceptions of them.

Such a view seems to me to be coherent. It requires that one conceive of the whole of history as preordained by God (or timelessly ordained—since we are considering only subjective atemporalism, all of this is consistent with God's being objectively either temporal or atemporal). Theological predestination is a view with both a long tradition within Christianity and an equally long history of debate about the problems it raises, which I am not going to consider here. For our purposes, it suffices to note that if one supposes that all events are reflections of the divine will, and if propositions about what God wills have truth-values, then all temporal propositions have truth-values. For example, if it is true that God eternally wills that I eat porridge for breakfast on Thursday, then it is true even now on Wednesday that I will eat porridge for breakfast on Thursday. And the proposition "I eat porridge on Thursday" is timelessly true. But that is simply the same thing as there being an objective fact of the matter about what happens on Thursday, even though it is in the future; and that, surely, is the same thing as that event existing.

I conclude, then, that premise (2) is true as well. It follows that, given basic Christian commitments, if God is objectively atemporal then God is subjectively atemporal, a tenseless ontology of time is true, and four-dimensionalism is true.[37]

In what follows, then, and particularly over the next two chapters, I shall for the most part assume the truth of these theories, though I shall sometimes consider endurantist alternatives. Also, when speaking of atemporality in relation to things other than God, I shall generally mean objective atemporality unless otherwise specified.

The possibility of atemporal objects

Are non-abstract atemporal objects, other than God, possible? There seems to me to be no obvious barrier to the theoretical possibility of subjectively atemporal beings, even if one has to turn to either science fiction or miracles to conceive of them. The possibility of objectively atemporal beings, though, is more problematic, especially if we are thinking (as we are) about particulars rather than universals. Could there be a *particular* entity, which is not a universal, but that is objectively atemporal?

---

37. R. Keith Loftin and R. T. Mullins, "Physicalism," argue that Christianity requires endurantism. If that is so, and if the argument I have just given is correct, then divine atemporality is incompatible with Christianity. And indeed Mullins has argued at length (*End*) against divine atemporality. I consider Loftin's and Mullins' argument in chapter 7 below, however, where I argue that it is unsuccessful.

What would such an entity be like? We might instinctively imagine it as frozen in time, statue-like—but of course a frozen object is not atemporal; it is merely unchanging. A closer analogy would be a photon. The faster an object travels from one point to another, the more slowly time passes for that object relative to other objects. As it approaches the speed of light, the amount of time spent on the journey approaches zero. So from our point of view, a photon takes eight minutes to travel from the sun to the earth; but no time at all passes "for" the photon.

Still, this is not really atemporality. The photon still has temporal relations with other things, in the sense that its leaving the sun is simultaneous (for some observer) with other events, such as the observer's observing it leave; and its arriving at the earth is simultaneous (for that same observer) with other events again, such as the observer's observing it arrive. It is tempting to try to imagine a photon that is forever voyaging, never beginning or ending its journey, passing through the whole of time without its personal clock advancing by a single second. But the finite nature of time itself still undermines such a thought experiment as an example of real objective atemporality.

Moreover, the special theory of relativity tells us that space and time are intimately connected, such that they are really elements of the same thing, spacetime. It would seem, then, that there could not be an objectively atemporal being that is located in space.[38] But perhaps this is only true for the universe as we know it. We might imagine different universes that follow exotic laws of physics, where spacetime as we know it does not exist, but something analogous to space does, such that objects in that universe can have internal structure and relations of some kind to each other, but these relations are not temporal in any sense, and perhaps not spatial either in any sense that we would recognize. Such a universe would clearly be so wildly unlike our own that we cannot really imagine it, but I do not see any obvious incoherence in the concept.[39]

As a partial analogy, imagine a "Flatland" universe where there are only two spatial dimensions, populated by Euclidean geometrical shapes. Such a universe would clearly be very unlike our own, but it does not seem

38. Robert Coburn states that "it is logically impossible that a non-temporal thing should possess spatial characteristics" ("Professor Malcolm," 154)—an extremely strong assertion for which he gives no argument.

39. Hud Hudson briefly floats the possibility of "a spatial-only (that is, non-temporal) world" (Fall, 83), but does not pursue the idea further. An alternative idea is that it is not a necessary feature of bodies that they be located in space. If this is so, there could be a universe that is physical, or at least bodily, without being spatial. And if that is so then one can deny that heaven is spatial without having to deny that the blessed are embodied. On this, see Davis, "Paradise . . . Lost?"

inherently incoherent, and it seems that it would be meaningful to talk about different entities in that universe, their relations to each other, their internal structures, and so on. That would be so even if this universe had no time either. What we are envisaging now would not be simply our universe with one dimension removed—it might have entirely different dimensions—but, by analogy, it could still have inhabitants with various properties.

So we have the concept of a different universe with different laws of physics, such that it can contain objects that are differentiated from each other, and that can contain internal structure (like our own), but where these objects do not exist in spacetime but rather in an alternative sort of structure that is wholly atemporal. Given this, could any of these objects be persons?

Answering that question fully would require a clear theory of person-hood, which is beyond the scope of this work. But we can appeal here to conceptions of God within the tradition of classical theism. For example, according to the Christian doctrine of the Trinity, God is three persons; there is thus distinction (if not division) within the atemporal God. According to scholastic philosophy, there exist within God an infinite number of ideas of creatures, both actual and possible; there is thus multiplicity of a sort within the atemporal God, despite the divine simplicity. And according to Calvinist theology, it is possible not merely to distinguish between the divine decrees but to order them, so that we can say that although God's decision to do x does not temporally precede God's decision to do y, it does nevertheless precede it in a non-temporal way.[40] God's desire to perform x is more fundamental to the divine nature than God's desire to perform y, perhaps, which God does only in order to bring about x. So there could be *sequence* within an atemporal being. And if such things are possible at all, I do not see why they could not be possible for an atemporal non-divine being.

Still, there is more to personhood than this. Suppose we narrow our question a little and ask whether atemporal entities could be *conscious*. In his discussion of whether God could be both a person and atemporal, William Lane Craig argues that (a) knowledge does not require time, and (b) consciousness should be understood as knowledge of a certain kind.[41] But

---

40. This view, that one divine decree can "precede" another, underlies the debates in early modern Calvinism about what order the decrees should be in. This was at the heart of the Amyraldian controversy, for example: Moïse Amyraut held that the decree to save precedes the decree to elect some people rather than others. Other Calvinists held that the decree to elect precedes the decree to save. For more analysis of this, see Crisp, *Deviant Calvinism*, 184–88.

41. Craig, "Divine Timelessness," 112–13. Although I argue here that Craig leaves

while I think (a) is correct, I am not so sure about (b). I would prefer to say that consciousness requires *phenomenal consciousness*, meaning experiences that have a quality of "what it is like-ness." So, for example, a camera can record images, but the camera (presumably) does not experience this process: there is a sense in which it perceives things, but it would be meaningless to ask what it is *like* for the camera to do so. Experiences of perceptual consciousness include immediate and primitive objects of sense perception, but they also include introspective experiences (thinking about things) and also the significance, to the observer, of what is perceived or introspected.[42]

However, philosophers and psychologists alike disagree about the nature of perceptual consciousness and its grounds. A common notion is that consciousness is extremely closely related to intentionality, that is, the property of being *about* something. The term was coined in the nineteenth century by Franz Brentano, who also gave his name to "Brentano's thesis," the claim that all conscious states are intentional states. That is, to be conscious at all is to be conscious *of something*.[43] Philosophers remain divided about whether this thesis is true, with focus particularly on the status of experiences such as pain, which may or may not be representative.[44] Even among those who accept Brentano's thesis, there is disagreement over whether intentionality or consciousness is the more basic feature, with some grounding consciousness in intentionality and others grounding intentionality in consciousness.[45]

What matters for our purposes is that whatever position one takes on the nature of consciousness and its relation to intentionality, neither time nor space seems to be a conceptual requirement. The nature of intentionality itself is controversial, but it is usually taken to involve two relations (either both of them or just one, depending on the analysis): *representation*

---

too much unsaid about consciousness, I think that most of his arguments in this paper are correct. In particular, he is right to identify most criticisms of the notion of atemporal personhood, such as Coburn, "Professor Malcolm," 155, as relying on assertion more than argument. Although Craig's focus is the concept of God, most of what he says is equally applicable to non-divine atemporal persons.

42. Mark Rowlands gives the example of seeing Muhammad Ali at an airport: "believe me, this was an experience which very definitely had a phenomenal character, one which could not be reduced to the aggregation of significances of patches of colour, shape, contours, and the like" (*Consciousness*, 2).

43. Rowlands, *Consciousness*, 198. The claim long predates Brentano, though. Nicolas Malebranche, for example, made the very similar claim that "to see nothing, not to see anything, is not to see at all" (*Three Letters*, I in *Oeuvres Complètes*, VI 202).

44. Rowlands, *Consciousness*, 198–201.

45. Chalmers, *Character*, 339–41.

and *causation*. Plausibly, both are required. Consider a painting of a vase of flowers. If the painting is truly "of" the flowers, then it must represent the flowers; and there must be a causal story in which the flowers are a part-cause of the painting. For example, the painting may *resemble* the flowers, and the artist may have been looking at them as she painted. Remove either of these elements, and the painting is not really "of" the flowers at all. A painting that resembles some object by pure chance is not a painting of that object, and a painting that does not represent its supposed object *at all* is not a painting of it either.[46]

Applying this to mental intentionality, we can say that my thought is "of" its object if (a) it represents that object in some way, and (b) the object is in some way a cause of my thought. But neither of these requires temporality. A proposition is atemporal, but it represents facts about the world. One common theory of representation is that of "mirroring": on this account, A represents B if and only if the structure of A is sufficiently similar to that of B. It is easy to see how this applies to pictorial representation, and one can apply it to linguistic representation too if one assumes that the grammatical structure of sentences mirrors the relations between the things to which they refer. In our imagined world of quasi-space without time, objects can have quasi-spatial structures, so they could certainly represent each other (or indeed temporal objects too).

What about causation? Here, things seem trickier: in what sense could an atemporal object be the cause of something else, or be an effect of an exterior cause?

Atemporality and causation

Once again, classical theism may seem to offer a resolution. The classical theist can point to God as an atemporal cause of temporal things, but again this has to be accompanied by the caveat that God is unlike created things. God may act causally upon other things in a way that differs from creaturely causation. And the very notion of atemporal divine causation is itself obscure, to the extent that its difficulty is one of the motivating factors behind the notion of divine sempiternity as an alternative to atemporality.

But it is worth taking a step back, and noting that causation *in general* is obscure. Phil Dowe, in a helpful discussion of the ways in which

46. It is important to recognize that although "representation" may involve pictorial *resemblance*, it does not have to do so. A written description of an event represents that event, but it does not resemble it. Similarly, an abstract painting may represent something without resembling it.

philosophers have approached the topic, distinguishes between two quite distinct kinds of analysis: "conceptual" and "empirical":

> [C]onceptual analysis is a meaning analysis that begins with our everyday, common sense understanding of the relevant concept. That is, the way in which we commonly speak and think provides the primary data for the analysis. . . . On the other hand, empirical analysis seeks to establish what causation in fact is in the actual world. Empirical analysis aims to map the objective world, not our concepts. Such an analysis can only proceed a posteriori.[47]

Some of the most influential philosophical accounts of causation fall, broadly, into Dowe's category of "conceptual analysis." Two of the most important theories of recent decades—David Lewis' counterfactual theory and James Woodward's interventionist theory—can be understood in this way. For Lewis, to say that X causes Y is to say that (very simplistically), if X had not happened, Y would not have happened.[48] But even if we accept this theory, it tells us only the circumstances under which we do (or, perhaps, under which we *should*) say that X is the cause of Y. It tells us nothing about how, or why, X actually causes Y.

Something similar can be said of the second major influential contemporary account of causation, the "interventionist" theory introduced by James Woodward in his *Making Things Happen*. In that book, Woodward attempts to capture the circumstances under which we say that one thing causes another, both in ordinary speech and in scientific description. He distances himself from Dowe's "conceptual analysis" category by pointing out that his concern does go beyond merely analyzing words: he also analyzes *practices*, particularly in scientific experimentation, and his account is also intended to be normative, in that it does not merely describe how people talk and act but also prescribes how they *should* act, again particularly in designing scientific experiments.[49] There is thus a pragmatic element to Woodward's account that is lacking in Lewis'. But like Lewis, Woodward does not seek to describe (in Dowe's words) "what causation in fact is." Woodward thinks (again to put it very simplistically) that to say that X causes Y is to say that there is a possible intervention upon X that changes Y.

47. Dowe, *Physical Causation*, 2–3.
48. Lewis, "Causation."
49. Woodward, *Making Things Happen*, 7–8.

Woodward defines a total cause (or TC) like this: "X is a total cause of Y if and only if there is a possible intervention on X that will change Y or the probability distribution of Y."[50] And he goes on to point out:

> the kind of realism that follows from this way of viewing matters is metaphysically modest and noncommittal. It requires only that there be facts of the matter, independent of facts about human abilities and psychology, about which counterfactual claims about the outcome of hypothetical experiments are true or false and about whether a correlation between C and E reflects a causal relationship between C and E or not. Beyond this, it commits us to no particular metaphysical picture of the "truth makers" for causal claims.[51]

Suppose we accept one of these accounts of causation, or any other which falls into the "conceptual analysis" category. Could an atemporal thing be a cause? Could it be an effect? That will depend on the account. One might, for example, construct an account of causation that dictates that the cause temporally precede its effect. Indeed, in early modern times, it was widely assumed that contiguity in both space *and* time was, analytically, part of the very concept of causation.[52] That would rule out both causation at a distance (unless cause and effect were linked by a chain of intervening mediate causes) and atemporal causes or effects. But more recent conceptual analyses of causation have been more modest in their spatiotemporal demands. This is, in part, a result of our increased scientific understanding of reality. Newton's theory of gravity led to a general acceptance of the possibility of action at a distance.[53] Later, scientists observed apparent action at a distance in the quantum realm, as in the Einstein-Podolsky-Rosen/Bohm experiment.[54] Most, though not all, theorists think that quantum mechanics does involve causation at a distance.[55] Even if they are wrong, the old assumption

50. Woodward, *Making Things Happen*, 51.

51. Woodward, *Making Things Happen*, 121–22; see also Woodward, "Interventionism," for a much more extended discussion of his metaphysical agnosticism.

52. Thus, for example, Hume listed spatiotemporal contiguity as the very first element of the concept of causation: "I find in the first place, that whatever objects are consider'd as causes or effects, are *contiguous*; and that nothing can operate in a time or place, which is ever so little remov'd from those of its existence. . . . We may therefore consider the relation of CONTIGUITY as essential to that of causation . . ." (*Treatise*, I.3.ii, p. 54).

53. Woodward, *Making Things Happen*, 149.

54. Bohm, *Quantum Theory*.

55. For example, Berkovitz, "Aspects of Quantum Non-Locality"; Maudlin, *Quantum Nonlocality*.

that spatial contiguity is, *analytically*, part of the concept of causation has certainly been undermined.

If spatial contiguity is no longer essential for causation, what of temporal contiguity? One argument for the necessity of temporal contiguity is that if there were a time-gap between the cause and its effect, something might in theory intervene during that gap to prevent the effect from occurring.[56] But any general causal statement contains at least an implicit clause along the lines of "assuming nothing intervenes"—e.g., throwing a brick at a window will cause it to smash *if* nothing deflects the flight of the brick. Similarly, suppose that events of type F cause events of type G with a time delay, and that a is an event of type F. The occurrence of a is sufficient to cause b—an event of type G—shortly afterwards. That is consistent with supposing that b's occurrence is dependent upon nothing occurring after a to block it, because when we say that "occurrence of a is sufficient to cause b" there is an implicit "assuming nothing intervenes to prevent it."

Perhaps unsurprisingly, given these considerations, philosophers have in recent years been inclined to send temporal contiguity the way of spatial contiguity. Indeed, Bertrand Russell attacked as incoherent the very *possibility* of temporal contiguity between cause and effect.[57] Others have been less confident, preferring to argue that causation is irreducible to other properties (including temporal contiguity).[58] Even among those who do not regard causation as irreducible, analytic theories tend towards neutrality on spatiotemporal relationships. Take the interventionist theory, for example. As Woodward points out, on his theory,

> it does not follow from the fact that a relationship is exploitable for purposes of manipulation that it must satisfy a spatiotemporal locality or continuity constraint . . . when spatiotemporal continuity or contiguity are absent but the relationship nonetheless supports manipulation, we may legitimately take it to be causal.[59]

That is, all that is needed for X to be a cause of Y is that there be a possible manipulation of X that would change Y. It is not necessary for X to be spatially or temporally adjacent to Y, or to be linked to it by a spatiotemporal chain. Why, then, must X or Y be temporal at all?

56. Chakravartty, "Causal Realism," 11–12.

57. Russell, *Mysticism*, 174–201.

58. E.g., Swinburne, "Irreducibility." The irreducibility of causation is also implied by the attempt by some philosophers to construct a metaphysics reducible to causal powers alone—e.g., Marmodoro, "Individuation."

59. Woodward, *Making Things Happen*, 148.

One apparent problem here is that atemporal things cannot change. Thus, suppose we have some atemporal object X. There is no possible intervention that anyone can perform on X to change it. Or, if X is temporal and Y is atemporal, we may perform interventions on X but the atemporal Y will not change as a result. The solution is to think modally, in terms of counterfactual interventions: if an intervention *had been* performed on the temporal X, then the atemporal Y would have been different, and similarly for an atemporal X and a temporal Y.[60] Indeed, talk of "performing interventions" upon X can be seen as equivalent to talk of counterfactuals concerning how X *might have been*, or how it is in different possible worlds.

So a conceptual analysis of causation like Woodward's seems to leave open the possibility that atemporal objects might be causally related, both to each other and to temporal things. This would suggest, among other things, that an atemporal being could be said to *act*, which at least some commentators have argued is essential if that being can be said to be alive.[61] They might even be acted upon. One puzzle that emerges from this is that one might have a temporal cause of an atemporal effect, which seems on the face of it a little like backward causation. However, an atemporal effect would of course not *precede* its cause—and indeed, if we accept the existence of (say) propositions as atemporal objects, they are affected by temporal events. For example, the proposition "Napoleon is defeated at Waterloo," though about a temporal event, is itself atemporal, and its truth is dependent upon a temporal event.

Conclusion

We are now in a position to say that, if objectively atemporal objects are possible, there is no reason in principle why atemporal persons could not be possible. They could meaningfully be said to be conscious, and to have thoughts that are genuinely of other things. Obviously an atemporal conscious being would be conscious in a very different way from us: it could not think discursively, for one thing, passing from thought to thought as we do.[62] It could, perhaps, have dispositions, if those are understood modally:

60. Woodward frames his theory in counterfactual terms—see *Making Things Happen*, 187–88. He distinguishes his account from Lewis' by noting that it sets more stringent conditions on causation: it is not enough for causation to say that if X had not occurred Y would not have done so (pp. 213–14).

61. For example, Kneale, "Time and Eternity," 99.

62. Ted Chiang's "heptapods," mentioned earlier as fictional examples of subjectively atemporal beings (n. 33), are again suggestive. Their written language is non-sequential, with symbols for different words being written over each other at the same time,

that is, one might say that it could be disposed to exist in a certain state giv-en certain conditions, whether or not those conditions actually obtain.[63] So one might be able to construct an account of atemporal beliefs, for example, if one thinks that beliefs are dispositions. One might even be able to say that the atemporal conscious being has some beliefs in virtue of having others.

The question now is whether a person who is temporal could *become* atemporal. Such a possibility may seem unpromising, but we shall consider it in the next chapter.

---

reflecting the fact that although they can combine concepts, they do so without any order. As the story makes clear, such a language would be wholly alien to us, but need not be incoherent.

63. See Craig, "Divine Timelessness," 112.

3 _____

Becoming Atemporal

A famous passage in the Babylonian Talmud tells of how Elisha ben Abuyah fell into heresy after seeing a vision of the angelic being Metatron:

> He saw that permission was granted to Metatron to sit and write down the merits of Israel. Said he: It is taught as a tradition that on high there is no sitting and no emulation, and no back, and no weariness. Perhaps,—God forfend!—there are two divinities![1]

Elisha was led to entertain this blasphemous thought by the fact that Metatron appeared to enjoy privileges granted to God alone, such as sitting down rather than standing in attendance. Some other sources identify Metatron with Enoch, who according to Gen 5:24 "walked with God; then he was no more, because God took him" (NRSV). In other words, Enoch was a normal human being, but instead of dying he was taken by God, and, so later sources claim, transformed into the quasi-divine Metatron.[2] Suppose

---

1. Hagigah 15.1, in Rabbinowitz and Epstein, *Ta'anith* (no page numbers).

2. The most famous passage identifying Metatron with Enoch is in 3 Enoch 4. The process by which he was transformed and glorified is described in chapters 6–15. In 3 En. 12.5 Metatron is given the title of "lesser God." On Metatron and his relation to the divine in Jewish literature, see Abrams, "Boundaries." On the identification of Enoch with Metatron, see Idel, "Enoch Is Metatron." However, exactly when and where this identification was made is a matter of controversy. Paz, "Metatron Is Not Enoch," argues that Enoch was first identified with Metatron as late as the eighth century CE. Schäfer, *Jewish Jesus*, 103–49 also gives a relatively late date to 3 Enoch, arguing that the Metatron/Enoch tradition arose as a response to post-Chalcedonian Christian beliefs about Jesus.

we imagine that one of the divine properties Metatron exemplifies is objective atemporality.[3] Enoch, of course, is temporal. Can we make sense of the idea that Enoch becomes Metatron?

On the face of it, such a scenario seems incoherent. If Enoch becomes Metatron, then Metatron has a temporal relation with Enoch, since he comes after Enoch. But if Metatron is objectively atemporal, this by definition is impossible. Moreover, Enoch has, during his lifetime, all sorts of temporal relations with other persons and objects. If Metatron used to be Enoch, then Metatron inherits versions of those relations. For example, Enoch (for part of his life) has the property of existing at the same time as Methuselah. If Metatron straightforwardly *is* Enoch then he has the property of *having* existed at the same time as Methuselah, and that would seem to rule out Metatron's being atemporal.

So we can express this basic problem like this:

(1) If a temporal being is to become an atemporal being, it must change from being temporal to being atemporal.

(2) It is impossible for a being to change from being temporal to being atemporal.

(3) Therefore, it is impossible for a temporal being to become an atemporal being.

However, such a conclusion would be premature. Let us grant (1) for the sake of argument.[4] (2) is where we will direct our attention.

---

3. Such a view is of course alien to the ancient and medieval Jewish traditions about Metatron. I do not pretend to be articulating what was actually believed about Metatron, merely using the name for this thought experiment.

4. (1) could be questioned in the following way: if one thinks that God is atemporal, and accepts the doctrine of incarnation, then one is committed to thinking that the Son is an atemporal person who becomes a temporal person, namely Jesus. But on the traditional understanding of incarnation, the Son does not literally change into Jesus. God cannot change at all, according to classical theism. Rather, the Son "assumes," or is united to, a human body and soul (his "human nature," understood as referring to a concrete particular), in virtue of which he can legitimately be called human. So here we have a case of an atemporal person becoming a temporal person, but without changing from being atemporal to being temporal. And if that is so, then a change in the other direction—from temporal to atemporal—should be coherent too. However, since this move is made possible only by distinguishing between the two natures in Christ, it does not really provide a good parallel to our question. Enoch does not acquire Metatron as a new additional nature: he is supposed to *become* Metatron. In the context of our discussion, then, we shall accept (1). For more on this understanding of incarnation, see below in the conclusion.

Personal timelines

To begin with, consider the distinction between different personal time-lines. Usually, events that are ordered in a certain way on one person's time-line are ordered similarly on another person's timeline. For example, if I have cereal for breakfast and sandwiches for lunch, the lunch is later on my personal timeline than the breakfast; and if you are watching me both times, the lunch will be later on your personal timeline as well. But it is possible to imagine scenarios where the same events might be ordered differently on different timelines—most obviously, in thought experiments involving time travel. If Marty practices the guitar in the morning, and then travels back in time thirty years and attends a school ball with his parents, then on his parents' timelines, his attending the ball precedes his practicing the guitar. But on his personal timeline, his practicing the guitar precedes his attending the ball. So the temporal relations that hold between these different events on one timeline do not hold between them on others, even though they are exactly the same events.[5]

If two events can, at least in theory, hold contradictory temporal relations to each other when considered under different timelines, perhaps it could also be the case that they hold temporal relations to each other on one timeline and no temporal relations to each other on another. Consider an event in Enoch's life, such as becoming the father of Methuselah, and an event in Metatron's life, such as writing down the merits of Israel. If Metatron is atemporal, then writing down the merits of Israel occurs at no time, and has no temporal relations with any other event. It is an "event" only in a loose sense of the word. It does not occur after (or before) Enoch's becoming the father of Methuselah. All of this could be true in the timelines of everyone other than Enoch—here using the word "timeline" loosely as well, because Metatron's writing down the merits of Israel is not a temporal event and therefore cannot really be said to be "on" anyone else's timeline at all, strictly speaking. But from the point of view of anyone else, Metatron's acts would be atemporal. However, all of this could be consistent with its being the case that on the personal timeline of Enoch/Metatron, becoming the father of Methuselah does precede writing down the merits of Israel. From Enoch's perspective, he performs all the acts of his earthly life, and then is taken into heaven, and then performs acts that are atemporal on the public timeline. From the perspective of anyone else, Metatron's acts are genuinely atemporal and have no temporal relations with anything—just as, from the

---

5. Brian Leftow makes use of this idea in constructing a time travel parallel to the Trinity—see Leftow, "Latin Trinity."

perspective of anyone other than Marty, his attending the school ball really does precede his practicing the guitar.

In this scenario, Enoch lives his life in the usual way, and then ceases to exist temporally. To an onlooker, perhaps he would simply vanish.[6] Also, to an onlooker, it would be true at every point in history that Metatron timelessly exists—though it would of course be true at no point in history that Metatron exists *then*. Enoch would be truly temporal, and Metatron would be truly atemporal. But Metatron would timelessly experience his acts, such as writing down the merits of Israel, as having occurred *after* his acts as Enoch, such as becoming the father of Methuselah.

But is even this coherent? One might say that if Metatron's existence is truly atemporal, then even *from his point of view* it could not come after anything else. If it did, Metatron's existence would have to have a beginning, at least from Metatron's point of view; but this is inconsistent with its being atemporal. I am not sure that this objection holds. As long as Metatron's existence is atemporal from the perspective of everyone else's timeline, it is not incorrect to say that Metatron is atemporal (just as it is not incorrect to say that Marty attends the ball before practicing the guitar). The scenario sketched above therefore does seem to me to offer a coherent picture of how a temporal person could genuinely become an atemporal one.

But is a stronger scenario possible, in which Enoch becomes Metatron and Metatron is atemporal on *all* timelines, including his own? That seems to be ruled out by the objection mentioned above. However, we may be able to find a way to allow it if we consider the structure of temporal relations.

Relations

David Vander Laan observes:

> The idea of a future atemporal state is incoherent. To be in an atemporal state is to lack temporal properties and relations. *Being later than* is a temporal relation, so no one in an atemporal state exists later than any temporal event.[7]

Vander Laan's objection rests upon a typically modern conception of relations.[8] On this view, relations are multi-place predicates (or, more ac-

---

6. According to 3 En. 6.1, he was taken up to heaven in a fiery chariot pulled by fiery horses, which presumably reflects an assumption that heaven is a physical location that can be reached by local motion alone.

7. Vander Laan, "Paradox," 159.

8. On the development of this view of relations, see Dipert, "Peirce, Frege."

curately, they are *expressed by* multi-place predicates). So, for example, "is bigger than" is a two-place predicate: two noun phrases need to be added to it to yield a meaningful sentence. This suggests a picture of relations as existing "outside" their relata, linking them together like chains strung from one subject to another. To put it rather crudely, if "is bigger than" is a two-place predicate expressing a relation that holds between x and y, then the "biggerthanness" is something distinct from both x and y and their monadic predicates, since it inheres in neither of them exclusively. And since it seems metaphysically extravagant to believe in real entities linking related objects in this way, it is common today to assume that relations are really abstractions. If x is bigger than y, then the two-place predicate "is bigger than" holds between them—but this is just a roundabout way of saying "x is size $s1$, and y is size $s2$." There isn't really a distinct entity hovering between them that corresponds to "is bigger than."

A corollary of this view of relations is that if x is related in some way to y, then y is related conversely to x. For example, if x is bigger than y, then y is smaller than x. This follows because, clearly, if a multi-place predicate is to express anything meaningful, all of its places must be filled. Applying this to our problem, if x is earlier than y, then y is later than x. So if Enoch is earlier (on his timeline) than Metatron, then Metatron is later (on that timeline) than Enoch. And if that is so, then Metatron is not truly atemporal.

But this is not the only possible way of conceiving of relations. Scholastic philosophers recognized another, in a way that built upon Aristotelian metaphysics. A key assumption in this metaphysics is that an accident cannot inhere in more than one subject. For these thinkers, consequently, multi-place predicates can have only "intellectual" existence—that is, they are mental abstractions that we imaginatively project upon external objects, but they have no real existence in them.[9] However, relations can also be conceived as properties inhering in *single* subjects, which can be expressed by *single*-place predicates. Suppose, for example, that Ernie is five feet tall and Bert is six feet tall. A modern philosopher might say that the relation "is shorter than" holds between Ernie and Bert, and that the relation "is taller than" holds between Bert and Ernie. She might also observe that these relations are merely abstracta. A scholastic philosopher would agree that the multi-place predicate "is shorter than" is an abstraction (or, in scholastic jargon, has a purely intellectual reality)—but would *also* hold that Ernie *really* has the monadic property of "being shorter than Bert," and Bert *really* has the monadic property of "being shorter than Ernie." So each has his

9. Peter Aureoli makes this position explicit. See Henninger, *Relations*, 153–54.

own property that "points to" or refers to the other.[10] For some scholastic philosophers, notably Duns Scotus, these properties are distinct from, but based upon, non-relational properties.[11] So Bert has the property of being six feet tall, and *also* the property of being taller than Ernie, but he has the latter property partly in virtue of having the former. Bert's height (a non-relational property) is the *foundation* for his property of being taller than Ernie (a relational property). Others, notably Henry of Ghent, are more metaphysically parsimonious. For Henry, the relational property is *intentionally* distinct from its foundation (we can distinguish between Bert's height and his being taller than Ernie) but it is not *really* distinct (it is not a property *in him* distinct from his height).[12] On this view, an object can become really related to something else without undergoing any change in itself: if Ernie grows taller than Bert, then Bert really does acquire the relational property of being shorter than Ernie, but this is not a real change in Bert because this "new" relational property is not something distinct from his height. Rather, the change in Ernie is sufficient to give Bert's height a different relational value.

Either way, though, it should be clear that this is, broadly, a realist approach to relations. The property of being taller than Ernie is a real relational property that Bert actually has. It is not simply an idea in the mind of some third-party observer, as multi-place predicates are. This is one of the points at which Aristotelian metaphysics slots neatly into Christian theology. The standard western view of the Trinity was (and remains) that the persons of the Trinity are distinguished from each other solely by their mutual relations.[13] As Gregory of Nazianzus, one of the chief architects of this view, reasoned, a name such as "Father" cannot represent an essence (because then each person would have a different essence, destroying the unity of the Trinity); but it cannot represent an action either (because then each person would be simply a different act of the same individual, leading to modalism); it therefore represents a relation.[14] For Thomas Aquinas, similarly, the divine persons are relations.[15] Such a view requires realism about relations: they are not purely mental beings, because if they were, they could

---

10. On this, see Henninger, *Relations*, 4–6.

11. Henninger, *Relations*, 71–78.

12. Henninger, *Relations*, 54–55. Whether Thomas Aquinas also holds this view is unclear as he does not explicitly consider it. See *Relations*, 29–31.

13. On the emergence of this idea in Cappadocian theology, see White, *The Trinity*, 138–53. For a recent defense of this view, see Nicolas, *Catholic Dogmatic Theology*, 172–99.

14. *Theological Orations*, III.16, in Gregory of Nazianzus, *God and Christ*, 83–84.

15. Aquinas, *ST*, I q. 40 a. 1, vol. 2, p. 153.

not constitute the distinctions between the persons of the Trinity. Anyone wanting to adhere to this traditional understanding of the Trinity as based on the mutual relations of the persons, then, will need to be a realist about relations in some way.[16]

Nonetheless, on the scholastic view, not all relations are real. Some relational properties themselves have only intellectual existence—that is, they exist only in the mind. Thomas Aquinas, whose views on this are typical, points out that "since relation has two extremes, it happens in three ways that a relation is real or logical."[17] If Ernie has relational property R1, and Bert has relational property R2, it could be that (1) R1 and R2 are both only intellectual properties, that (2) both of them are real properties, or that (3) one is real and the other only intellectual. For (1), Aquinas gives the example of when we compare an object to itself, since we imagine it as two-fold when it is really only a single thing. For (2), he gives the example of relations of quantity, as when one object is taller than another, and also causation.

(3) is most relevant to our purposes. These are "non-mutual" relations, where one of the related things really bears a relation to the other, but not vice versa. Aquinas gives the example of perception and knowledge. If I see a tree, or think about a tree, I have the relational property "thinking about the tree." This is a property that I really have. But although the tree can be said to have the property "being thought about by me," that is not a property that the tree itself really has. It is an intellectual property, or a "relation only in idea," that is, something we falsely ascribe to the tree.[18]

Armed with this metaphysics of relations, Aquinas and other scholastic philosophers could explain how God relates to creatures when God is not supposed to have any accidental properties, or indeed any properties that require other things to exist. How, for example, can God properly be called "Lord"—a term that implies the existence of something over which God *is* Lord, and which is therefore inherently relational—if God has no dependencies upon anything else? The answer is that all relations between

16. Thus, even William Ockham, who holds that as a general rule relations are only intellectual beings, still admits that revelation tells us that in at least some cases—notably the Trinity, the incarnation, and the Eucharist—they have extra-mental reality. See Henninger, *Relations*, 140–45.

17. Aquinas, *ST*, I q. 13 a. 7, vol. 1, p. 165.

18. Aquinas also gives a second kind of example, which is rather more puzzling: an animal moves to the left of a column, and as a result the animal really has the property of "being to the left of the column" but the column does not have the property of "being to the right of the animal." Presumably the reasoning here is that since the column does not move, there is no real change in it, and therefore it cannot acquire a real relational property—for Aquinas thinks that a thing cannot change unless there is a change *in* that thing. On this, see Henninger, *Relations*, 21.

God and creatures are real on the part of creatures, but not on the part of God:

> Since therefore God is outside the whole order of creation, and all creatures are ordered to Him, and not conversely, it is manifest that creatures are really related to God Himself; whereas in God there is no real relation to creatures, but a relation only in idea, inasmuch as creatures are referred to Him. Thus there is nothing to prevent these names which import relation to the creature from being predicated of God temporally, not by reason of any change in Him, but by reason of the change of the creature; as a column is on the right of an animal, without change in itself, but by change in the animal.[19]

So, for example, to say that God is Lord is to say that all creatures have the property of being properly subject to God. But God does not have any corresponding property that refers to creatures, because if that were so then either God would acquire that property after the point of creation, or God would necessarily create from all eternity, and neither of those is acceptable to classical theism.[20]

Notably, the same reasoning applies to the incarnation. For medieval theologians, when the divine Son becomes human, he "assumes" (or acquires) a human body and soul (the "human nature"). However, although the Son and the human nature are united more perfectly than any union found in nature, this union consists of relational properties only on the

---

19. Aquinas, *ST*, I q. 13 a. 7, vol. 1, pp. 166–67.

20. William Lane Craig describes this view as "prima-facie incredible," "startling," and "extraordinarily implausible" ("Tensed," 224, 225, 226), largely on the grounds that it is incoherent to suppose that there can be a real property in the object affected without there being a real property in the agent doing the affecting. Craig appeals, in particular, to a modal argument (p. 229): if all relations between God and creatures involve a property in the creatures but not in God, then God would have exactly the same properties in a universe where God created a different universe, or one where God created nothing at all. But this is inconsistent with the belief that God has genuine knowledge of and love for the creatures that are actually created. However, Craig's argument misunderstands Aquinas' position. Aquinas is not committed to the view that God has *no* properties that, in theory, could be different in a universe with different creatures. He is committed only to the view that whatever properties God has do not constitute foundations for relational properties. It would be consistent with this for Aquinas to hold that, in a universe where God created Bob, God has properties that differ from the properties God has in a universe where God created Bill instead. (All of this assumes that it makes sense to talk about God having different properties in different possible worlds, which Craig assumes is required by the belief that God knows, loves, etc. God's creatures, but which seems hard to reconcile with the view that God is a necessary being.)

part of the human nature. That is, the human nature has the property of "being hypostatically united to the divine Son," but the divine Son has no corresponding property of "having assumed the human nature" or anything like that. If we use such language of the Son, it should be understood as an abstraction or figure of speech. The Son cannot acquire such properties or indeed bear such properties to anything created, even his own human nature.

Suppose we accept a metaphysical account of relations along these lines. Could they be applied to Metatron? The conceptual distinction between x's relation to y (conceived as a property of x alone) and, conversely, y's relation to x (conceived as a property of y alone) allows us, at least in theory, to hold that one of them truly inheres in its subject and the other is a mental abstraction. So then, we could say that, on his personal timeline, Enoch really has the relational property of "being earlier than Metatron," but Metatron does not really have the relational property of "being later than Enoch."

A scholastic approach to relations certainly allows us to *say* this without any explicit incoherence. In standard predicate logic we might represent a temporal relation (or any other relation) with a two-place predicate, like this: Rab—where Rxy means x is temporally prior to y. On this logic, both a and b are temporally related to each other, because they are both terms of the same temporal relation. We don't even need to consider the converse of this relation (say Sxy, meaning x is temporally posterior to y) to know that both a and b exist in a temporal relation to each other.

But suppose we devise a new logic based on the scholastic approach. In this logic, we attempt to express only real properties. That means that all multi-place predicates are banned, because those are entities of reason alone. If we want to say that a is temporally prior to b, we cannot plug a and b into a two-place predicate. Instead we have to create a bespoke predicate specifically to express "being temporally prior to b," and plug just a into that. Call this relation Rb, so we can say Rba to express the proposition that a is temporally prior to b. Crucially, b itself is not a term in this formula. The relation Rb "points" to b, but it is a single-place predicate, applied to a alone. For all we know, b has no real relational predicates at all. We might, of course, create the relation Sa to express "being temporally posterior to a," and state Sab. Taken together, Rba and Sab express the same state of affairs that Rab expresses in ordinary predicate logic. But because it is now separated out into two statements, there is at least no logical contradiction in holding Rba to be true while not affirming, or even while denying, Sab.

I think that this is enough to show that the claim that temporal Enoch becomes atemporal Metatron is not inconsistent, in the sense that it can be stated without formal contradiction—and that might be all we need. However, we may still seek a *justification* for saying that, although Enoch has the property of temporally preceding Metatron, Metatron does not have the property of temporally succeeding Enoch.[21] What, to put it another way, are the truth-conditions for Enoch's really having the relation of preceding Metatron and Metatron's not really having the relation of succeeding Enoch? After all, in all other known cases of temporal relation, if a has the property of preceding b, b has the property of succeeding a. We are therefore surely entitled to ask what is different in this case.

One possible answer might use Aquinas' explanation of non-mutual relations. He holds that if x and y bear mutual relations to each other, this is because the foundations of those relations in both x and y must be of the same type.[22] For example, if Bert is taller than Ernie, and Ernie is shorter than Bert, in each case the relational property is based upon their height. Consequently, each one bears a real relation to the other. But if I know a tree, then this is, on Aquinas' view, through a non-material action on my part; but there is no corresponding non-material passion on the part of the tree. So I really have the relational property of "knowing the tree," but the tree's relational property of "being known by me" is an intellectual relation only, and not something that is really in the tree.[23] This explains why Aquinas thinks that all relations between God and creatures are non-mutual: God has no properties of the same kind as creatures' properties. So if a creature bears a certain relation to God on the basis of some property, God cannot bear a reciprocal relation back to the creature, because God cannot have any property of that type.

We might apply this to Enoch and Metatron. Enoch has the relational property of "being earlier than Metatron," which is founded upon the non-relational property of existing at time t.[24] But Metatron does not have the

21. This result is similar to the use of relative identity as a way of articulating the doctrines of the Trinity and the incarnation. As Peter Van Inwagen has shown, it is straightforward to formalize these doctrines using a logic of relative identity that results in no contradictions (Van Inwagen, "Not Three Gods"; "Not By Confusion"). As he also notes, though, such a strategy at best only shows that the doctrines need not involve formal contradiction (provided one accepts the logic of relative identity)—it does not show *how* they avoid contradiction ("Not By Confusion," 202).

22. *De Potentia*, q. 7 a. 10, in Aquinas, *Power of God*, 222–23; see Henninger, *Relations*, 34.

23. Henninger, *Relations*, 36.

24. I am aware that, plausibly, the property of existing at time t is itself relational. For the sake of simplicity I am ignoring this, but I see no reason why the foundation of a relational property could not itself be a relational property. For example, ratios are relations, but they can be compared to each other—e.g., the ratio 2:1 is equal to the ratio 4:2.

relational property of "being later than Enoch," because to have such a relational property he would have to have a temporal property, which he cannot do.

However, while this successfully explains why Metatron lacks the property of being later than Enoch, it leaves us in the dark about why Enoch has the property of being earlier than Metatron. This case does not really parallel that of the tree and the knower, because we can understand how it is possible for me to know a tree without the tree having any epistemic properties, but we cannot understand how it is possible for Enoch to be earlier than Metatron without Metatron having any temporal properties.

This does not mean, in itself, that it is not possible for Enoch to be earlier than Metatron without Metatron having any temporal possibilities, only that we cannot understand why and how it is so. That might be enough (some mystery, surely, is to be expected!). But such a conclusion does seem unsatisfying. However, we might, alternatively, construct an account in which Metatron's existence succeeds Enoch's, but in a non-temporal way.

Identity, temporal and atemporal

If one favors endurantism, then identity over time is irreducible; so plausibly one could say the same about identity across time and atemporality too. Although not couched in terms of endurantism and perdurantism, George Mavrodes gave an answer rather like this to the problem of how we could be identical with our future resurrected selves.[25] Mavrodes frames the problem in terms of the criteria for identity over time. The objector to the doctrine of resurrection, as he sees it, points out that whatever the criteria are for saying that a future person P2 is identical with a past person P1 (e.g., continuity of material composition), those criteria are not met by resurrected persons, and consequently they cannot be identical with earthly persons. Mavrodes' response is to reject the notion of criteria for identity over time at all. Rather, identity over time is a simple, unanalyzable concept. Consequently, the identity of the earthly person with the resurrected person could be an unanalyzable fact. It could be true that x, who lives now, is identical with y, who lives in the future, even though x and y have numerically distinct bodies. Any argument to the contrary, he suggests, will ultimately involve an appeal to some unanalyzable notion of identity—for example, it may be said that identity of personhood requires identity of bodies; but what makes a body at one time identical with a body at another time? Perhaps it has to be composed of the same particles, or have the same overall

25. Mavrodes, "Life Everlasting."

structure—but what makes a particle or a structure at one time identical with one at another?

More generally, Trenton Merricks questions the notion of there being *criteria* for identity over time at all. He observes that, if one rejects "criterialism," all kinds of possibilities are opened up:

> Can an object "jump" through time? Suppose I affirm that this is possible. One could, of course, deny this. But one could not pretend to defend this denial by arguing that objects which cease to exist entirely and then come back into existence cannot satisfy any reasonable criterion of identity over time. Nor can I defend my affirmation by suggesting a criterion that would make such jumping possible. I think these remarks about "jumping" through time illustrate a more general point. Because there are no criteria of identity, one may not build into one's thought experiments the claim that some criterion of identity has been satisfied (or violated), and then go on to conclude that identity over time has (or has not) been preserved.[26]

I am sympathetic to this view. An omnipotent God should be able to bring about any logically possible situation, and it certainly seems to me logically possible that a future resurrected person is identical to me. This is because I am by nature skeptical about metaphysical claims, such as claims about the criteria of identity over time. To insist that it is *logically impossible* that the future resurrected person is identical to the earthly me, I would need to be absolutely certain that (a) some relation (or relations) R fails to hold between the present and future persons, and that (b) this relation R really is essential to identity. But even if I could be certain of (a), which itself seems unlikely, I do not see how I could ever be certain of (b). So there seems to me to be no compelling reason to think that a scenario in which I—really *I*—awake on the day of judgment (despite having died a long time previously and not existed in the meantime) is logically impossible; and, consequently,

---

26. Merricks, "No Criteria," 120. For a more recent defense of this position, see Langford, "Anti-Criterialism." Langford points out that part of the anti-criterialist position is that exotic cases of identity over time are conceptually possible—for example, that where normally a cat persists from one moment to the next, there is a "weird possible world" in which it does not even though another cat, "biologically continuous" with the first, takes its place (p. 614). The ability of anti-criterialism to accommodate such possibilities may be an argument against it: how do we know that such things do not happen sometimes in the actual world, in which case, how can we be confident that any given thing has persisted? (Langford's answer is that it is simpler to suppose so—pp. 621–24). But this feature of anti-criterialism also makes it well suited for Christian eschatology.

there is no compelling reason to think that an omnipotent God could not bring it about.[27]

If this is so, we can apply the same reasoning to the case of Enoch and Metatron. Suppose we take an endurantist view, and hold that identity over time is basic and cannot be reduced to any other relation. Why not suppose that the same thing could hold for identity of a temporal object and an atemporal one? In the absence of any clear reason why Metatron *couldn't* be identical with Enoch, an omnipotent God could make it the case that he is.

But although this would allow us to say that Enoch and Metatron are the same person, it is hard to see how it could allow us to say that Enoch is *earlier* than Metatron. God cannot simply decree that he is, if this would be incoherent. Perdurantism, however, may give us a way forward. On this view, there *is* some criterion by which an object at one time is (or is not) identical with an object at another time, and if God is going to make Metatron identical with Enoch then God has to respect that criterion. As noted earlier, there are different varieties of perdurantism. At one extreme, a very loose stage theorist might hold that there is no real identity between the different stages of a persisting object at all, to the extent that there *is* no persisting object. Such a view would be radically problematic, since it would entail (among other things) that nobody could be justly praised or blamed for their past acts. At the other extreme, a worm theorist may hold that the different temporal parts of a single individual form a coherent, unified whole just as the different spatial parts of an organism do.

One common answer, at least among philosophers of religion, is to appeal to identity-making causative relations. On this view, what makes me-at-$t2$ identical with me-at-$t1$ is that me-at-$t1$ causes the existence of me-at-$t2$. Clearly, not all causal relations constitute identity. If I build a chair, the chair is not me. So philosophers taking this approach must set out what

---

27. Peter Van Inwagen argues otherwise. In response to Mavrodes, he suggests the scenario of a monastery that claims to possess an original autograph of St. Augustine, which was known to be destroyed in a fire. The monks claim that it was destroyed, but God has miraculously restored it. Van Inwagen writes: "Now suppose our monks were to reply by simply asserting that the manuscript now in their possession did know the impress of Augustine's hand; that it was a part of the furniture of the world when the Saint was alive; that when God recreated or restored it, He (as an indispensable component of accomplishing this task) saw to it that the object He produced had all these properties. I confess I should not know what to make of this. I should have to tell the monks that I did not see how what they believed could possibly be true" ("Possibility," 117). Van Inwagen's justification for this is that, while there may be unknowable mysteries concerning the divine nature, there cannot be concerning the survival conditions of manuscripts. And, by extension, the same thing applies to human beings. As should be clear, though, I do not think that we can be so confident about survival conditions. The monks' story does not seem to me to be *incoherent*, however unlikely it might be.

the *special* causal relations are that hold between an object at one moment and that same object at the next moment. If this can be done satisfactorily, though, one can simply envisage that these causal relations exist between my earthly body at the point of death and my heavenly body at the point of creation.

As I noted in the introduction, Dean Zimmerman and Kevin Corcoran both build upon earlier suggestions by John Hick and Peter Van Inwagen to suggest that God might cause the fission of the particles of my body at death—so that one set remains on earth in a dead state while the others live on in heaven.[28] Luckily for me, the second set of particles constitutes me, the same me who died. Why is this? Because the heavenly particles are not simply a new creation that God produces out of nothing. Rather, God brings it about that the new body is actually brought into existence by the old one, just as my body at each moment causes its successor to come into existence. In other words, rather than create the heavenly me directly, God gives my dying body the power to cause its heavenly duplicate to come into existence. Zimmerman dubs this the "falling elevator" model of resurrection,[29] because when it seems that all is lost, God whisks the dying person away to a new body in a new place.

Surely, one might say, a new copy of me is not identical with me. I can tolerate having my particles replaced gradually over a long period, but not all at once. But it is important to recognize that this model depends for its viability upon a version of perdurantism where alarmingly complete changes of particles happen *at every instant*. What happens at death is no more metaphysically dramatic than what is happening all the time anyway.

However, this overlooks problems with the notion of fission itself. Either God deceives the mourners on earth by creating a fake corpse and whisking the real one away—"body-snatching," as Zimmerman calls it[30]—or *both* the corpse and the resurrected person in heaven are identical with the person who died. This has attracted considerable criticism. Among other things, it seems to violate the transitivity of identity, since the corpse and the resurrected person are not identical with each other even though they are both identical with the pre-death person.[31]

Rather than retreading ground that has been extensively explored in the literature, I shall confine myself here to observing that if the "falling

---

28. Van Inwagen, "Possibility," 121; Zimmerman, "Compatibility," 205–7; Corcoran, *Rethinking*, 210–13.

29. Zimmerman, "Compatibility," 196.

30. Zimmerman, "Compatibility," 196.

31. For criticism of models of this kind, see e.g., Hershenov, "Materialist Conception," 459–63.

elevator" model has any plausibility, I think it has *more* plausibility if we apply it to the Enoch/Metatron case. Suppose that, at the moment of translation, Enoch's body has the same causative relation to Metatron's that any body has at any moment with its immediate successor. As we have seen, there is no problem with supposing that an atemporal entity can have causal relations with a temporal one. Moreover, in this case there is no inconvenient dead body after the crucial moment, leading to problematic multiple contenders for the identity of Enoch. Enoch does not "die" but disappears. He no longer exists in any time. He is, timelessly, identical with the atemporal Metatron.

Conclusion

With all this in place, we can sketch out our metaphysics of Metatron like this. An atemporal person could, in theory, exist in a universe that contains complexity but no temporal relations. Such a person could not think discursively, let alone carry on a conversation; but they could have conscious awareness, with thoughts of external (or internal) objects, as well as beliefs about those objects. They might also have states qualitatively similar to memories. These "memories" could be of a temporal existence. A number of relations are possible between the temporal and atemporal existences:

(1) The atemporal existence could be temporally posterior to the temporal one on the individual's own timeline, but atemporal on everyone else's. (But would it then be genuinely atemporal?)

(2) The temporal existence could be really prior to the atemporal one, without the atemporal one being really posterior to the temporal one. This option can be subdivided:

   (a) We can appeal to a medieval logic of relations to ensure that there is no formal contradiction in the claim. (This is coherent on paper, but unsatisfying.)

   (b) We can appeal to an endurantist and anti-criterialist view of identity over time, coupled with divine omnipotence.

   (c) We can appeal to a perdurantist and causative view of identity over time.

I think that all of these are viable options, to varying degrees. The most satisfying is (2)(c), since not only does this fit well with my argument in the previous chapter that divine atemporality entails perdurantism, but this is the only answer that can really explain *why* the temporal and atemporal persons are one and the same even though no temporal relations at all hold between them. On such a scenario, the temporal existence would not *temporally* precede the atemporal state, but it would *causally* precede it, and the causative relations between the temporal state and the atemporal state could be such as to constitute identity. In such a case, the "memories" experienced by the atemporal person, although not of experiences temporally prior to their atemporal existence, could be of experiences causally prior to it. In such a situation, it would be coherent to say that the temporal person has "become" atemporal, despite all the caveats that must be put in place around such a statement.[32]

And what goes for Metatron goes for everyone. If the situation just described is coherent, it could be the case that heaven works like this. We shall consider what that might be like in the next chapter.

32. If it is coherent to suppose that a temporal person can become atemporal, does this mean it is also coherent to suppose the reverse—that an atemporal person could become temporal? If so, this could have implications in Christology, if one wanted to combine atemporalism about God with a transformationalist model of incarnation according to which the (atemporal) divine Son is transformed into a (temporal) human being. Elsewhere (Hill, "Incarnation, Timelessness," 22–24) I have argued that such a view is incoherent, but in light of the arguments in this chapter I am now not so sure. Robin Le Poidevin, *And Was Made Man*, 194–213, defends the coherence of such a view, although he conceives of God as trans-temporal rather than as strictly atemporal.

4

Heaven without Time

I n Shakespeare's *Hamlet*, Claudius, who murdered his brother to become
king, is overcome with guilt and kneels down to pray. Hamlet, who is trying to drum up the nerve to kill Claudius to avenge his father, comes upon
him, and realizes that at last he has a chance to act:

> HAMLET: Now might I do it pat, now a is a-praying,
> And now I'll do't.
>   And so a goes to heaven,
> and so am I reveng'd. That would be scann'd:
> A villain kills my father, and for that,
> I, his sole son, do this same villain send
> To heaven ...
>   And am I then reveng'd
> To take him in the purging of his soul,
> When he is fit and season'd for his passage?
> No.
> Up sword, and know thou a more horrid hent:
> When he is drunk asleep, or in his rage,
> Or in th'incestuous pleasure of his bed,
> At game a-swearing, or about some act
> That has no relish of salvation in't,
> Then trip him, that his heels may kick at heaven
> And that his soul may be as damn'd and black
> As hell, whereto it goes.[1]

Hamlet believes that Claudius' final destination is entirely determined by
his spiritual state at the moment of death. If Claudius dies while praying,

1. *Hamlet*, Act III, scene 3, 77–100, in Shakespeare, *Complete Works*, 315.

then his soul is "fit and seasoned" to go to heaven, despite the crimes he has committed in the past. If, conversely, Claudius dies later on while doing something mundane, he will go to hell, despite having previously had this moment of repentance and prayer.

The notion that one's spiritual state at the precise moment of death trumps the rest of one's life in determining one's final destination was a common one in early modern times. Much spiritual literature of the period revolved around the importance of dying properly, and focused on how to prepare oneself to be sure of being in the appropriate state of mind at this most significant moment.[2] In 1651, Jeremy Taylor, one of the most well known authors in this tradition, warned his readers starkly:

> He that would die well must all the dayes of his life lay up against the day of death, not only by the general provisions of holinesse and a pious life indefinitely, but, provisions proper to the necessities of that great day of expence, in which a man is to throw his last cast for an eternity of joyes or sorrows; ever remembering, that this alone well performed is not enough to passe us into Paradise, but that alone done foolishly is enough to send us to hell. . . .[3]

Even today, this notion of the supreme importance of one's state of mind at the moment of death—and the practice of dwelling upon it for the purpose of improving one's life in the here and now—has been retained and secularized. Now we are urged to consider our future regrets as we die. In one advert for a travel company, a famous actor asks us: "Do you think any of us will look back at our lives and regret the things we didn't buy . . . or the places we didn't go?" The implication is that, on your deathbed, you somehow enjoy perfect mental clarity and perceive what in your life was truly important. Thus, even while we enjoy good health, we can imaginatively project ourselves into our last moments and access that moment of clarity *in extremis*, just as our ancestors were exhorted to spend their lives imagining themselves to be on the point of death.[4]

2. On this *ars morendi* genre and its great popularity in the fifteenth to seventeenth centuries, see Atkinson, "English Ars Morendi."

3. Taylor, *Holy Dying*, 2.1, p. 50 (italics original). Clearly, Taylor's theology of death is less generous than Shakespeare's: a bad death will counteract a good life, but a good death will not counteract a bad life.

4. I would argue that there is no reason to think that imminent death really makes the scales fall from our eyes in such a way. Right now, I might plausibly wish that I had spent my life up to this point working so hard that I could now retire early with a hefty pension. But although I might benefit now from having done that, it does not follow that it would have been a wise course of action, all things considered. The suffering I

It seems to me, though, that such an emphasis on the importance of one's final moments is not only unhealthily morbid but theologically deeply problematic. It makes salvation into little more than a matter of luck. Presumably it is the case that one and the same person might sometimes be spiritually fit to go to heaven and sometimes not (if not, then why try to improve oneself spiritually at all?). But if going to heaven is dependent upon one's spiritual state at the moment of death, then whether a person actually goes to heaven is entirely down to whether they have the good fortune to die at precisely the right moment. According to Taylor, at least, a good person who has led a holy life may go to hell if she happens to die during her one moment of sin, but would have gone to heaven if she had died at any other time. That does not seem just.[5]

More broadly, there is a tension here, pulling us in two different directions. On the one hand, we want the bulk of a person's life to make a difference. If, like Claudius, someone has spent their whole life committing terrible sins, and has a convenient conversion only on their deathbed, it seems wrong that most of their life has no bearing on their final destination. On the other hand, we want a *genuine* change of heart to matter. If I really do repent of my past sins and want to lead a better life, would that count for nothing?

In my view, this is an inevitable problem if we think of heaven as temporal. To see why, consider what a *temporal* conception of heaven involves.

What is temporal heaven?

A temporal conception of heaven is one according to which time passes in heaven. Time in heaven may be very unlike time on earth, and the blessed may experience its passage in a very different way from how we experience it, but if heaven is temporal we may still meaningfully talk about sequences of events there that are ordered in time. The blessed may perform one activity after another, for example.

---

would have endured through excessive overwork in the past might have outweighed the happiness I would enjoy now. Similarly, on my deathbed I may well wish that I had spent my life doing things that make me happier *when I am on my deathbed*, but that does not mean that that would have been a better life overall.

5. A possible answer to this might be to adopt a version of the doctrine of the perseverance of the saints, according to which a person who is elect (i.e., destined for heaven) cannot become un-elect. One might say, for example, that at the moment of conversion a person becomes spiritually fit for heaven and can never stop being spiritually fit for heaven, thus making their salvation assured no matter when they die.

Such a view has always been dominant in Christian theology. Certainly the imagery at the end of the book of Revelation—of the blessed "walking," "worshipping," and "reigning"[6]—strongly suggests temporal activities. Accordingly, in the early Middle Ages, a large and complex literature arose concerning the nature of life after death. Much of this was concerned with what people could expect to experience after their death: journeys from one part of the afterlife to another, battles between angels and demons for their souls, prayerful interaction with the living, intercession on their behalf by Christ, various judgments, and so on.[7] While there was little overt discussion about how life after death related to time, all of this literature presupposed—at least on a literal reading—that it would be temporal. *Events* occur to the dead, and are ordered in such a way that *narratives* about their postmortem experiences can be constructed. Unless all of this is to be read solely figuratively, it is testament to a widespread assumption that life after death is temporal, just like life on earth.

How would time in heaven relate to time on earth? We may distinguish between three different possibilities:

(1) Heaven comes at the end of earthly time.

(2) Heaven has its own timeline quite distinct from earthly time.

(3) Heaven runs parallel to earthly time, sharing its timeline and interacting with it.

On (1), heaven will come in the future. So everyone will enter heaven together, at the end of earthly time. This would include, for example, the traditional Christian conception of the general resurrection of the dead, as described in passages such as 1 Thessalonians 4:13–18. On this conception, the timeline of heaven is a continuation of the timeline of earth.

The most notorious problem with (1) is that it introduces a temporal gap into the lives of the blessed. If I die now, and will not enter heaven until I am resurrected in the far future, then there is a long period of time during which I do not exist.[8] Even if temporal gaps in the life of a single individual are conceptually possible at all, which is dubious,[9] it is hard to see why we

6. Rev 21:24; 22:3, 5.

7. On this, see Forbes, "Theology of the Afterlife."

8. The traditional way around this is to appeal to the soul as the principle of personal identity: when the body dies, the soul survives, to be reunited with the body at the point of resurrection, and this is what guarantees personal identity. However, this concept of the soul brings with it all the baggage of dualism and is not fashionable among either theologians or philosophers of religion at the moment.

9. For an argument that such things *are* conceptually possible, see Hershenov, "Materialist Conception," 463–65.

should consider this a case of a temporal gap and not simply two distinct individuals existing at different times.

To avoid this, a number of contemporary philosophers of religion have hinted at an alternative conception of heaven (2), where heaven does not come in the future but is like a parallel universe with its own timeline.[10] Here again everyone enters heaven together at the beginning of its timeline. But instead of having to wait for that timeline to begin, as in (1), a person who dies could be instantly transported to the beginning of heavenly time. It is a spatial, or inter-dimensional, move rather than a temporal one. A conception of heaven rather like this is at least implied by Peter Van Inwagen's suggestion that, when I die, God might remove my body and transfer it somewhere else (to be resurrected) while replacing it with a replica.[11] A different conception of heaven, though related to this, is Hud Hudson's suggestion that heaven lies not in the future but in the hyper-future.[12] On this view, heaven is temporal, but it is only hyper-temporally, and not temporally, related to our earthly timelines.

An alternative might be to reject the notion of bodily resurrection in a parallel universe heaven, and instead posit a soul that travels to heaven instead. This accounts for the continued presence of the corpse on earth without making God resort to any dubious sleight of hand and without raising difficult questions about personal identity. In fact, souls are normally associated with a slightly different conception of heavenly time, which I am numbering (3). (3) places heaven closer to earth than (2) does by having heaven and earth share the same timeline. On this conception, one can meaningfully talk about what is happening "now" in heaven just as one can talk about "now" in distant countries. Moreover, with (3) it is not the case that everyone enters heaven at the beginning of the heavenly timeline. Someone who died last year entered it last year, while someone who dies tomorrow enters it tomorrow. This raises the possibility of the blessed having to wait for their loved ones to join them, as envisaged by the spiritual "Save a Seat for Me" by the Five Blind Boys of Mississippi:

> I'm going to keep on pressing on the Word
> Till my battle is fought, my victory is won.
> But if you make it in glory before I do,
> Save a seat for me!

10. The relation between earth and heaven, on this account, is like that between the two universes "Alpha" and "Beta" in Herbert Nelson's thought experiment. See Nelson, "Time(s)," 4–7.

11. Van Inwagen, "Possibility," 121.

12. Hudson, "Resurrection."

This is the traditional Christian conception of heaven as the temporary resting place of the souls of the saints while they await the resurrection of their bodies. Not only does it avoid the temporal gap problem of conception (1), it has great pastoral and emotional power, as it allows the believer to say that their departed loved ones are in heaven *right now*, something that no other conception of heaven allows to be literally true. Thus, in 1336, Pope Benedict XII issued the constitution *Benedictus Deus*, stating that the souls of the blessed "*immediately [mox]* after death, . . . already before they take up their bodies again and before the general judgement, . . . *have been, are* and *will be* with Christ in heaven, in the heavenly kingdom and paradise, joined to the company of the holy angels."[13] The repeated use of temporal language here makes it plain that the place of the blessed shares the same timeline as earth.

Temporal heaven and the bottleneck problem

All of these different conceptions of heaven as temporal share a common feature. Each one presents an individual's personal timeline as a single thread: it extends throughout their earthly life, and then beyond it, through their death and into their heavenly life. This is so even on conception (1), where there is a temporal gap between a person's death and their entry into heaven, and on conception (2), where there is what one might call a dimensional gap at the same point. On these conceptions, the thread has a gap in it, but it still passes *from* an earthly past *into* a heavenly future, *through* the crisis of death.

Now consider again the idea that we saw in the last chapter, that assuming a perdurantist approach to identity over time, an object (or, at least, a person) at any given time can be considered the immediate cause of that person at the immediately succeeding time. Me-at-t_1 is the cause of me-at-t_2, and this is why these two distinct temporal entities can be legitimately considered temporal *parts* of the same individual. Now me-at-t_1 is, presumably, caused by the even earlier me-at-t_0. Me-at-t_0 is, therefore, the cause of me-at-t_2, but not immediately: me-at-t_1 interposes itself. Any causative power that me-at-t_0 has over me-at-t_2 is entirely mediated by me-at-t_1.

Suppose that heavenly-me is caused by earthly-me in such a way that heavenly-me is the same person as earthly-me, just as me-at-t_1 and me-at-t_2 are the same person. On the views we looked at in the last chapter, associated with Kevin Corcoran and Dean Zimmerman, the immediate cause of heavenly-me is not earthly-me considered as a whole—it is the *very last moment* of earthly-me. At the moment of death, God gives my body the

13. In Dupuis, *Christian Faith*, 943 (my italics).

power to cause a heavenly version of myself to come into existence, in such a way that this heavenly version of myself is a continuation of me. Me-at-the-moment-of-death is therefore the immediate cause of my heavenly self. Any earlier state of my being has causative power over my heavenly self only *through* my moment of death—just as, in more mundane cases of identity over time, me-at-t_0 has causative power over me-at-t_2 only *through* me-at-t_1. In other words, me-at-the-moment-of-death functions as a kind of bottleneck. Whatever influence my earthly life has over my heavenly state must pass through that moment.

But this leads, inevitably, to the Hamlet view of salvation. If my heavenly self is wholly caused by me-at-the-moment-of-death, then me-at-the-moment-of-death has spiritual significance that dwarfs all the rest of my life put together. This is so even if my spiritual state at that moment is an uncharacteristic aberration. If I happen to die at the one moment in my life when I give in to temptation—well, too bad.[14]

14. There is a possible objection to this, which is that the transition from one's earthly life to one's heavenly life is not a purely natural process. God is involved. Suppose I had led a mostly good life with one lapse at the end. Couldn't God review the whole of my life and decide to admit me to heaven, despite my poor spiritual state at the moment of death? (I am grateful to Robin Parry for this objection.) Well, perhaps God could do that. But Christian theologians typically want to say that the identity of my heavenly self depends, in some way, upon continuity with my earthly self. As we shall see later in this chapter, theologians traditionally hold the composition principle, according to which identity of a body over time requires either the persistence of the same component parts or organizational continuity. Contemporary philosophers of religion who reject this principle for heavenly selves, such as Dean Zimmerman and Kevin Corcoran, appeal to continuity in causative terms. If we accept any of these accounts of what makes the heavenly person identical with the earthly one, then even if we grant that God can overlook lapses late in life when deciding whether to admit someone to heaven, the identity of that person depends disproportionately upon who they were at the moment of death. For it is the particles that composed them then, or the organizational principle that characterized them then, or the causative power they had then, that determines not merely who the resurrected person is, but what they are like. One way out of this might be to deny not only the compositional principle but any notion of criteria of identity. As I discussed in chapter 3, George Mavrodes and Trenton Merricks both argue for such a view. If this is the case then the identity of the earthly and heavenly persons is basic, and it does not depend upon any properties or powers of the earthly body at the moment of death, or at any other moment. This could provide a way of avoiding the bottleneck problem. But while I am sympathetic to such an account of identity in itself, it seems to me to abandon too readily a key element of traditional Christian belief in the resurrection, as we shall see later in this chapter. We can therefore say that the bottleneck problem has two possible solutions. One is to abandon traditional notions of the criteria of identity, and the other is to abandon the notion of heaven as temporal. Those who do not wish to adopt the latter solution therefore seem obliged to adopt the former, but for some, that may be too great a metaphysical or theological price to pay.

Atemporal heaven

But suppose instead that the heavenly existence is atemporal. The notion is, historically, bound up with Platonism and its fundamental distinction between the changeable world of Becoming and the unchanging world of Being. Time is a feature of Becoming, not of Being. For Platonists, the unchanging is superior to the changeable, so there is a natural tendency to want to conceive of heaven as timeless.

Augustine was the most prominent Christian theologian to incorporate this Platonic outlook into the doctrine of heaven. As Caroline Bynum observes, he "seems unable to imagine a case of growth or change that is not in some way a deterioration or loss of identity."[15] For example, in one famous passage, he writes:

> Finally, when the fullness of time came, he who was to free us from time (*ille qui nos liberaret a tempore*) also came. For, freed from time, we shall come to that eternity where time is not (*aeternitatem illam ubi non est tempus*). And there it is not asked, when will the hour come? For the day is everlasting and is not preceded by a yesterday nor closed out by a tomorrow. But in this age the days turn, and some pass away, and some come. No day remains, and the moments in which we are speaking drive one another away, and the first syllable stays not, so that the second syllable may be able to make its sound. Since we began to speak, we have grown a little older, and without any doubt, I am now older than this morning; thus nothing stays still, nothing remains fixed in time. And so we ought to love him through whom times were made, that we may be freed from time and fixed in eternity (*ut liberemur a tempore et figamur in aeternitate*) where there is no longer any alteration of time (*nulla est mutabilitas temporum*).[16]

Here and in some other texts, Augustine envisages a heavenly state that is not simply everlasting, for that would involve the succession of moments that he regards as a sign of the inferiority of our current state. Rather, salvation consists of being taken out of time altogether, and no longer experiencing any succession of moments. But neither here nor elsewhere does he explain why this is desirable, apparently taking it for granted.[17] The undesirability of time seems to be a fundamental value for Augustine, of the kind I discussed

15. Bynum, *Resurrection*, 101.

16. Augustine, *Tractates*, 31.5, p. 34.

17. On this, see Teske, "Vocans Temporales."

briefly in the introduction, since he is not able to give a clear justification for it, or a coherent explanation of how it works. For example, Augustine seems to think that the heavenly state will involve motion, but does not explain how this is compatible with a lack of time.[18]

Perhaps unsurprisingly, then, later theologians have rarely adopted Augustine's idea of heaven as salvation from time despite his weighty influence in other areas. One possible exception is Meister Eckhart, who states that the heavens lie outside both space and time, and that only through abstraction away from space and time can the soul reach God.[19] For Eckhart, our temporal existence is only a foreshadow of the existence we shall enjoy after time.[20] As he puts it:

> The aim of man is beyond the temporal—in the serene region of the everlasting Present. . . . All time strives towards eternity or the timeless Now, out of which it issued at creation. The merely temporal life in itself is a negation of real being. . . . It must through grace be lifted to the highest sphere of existence, and attain to freedom outside the narrow confines of the natural. . . . Only by grace man comes from the temporal and transitory to be one with God.[21]

But Eckhart does not explain how this works, or how it is possible for temporal creatures to become atemporal—if indeed he means this language to be taken literally at all.[22] Something similar may be said of Karl Rahner, who

18. Jason Carter argues that Augustine does have the resources to reconcile these apparently inconsistent claims, because of his view that change is the acquisition or loss of accidental properties. He writes that in heaven, for Augustine, "any 'change' that occurs will not be a change from something we have to something different that we do *not* have, but rather a 'change' from something we have to something else we *already* have, without the loss of any possession. In this sense, and in this sense alone, time as we know it, for Augustine, will not occur (at least not in a linear sense) in eternity. However, practically speaking, a form of temporality will remain in eternity, since motion will continue to occur; it will just not be the sort of temporal motion coordinate with the loss or gain of desired things" ("St. Augustine," 323–24, italics original). I have to admit, though, that I cannot make any sense of a notion of change that involves the acquisition of properties one already has, so I am not convinced that Augustine's account is coherent.

19. Eckhart, *Sermons*, 22, 31.

20. Eckhart, *Sermons*, 40–41.

21. Eckhart, *Sermons*, 59.

22. The suggestion that the notion of heaven as salvation from time might be more poetic than literal fits well with the trope in some traditions of fantasy writing, where the realm of elves or fairies is characterized as timeless. Probably the most influential example is Lord Dunsany's "Elfland," which is so uniformly static that its inhabitants are amazed by the succession of day and night on earth (Dunsany, *King*). It can also be

states that "the one total person is removed from empirical time through his death," but without explaining how this is possible.[23]

There exists, then, an Augustinian tradition of conceiving of heaven as atemporal, though it has always been a minority view and never properly fleshed out. However, the notion of atemporal heaven does not derive solely from philosophical considerations.[24] Another, less well-known, source is a

---

found in J. R. R. Tolkien's conception of Lothlorien and Rivendell as preserved by the elven rings of power, whose wearers "could ward off the decays of time and postpone the weariness of the world" (Tolkien, *Silmarillion*, 288). Throughout his enormous oeuvre, Dunsany in particular consistently portrays time as a hostile force. *In the Land of Time*, for example, tells of Karnith, king of Alatta, who vows:

> [W]e will go forth and conquer Time and save the gods of Alatta from his clutch, and coming back victorious shall find that Death is gone and age and illness departed. . . . There shall be neither fading nor forgetting, nor ever dying nor sorrow, when we shall have freed the people and pleasant fields of the earth from inexorable Time. (*Time*, 75)

The attempt proves tragic, as Karnith finds that while he journeys in search of Time, Time is at work in his own kingdom, to devastating effect. In Tolkien's work, Ar-Pharazôn, king of the Numenoreans, embarks on a similar expedition to wrest eternity from the Valar, but for Tolkien this is an act of hubris which brings deserved destruction upon his people. The villainous portrayal of Ar-Pharazôn, compared to the more sympathetic Karnith, reflects Tolkien's greater ambivalence towards the ideal of unchanging eternity. Although his elves are the "fairest of all earthly creatures" (*Silmarillion*, 41) and embody the Platonic ideal of immortality and changelessness, Tolkien also presents their attempts to halt the advance of time as "a kind of embalming" (*Letters*, 151). As Anna Vaninskaya, *Fantasies*, has shown, this ambivalent opposition between eternity and time in early twentieth-century fantasy literature has its roots in poetic tropes going back centuries. As such, we can see it as both a highly dramatized version of the same Platonism that underlies Augustine's desire to be "delivered from time" and share God's eternity, and an implicit criticism of it.

23. Rahner, *Theological Investigations XVII*, 118.

24. The economist and philosopher of science Scott Gordon advanced a philosophical argument for an atemporal heaven (or something very like it), without appealing to any kind of Platonism. He argued that if heaven is conceived as a state entirely lacking in scarcity, time must work there very differently from on earth. This is because (1) a true lack of scarcity is incompatible with the need to prioritize one activity over another, and (2) even in an infinitely extended time in which one can do everything, one still has to choose what order to do them in. Gordon argues:

> Let us assume that Heaven time, in addition to being infinite in length, is also infinite in width. Instead of being represented by a Euclidean line which has length but no width, a Heaven time line would have both length and width and would be infinite in both dimensions. In such a regime, there would be no time constraint upon actions or experiences. This would be a condition of no scarcity, since at every instant there is an infinite amount of time. ("Economics of the Afterlife," 213)

And he concludes that given infinitely "wide" time, infinitely lengthened time would no longer be necessary, resulting in a heavenly existence that is "exquisitely *intense* in experience but fleetingly *brief*" (p. 214, italics original). I am not sure how seriously

tradition of interpretation surrounding Revelation 10:6, which states that at the eschaton "time shall be no longer" (my literal translation of χρόνος οὐκέτι ἔσται). The NRSV renders this as "there will be no more delay," on the assumption that χρόνος refers not to time in general but to the time of waiting, and most contemporary commentators follow this interpretation.[25] The French Catholic liturgical translation, however, gives the more literal (and dramatic) "Du temps, il n'y en aura plus!"[26] In doing so, it follows a tradition of interpretation that goes back to the early seventh-century commentator Andrew of Caesarea,[27] who wrote concerning this verse:

> They swear an oath that there would *no longer be time*, <meaning> either in the future when time is not to be measured by the sun but eternal life, which is beyond the measurement of time, or <meaning> that there will not be a long time after the six voices when the things prophesied by the angel will be fulfilled.[28]

Andrew's uncertainty over the interpretation of this verse is reflected in his assumption elsewhere in his commentary that the kingdom of the saints would be everlasting, rather than timeless.[29] However, some subsequent commentators, such as Bede, would take up his suggestion that this verse teaches a literal end to time.[30] This remained a minor tradition. It is not found in the most popular medieval commentary on Revelation, that of Beatus of Liébana. But we do find Thomas Aquinas appealing to this verse to support the claim that there will be no time after the general judgment.[31] Thomas' use of this verse is rather limited: he appeals to it only to support the claim that there will be no movement of the heavens, suggesting that he interprets it as teaching a state of changelessness rather than atemporality. Elsewhere, he does argue that, as part of the beatific vision, the blessed will

---

Gordon meant this argument—which was presented in a paper of only a page and a half—to be taken. Certainly his readership of economists must have found it curious. I think it is reasonably convincing provided one accepts the premise that heaven must be a state of no scarcity whatsoever, but such a premise is tendentious, to say the least.

25. See, for example, Fee, *Revelation*, 141; Beale and Campbell, *Revelation*, 164; Brake, *Visions*, 127.

26. Quoted in Berder, "Du Temps," 319.

27. On this tradition, see Aune, *Revelation*, 568; Fair, *Conquering*, ch. 7. On Andrew and his influence, see Constantinou in Andrew of Caesarea, *Apocalypse*, 3–42; Hernández, "Andrew of Caesarea." On the differing interpretations of this verse of Revelation, see Berder, "Du Temps."

28. Andrew of Caesarea, *Apocalypse*, 128–29.

29. E.g., in Andrew of Caesarea, *Apocalypse*, 187.

30. In Bede, *Commentary on Revelation*, 178.

31. Aquinas, *ST*, Supp. q. 91 a. 2 ad contra, vol. 21, pp. 31–32.

share in the divine eternity.[32] They do not actually become atemporal, which Aquinas thinks is impossible,[33] but they engage in an activity (beholding God) that involves no succession or change and therefore constitutes participation, albeit creaturely, in the divine life.[34]

How can a broadly Augustinian conception of heaven as atemporal help with the bottleneck problem? As we saw in the previous chapter, we can conceive of an atemporal being whose existence is causally dependent upon a temporal being, with this causal relation being such as to constitute identity. But we can distinguish between two ways of conceiving this, which I shall call *final-state-determining* and *whole-state-determining*. On the final-state-determining version, the state of the atemporal being is causally dependent upon just the final state of the temporal being. So this conception mirrors the conception of heaven as temporal, where the moment of death functions as a bottleneck for any causal relations between the earthly and heavenly selves. The whole-state-determining view, by contrast, conceives of the heavenly state as caused by the *whole* of the earthly existence. In other words, if the heavenly existence is atemporal, there is no reason to suppose that it is more closely tied to the end of the earthly existence than it is to any other section. Death is no longer a bottleneck through which the causal story of a person's entire earthly and heavenly career must pass: any given moment in a person's earthly life could be a *direct* part-cause of their heavenly existence, because that existence is atemporal, and so this causation does not have to be mediated by subsequent earthly moments.

We can picture the whole-state-determining view like this. Suppose a four-dimensionalist picture, under which every individual is a four-dimensional spacetime worm,[35] as I have argued is entailed by the supposition of divine atemporality. We can imagine my earthly life as a spacetime worm stretching from t_1 to t_n. On a temporalist conception of heaven, the worm either extends to t_{n+1} and beyond, or it stops at t_n and starts again at t_{n+x},

32. Aquinas, *Commentary on the* Sentences of Peter Lombard, IV d. 49 q. 1 a. 2. On this, see Brown, *Eternal Life*, 167–79.

33. Aquinas, *Commentary on the* Sentences of Peter Lombard, IV d. 49 q. 1 a. 2 qa 3 obj. 3 and ad obj. 3, in Aquinas, *Love and Charity*, 359, 360–61.

34. Aquinas, *ST*, I q. 10 a. 3, vol. 1, p. 102; see also *ST*, IIa q. 5 a. 4 ad obj. 1, vol. 6, p. 77.

35. On four-dimensionalism, every individual is spread throughout time as well through space. The three-dimensional object occupying my chair right now is not the whole of me. It is only a single temporal slice of an object that extends back into the present and (perhaps) into the future as well. Since one can imagine that this temporal extension is quite long, and different parts of it are at different points in space (because I move about from time to time), it is tempting to imagine it with a long, sinuous appearance—hence the commonly used term "spacetime worm."

some time in the future. The defender of such a conception of heaven therefore has to explain how the worm can extend beyond tn, despite apparently ending there, or how it can really end there and yet restart at the later $tn+x$ without being a different worm. Either way, the point at tn is a bottleneck through which my timeline must pass if I am to reach heaven.

On the atemporalist conception, by contrast, there is no extension to the spacetime worm in time. It stops at tn and does not start again. On the final-state-determining view, the final slice of the worm is extended in a completely different direction, orthogonal to the temporal axis. And on the whole-state-determining view, *the entire worm* is extended in this way. Suppose we represent the worm as a one-dimensional line, with $t1$ at the left and tn at the right. Instead of extending the line further to the right, as on the temporalist conception of heaven, we extend the entire line upwards, creating a two-dimensional figure.[36]

This makes possible an answer to Joseph Ratzinger's objection against atemporal conceptions of heaven:

> Is it even logically possible to conceive of man, whose existence is achieved decisively in the temporal, being transposed into sheer eternity? And in any case, can an eternity which has a beginning be eternity at all? Is it not necessarily non-eternal, and so temporal, precisely because it had a beginning? Yet how can one deny that the resurrection of a human being has a beginning, namely, after death?[37]

On the atemporal conception, one can deny precisely this. The earthly life has an end, but the heavenly life does not have a beginning. But this does not mean holding that "man has always existed in the risen state, in an eternity without beginning,"[38] as Ratzinger goes on to insist is the only possible alternative, because if the risen state is atemporal it is not the case that it "has always existed." It exists atemporally, though it has always been true that it exists atemporally.

The whole-state-determining conception also side-steps some of the key traditional issues bedeviling belief in life after death at all. The most basic of these issues is how to reconcile the presence of a dead body with the belief that a person who has just died is now in heaven. Belief in an immortal soul is one obvious way to do this. Another is to hold that the dead body will be resurrected in the future. Other, less traditional answers are

36. This imagery goes back to C. S. Lewis, who also held an atemporalist view of heaven (and hell); see Lewis, *Problem of Pain*, 111–12.

37. Ratzinger, *Eschatology*, 109.

38. Ratzinger, *Eschatology*, 109–10.

available, such as Zimmerman's "falling elevator" model, mentioned earlier. But if heaven is atemporal, then the problem itself rests on a category mistake. Once I die, I do not persist temporally at all—either immediately as a disembodied soul or as a duplicate in another dimension, or at a future time. My spacetime worm does not extend on that axis. Rather, it extends orthogonally. Those who look to the temporal end of my spacetime worm at *tn*, expecting or hoping it to grow further in time, are looking in the wrong place. My spacetime worm is extended in a completely different direction, one that is not perceptible to any temporally based observers.

Some philosophers of religion have suggested a view of heaven similar to this, in which it is conceived as orthogonal to the spatiotemporal dimensions with which we are familiar. Hud Hudson, for example, appeals to the notion of hyperspace and the theoretical possibility of spatial directions such as "ana" and "kata" that are orthogonal to the familiar ones:

> Perhaps [heaven and hell] are arbitrarily close both to New York and to the spot on which you are currently standing in the directions ana and kata; compare a two-space of milk-slices and honey-slices that could be hovering just millimeters above Flatland. [That is, a two-dimensional heavenly reality with no thickness.] Why don't we take a spaceship for a blissful vacation in Heaven or on a bold and daring rescue mission to Hell? Perhaps because our modes of transportation are confined to the directions of our three-space prison; whereas we can travel up, down, left, right, forth, and back, no spaceship can take us ana or kata.[39]

Cruz Davis has attacked conceptions of heaven of this kind as susceptible to what he calls "technological Pelagianism."[40] The reasoning behind this is straightforward: if heaven exists somewhere in space, we could in theory get there via our own efforts. One might think that Hudson's heaven, located in an exotic direction, is safe from invasion—but Davis argues that even if it is physically impossible for us to travel from one dimension to another, this is a purely *contingent* impossibility. To avoid Pelagianism, it must be a *necessary* impossibility. As Davis puts it, the proponent of such a heaven must secure "not just the physical impossibility of making a trip into heaven without divine grace, but the metaphysical impossibility of such a trip as

---

39. Hudson, *Metaphysics*, 187–88. David Wilkinson, *Christian Eschatology*, 126–27, proposes a similar idea. His formulation involves additional temporal dimensions rather than spatial ones, though precisely how that differs is not spelled out in detail.

40. Davis, "Paradise . . . Lost?," 83.

well"—and as long as heaven is located in some other dimension, this is not secured.[41]

I am not convinced that the failure to meet this demand entails Pelagianism, simply because the historic condemnations of that doctrine asserted only that it is impossible for human beings to achieve salvation by their own means, without considering what *kind* of impossibility was meant.[42] But the prospect of human beings being able, even in theory, to travel to heaven unaided does seem very worrying.

Is the account I am suggesting vulnerable to this worry? Although Hudson uses analogies similar to those I have appealed to, his conception of heaven is different in one key respect: there is nothing in his account to suggest that it is *atemporal*. Indeed, it may even be on the earthly timeline, making this a temporal heaven of type (3).[43] Accordingly, it does seem that although on his account heaven lies in an exotic direction, it is not metaphysically closed off to us. We could at least coherently imagine traveling there.

But this is much harder to suppose with an *atemporal* heaven. It is one thing to suppose that we might, at least in theory, be able to travel or extend ourselves in exotic spatial directions without divine aid. But it is quite another to suppose that we might be able to enter an atemporal state by our own power. This is particularly so if we take atemporality to be a peculiarly divine property, an idea we will consider in more detail in chapter 6. For now, we can observe that to pass from a temporal state to an atemporal one (with all the caveats surrounding this kind of language that we have already noted) would be far more than a simple shift in space or even in time. It would involve a radical transformation of the traveler. As we saw in chapter 2, although the concept of an atemporal person is coherent, it would be a

41. Davis, "Paradise . . . Lost?," 87. Davis does not explain why a heaven that is not located in space is not subject to the same worry. If one accepts a "metaphysical possibility" of traveling to a spatial heaven without divine aid, why could there not be an equally problematic metaphysical possibility of entering a non-spatial heaven without divine aid?

42. Also, Davis' argument equivocates between *achieving salvation* and *entering heaven*. The condemnation of Pelagianism was concerned with the former, not the latter. But they are, at least conceptually, not the same thing. It *could* be the case that heaven is, after all, a physical location that we can travel to by ordinary means, but that doing so does not secure salvation—we would merely be visitors there, like Dante. Perhaps salvation would require a personal transformation that could not be achieved by ourselves, such as being embodied in an imperishable and incorruptible form. In that case, even entering heaven by our own means would not ensure salvation, in which case a view of heaven that entertains such a possibility need not be Pelagian.

43. Davis seems to interpret it in this way, categorizing Hudson's view as a "contemporaneous" account of heaven.

very different kind of person from the kind we are. It is not implausible to suppose that such a transformation, from a temporal to an atemporal existence, would require divine power, especially if atemporality is an inherently divine property.

Atemporality and succession

This picture raises an immediate problem. Life after death is, more or less by definition, supposed to come *after* a person's death. But this atemporal conception of heaven explicitly denies this. If heaven is atemporal, then it is no more true to say that I *will* be in heaven after my death than it is to say that I *was* in heaven before my birth. As we saw in the last chapter, however, there are multiple possible answers to this. One is to distinguish between different timelines, and say that my heavenly existence succeeds my earthly existence on my personal timeline, though it is atemporal from the point of view of everyone else's timeline. However, even if this works in a scenario where only one person is translated into an atemporal existence, it is much harder to apply to a scenario where many—perhaps *all*—people undergo such a translation. In that scenario, there is no timeline in which my heavenly existence is atemporal, because everyone else's timeline extends into heaven as well. Alternatively, we might appeal to a scholastic-style metaphysics of relation, and hold it to be coherent that my earthly life precedes my heavenly life even though my heavenly life does not succeed my earthly life.

As we have seen, a more satisfying answer is to appeal to causal dependence as constitutive of identity, at least under certain conditions, and to make the relation between the earthly and heavenly lives one of dependence, not a temporal relation at all. So a heavenly-me exists *because* an earthly-me does; moreover, the heavenly-me has the properties he does *because* of the properties that the earthly-me has.

There is a possible problem with this. Suppose my going to heaven is dependent upon my performing some specific act during my lifetime. Then it is true even before I perform that act that I am atemporally in heaven. And that, of course, raises issues not only of incoherence (this looks like backward causation) but of free will, since it seems that I lack the ability *not* to perform that act. I do not propose to spend much time on this problem since it so closely parallels the problem of reconciling divine omniscience with humanly freedom, which has been extensively discussed.[44] As I discussed in

44. For this discussion, see (among many others) Plantinga, "Ockham's Way Out"; Fischer, *God*; Hasker, *God*; Zagzebski, *Dilemma*; Warfield, "Divine Foreknowledge"; Flint, *Divine Providence*; Rogers, *Perfect Being Theology*, 71–91; Johnson, "God, Fatalism"; Merricks, "Truth and Freedom" and "Foreknowledge and Freedom"; Fischer and

chapter 2, I am assuming divine atemporality, which includes divine *subjective* atemporality and therefore knowledge of the whole of time. I therefore assume, for the sake of brevity, that divine atemporality can be reconciled with causation and with creaturely free will (assuming one wishes to affirm free will), and that the same solution, whatever it may be, can be applied to heavenly atemporality.

However, one way of getting around this problem is to appeal to divine action. We might suppose that events on earth do not directly cause effects in heaven, but God causes events in both heaven and earth, such that the former are dependent upon the latter. For example, if I lead a good life and go to heaven as a result, it is not the case that my goodness has directly caused my blessedness by some kind of quasi-natural causation.[45] Rather, God rewards me for my goodness by ensuring that I am (timelessly) in heaven. In this scenario, we can preserve the idea that my presence in heaven is dependent upon my behavior in this life even though heaven is atemporal and my heavenly life does not come "after" my earthly one in a temporal sense. My earthly life has logical priority to my heavenly life rather than temporal priority. God has chosen to actualize both of my lives in this way, such that God's decision to place me in heaven requires God's decision to have me fulfill the criteria for heaven in my earthly life. Throughout, God is the agent who causes both my meeting the criteria for heaven and my being in heaven. And it may be, of course, that God creates creatures who lead their earthly lives in certain ways specifically *because* God wants creatures to be in heaven, and the former are required for the latter—just as, to use the old example, God creates treacherous Judas because he is necessary for salvific Jesus.

If either of these conceptions of the atemporal heaven—as depending directly upon events on earth by quasi-causal laws, or as created together with earth by God in the way just described—is plausible, then we have a

---

Todd, "Truth about Freedom"; Fischer and Tognazzini, "Omniscience." On the particular question of divine *atemporality* and freedom, see also McArthur, "Timelessness"; Cook, "God, Time, and Freedom"; Yates, *Timelessness*, 235–68; Robinson, *Eternity and Freedom*; De Florio and Frigerio, "Timeless Solution."

45. For simplicity's sake, I am assuming a simple system of cosmic reward under which people who do good deeds go to heaven. Clearly, many Christian theologians would reject such a system, preferring instead to think in terms of God's grace as the criterion for entry to heaven. For many of them, however, entry to heaven would still depend upon the person doing *something*, even if it is only to respond positively to divine grace, in which case the discussion here can be recast in those terms. For those particularly Calvinist theologians who hold that divine grace is *wholly* determinative of salvation, the problem discussed above does not arise, because there is no need to suppose that *any* event in my life has to precede my entry into heaven—my salvation has been eternally decreed anyway.

way of saying that the heavenly life comes "after" the earthly life—not "after" in a temporal sense, but "after" in a logical or aetiological sense.

Atemporality and anticipation

However, would a heaven like this really give me something to look forward to? Even if it is true that my actions here on earth cause (in some mysterious way) an entity to exist in the atemporal realm of heaven, and so that entity's existence and nature is dependent upon my own, this does not give me any reason to hope that that entity's experiences are *mine*. If they are atemporal, I never have experienced them and I never will.

This objection rests upon the following principle, which I will call *the anticipation principle* (AP):

> AP: If I am rationally to anticipate a state of affairs, I must justifiably believe that state of affairs to lie in the future.[46]

But is the AP true? Consider again the different views of identity over time discussed in chapter 2. An objection to perdurantism is that it makes anticipation irrational. If I have temporal parts, then me-at-t_1 is not identical with me-at-t_2, in which case what happens to me-at-t_2 does not directly concern me-at-t_1.[47] It would make no sense (barring altruism) for me-at-t_1 to do anything to benefit me-at-t_2. Why should I give up alcohol, for example, if the only person to enjoy the health benefits is some future me who is not identical with me now? This problem is especially acute for stage theorists, who stress the distinction between the temporal parts to such a degree that they are distinct entities in their own right.[48]

Typically, perdurantists do not think that entities such as me-at-t_1 are persons at all. They are merely person-stages, proper (temporal) parts of persons.[49] So if I give up alcohol now in order to reap the health benefits

46. I frame this in terms of "justifiable belief" rather than of the event's actually lying in the future, because one can rationally anticipate events that turn out not to occur after all.

47. For a version of this criticism, see Zimmerman, "Material People," 502.

48. This problem is distinct from another objection to perdurantism based on its ethical consequences, which is that if I *do* do something unpleasant now in order to reap the rewards in the future, I am unethically coercing the "personites" or temporal slices of my four-dimensional self that overlap with the unpleasant hard work but not with the pleasant reward. For this objection, see Olson, "Ethics"; Johnston, "Personite Problem."

49. For example, in an influential paper David Lewis defines a person as a "maximal I-related aggregate" of person-stages, where "I-related" means that they constitute a single "I" (Lewis, "Survival and Identity," 59). This would rule out any subset of such

in the future, the "me" who is performing this action is not me-at-t_1. The person who gives up alcohol is *me* simpliciter—and *I* am a four-dimensional entity that extends across all of my temporal parts. Such a four-dimensional answer, however, entails an abandonment of the AP. For on this view, the person who acts is not temporally located uniquely at t_1 at all, but is temporally located equally at all times at which they have temporal parts. So the healthy state at t_2 is not a future state from the point of view of the acting person.[50]

So a perdurantist must reject the AP. What of endurantism? I argued in the previous chapter that if endurantism is true, then identity over time is basic and cannot be reduced to any other properties, in which case it is (for all we know) possible for an omnipotent God to see to it that an atemporal entity is identical with a temporal one. By the same reasoning, if identity over time is basic, then so too is the unidirectionality of time—the fact that we anticipate the future but look back on the past. An omnipotent God could make it the case that not only is the atemporal person in heaven identical with me, but that the atemporal state is one I anticipate rather than look back on. So for example, God could cause the atemporal person to have "memories" of my earthly life that are genuine, even though the atemporal life does not temporally succeed the temporal life.

I conclude, then, that the AP is false. Even if heaven were atemporal, and did not temporally succeed my earthly existence, I could still rationally *look forward* to it—not as something that will come in my future, but as something which succeeds my earthly existence in a non-temporal way. It is, for example, causally posterior to my earthly existence. It is also phenomenologically posterior, in that my heavenly self may have (genuine) memories of my earthly life, whereas my earthly self has no memories of my heavenly life.

Resurrection of the body

How are we to square all of this with the requirement of orthodoxy that the *body* be raised from the dead? It seems, after all, as if this requirement is not met. On the scenario we are imagining, the body dies and is buried, and

---

an aggregate as counting as a person. (Note, though, that Lewis does not provide any justification for this ruling.)

50. This, it seems to me, is itself a deeply implausible consequence of four-dimensionalism. If "I" am not a person-stage but a four-dimensional entity existing at a number of different times, why does it seem to me that I am located at one particular moment *right now*? How can four-dimensionalism account for the fact that we experience time as a succession of moments?

there is no future time at which it rises again. But in my view, it is actually *easier* to satisfy this requirement on the atemporal conception of heaven than it is on the temporal conception.

It is a commonplace, almost to the point of cliché,[51] in philosophical discussions of the doctrine of resurrection, of the kind we touched on in the previous chapter, to focus on the question: What makes the future resurrected person identical with the person who died, and not simply a sort of clone? But such a focus is not really biblical. Paul's discussion of the resurrection in 1 Corinthians 15 focuses on the fact of the resurrection and on the nature of the resurrection body, but shows no awareness of any uncertainty about the identity of the resurrected person.[52] Indeed, no Christian authors for nearly two centuries after Paul was writing seem aware of this issue.[53]

Only at the end of the second century do we find Christian authors showing any concern for this matter, with a succession of writers stressing that if God can create a person in her mother's womb, God is quite capable of re-creating *that same person* after her death.[54] These authors' answer to the problem of what makes the resurrected person identical to the one who died is material continuity: God gathers *numerically the same particles* that constituted the earthly body and reconstitutes them, so that they are numerically one and the same body.[55] As Tatian put it, even if my body is destroyed by fire, the matter that constituted my body is not annihilated but only dispersed throughout the universe, and God retains the ability to reassemble it.[56] (Pseudo-)Athenagoras, meanwhile, is quite explicit that the identity of the resurrected person depends upon numerically the same body and the same soul being reunited.[57]

This notion that identity of the body is based on identity of the components of the body, and the corresponding claim that the resurrection will involve God reassembling the dispersed particles that once composed our

51. Hewitt, review of *Paradise Understood*, 445 (quoted above, in the introduction), draws attention, rather sardonically, to the universality of this question in discussions of the topic.

52. On the range of interpretations of Paul's understanding of the resurrection body in 1 Corinthians 15, see Ware, "Paul's Understanding." Ware defends an interpretation like the one sketched above, in which Paul stresses the numerical identity of the earthly and resurrection bodies, the latter being genuinely physical.

53. Bynum, *Resurrection*, 24–26.

54. On this, see Bynum, *Resurrection*, 27.

55. On this, see Daley, "Hope for Worms," 147–51.

56. Tatian, *Oratio ad Graecos*, ch. 6, pp. 11–13.

57. (Pseudo-)Athenagoras, *De Resurrectione*, ch. 25 (*Legatio and De Resurrectione*, 146–47).

bodies, would remain the standard Christian view well into modern times. God will, at the end of time, gather together all of the particles that once made up my body, and put them back together, so that I have numerically the same body that I had in life. That is why I can be confident that I will be *me*.

Christian theologians, in other words, traditionally appeal (at least implicitly) to what we can call the *composition principle* (CP):

> CP: A body at time t_1 is identical with a body at a later time t_2 if and only if either (a) the body at t_2 is composed of the same parts as the body at t_1 or (b) there is organizational continuity between the body at t_1 and the body at t_2.

The clause about organizational continuity is needed because a living body is not composed of the same parts throughout its existence, which means that if only criterion (a) is adopted then my body now is not identical with the body I had ten years ago (alas).

There is an immediate problem with this principle, because any part of a body is presumably a body itself, in which case the principle becomes circular: what makes any given part of the body at t_2 identical with a part of the body at t_1? Do we have to appeal to parts *of* parts, and so on, ad infinitum? Perhaps not, if we reject the infinite divisibility of matter. Perhaps identity across time is basic for the most fundamental subatomic particles—whatever they may be—and for compound bodies, identity across time is parasitic upon the identity of the fundamental particles. So "body" in the principle should be taken to mean *not* "any physical object" but "a compound object," or, better, simply "a living organism." It is, after all, only living organisms that we are interested in here, so whether this principle applies to any other entities does not concern us.

The reliance on this principle is why traditional objections to the doctrine of resurrection, such as the cannibal scenario, were such a problem for theologians.[58] If what makes my resurrected self *me* is that my body will be made of the same stuff as it is now, then the prospect of some of that material getting hijacked by other claimants to it is a serious worry. It is noteworthy,

---

58. The objection is that if a cannibal eats another person, then some of the victim's flesh is transformed into the cannibal's flesh—so who gets that bit in the resurrection? The earliest version of this argument, as far as I know, is in the second-century (Pseudo-)Athenagoras' *De Resurrectione*, ch. 4, *Legatio and De Resurrectione*, 96–97. Like later discussions of this problem, the author points out that the problem goes beyond literal cannibalism, since the particles of a body that is decomposed and eaten by worms or fish may eventually become part of other people even if their dietary habits are mundane. On this, see Grant, "Resurrection," 195–98; Strickland, "Doctrine," 165–66; Bynum, *Resurrection*, 32–33.

however, that the medieval and early modern Christian philosophers who addressed this problem never did so by abandoning the composition principle.[59] A number of proposals were made: for example, that human beings cannot digest human flesh and therefore the same material is never shared by different people;[60] or that it is acceptable to lose some of the body's material as long as some particular, uniquely essential subset of that material is present in the resurrected body; or that as long as *any* of the original material is present, it still counts. None of these solutions abandons the CP, though some seek to modify it.

Today, philosophers of religion who defend the doctrine of resurrection usually reject that principle.[61] This is partly because of difficulties such as the cannibal problem, but also, at least in some cases, because of a suspicion that even if one could identify the "correct" particles to reassemble, and reassemble them, this would not be sufficient for the same body to be present. This argument goes back at least to Lucretius,[62] but its modern form derives primarily from Peter Van Inwagen.[63] Van Inwagen's central argument is that for the particles that constitute my body to constitute *my body*, it is not enough for them to bear the correct spatial relations to each other. They must bear these relations *as a result* of the correct causal story, and that story is violated if they are dispersed and then gathered back together.[64]

In the face of such objections, contemporary defenders of resurrection appeal to other relations that might hold between the earthly and the resurrected body, or (as we have seen in the case of Mavrodes and Merricks) to the brute fact of identity. As I have indicated, I am sympathetic to this

59. On this, see Strickland, "Doctrine," 16–79.

60. This suggestion goes back to (Pseudo-)Athenagoras, *De Resurrectione*, ch. 8 (*Legatio and De Resurrectione*, 106–7).

61. On this general rejection and the reasons behind it, see Davis and Yang, "Compositionalism," 214–16; Mooney, "Possibility," 273–75. The authors of these two papers buck the general trend by defending the notion of resurrection as reassembly. Lynn Rudder Baker, "Persons," 341–43, rejects the possibility of the resurrection body being identical to the earthly body on *any* criterion of identity. Mugg and Turner argue against Baker (I think correctly) that the resurrection body needs to be identical to the earthly one, but (I think incorrectly) reject the notion that this would require the reassembly of the original parts, or "mereological essentialism" ("Bodily Resurrection," 137). Stewart Goetz, "Human Persons," 303, in turn, argues against Mugg and Turner precisely on the grounds that sameness of body *would* require the reassembly of the original parts, and that this is impossible. He appeals to the traditional problems with the notion, which, as I discuss below, I think the atemporal account can resolve.

62. Lucretius, *De Rerum Natura*, III.947–61, pp. 266–67.

63. Van Inwagen, "Possibility," 118–19.

64. Trenton Merricks, "How to Live Forever," 187–88, presents this as the primary objection to the notion of resurrection by reassembly.

latter strategy, but it is hardly very satisfying. Indeed, I would go further: by abandoning the notion that the resurrected body is *numerically* identical with the earthly body—in the sense of being composed of the same stuff—these philosophers of religion have lost a key element of traditional Christian belief.

But all of this presupposes that the resurrection is something that happens in the future. The problems all arise from an apparent incompatibility between the doctrine (the body will arise in the future) and observable events (phenomena such as the decomposition of the body). If we abandon the doctrine that the body will arise *in the future*, and replace it with the doctrine that the body *arises atemporally*, then there is no inconsistency with the observable events, because the latter all occur within time but the former does not. To put it another way, we can accept that the body dies, is buried, and decomposes without again rising in the future, because resurrection does not consist of the body's particles re-combining (or being supplanted by suitable replacements) *at a future date*. Rather, resurrection consists of the entire body throughout its earthly career being extended out of time altogether.

To repurpose a much-used analogy, imagine a cube resting on a Flatland-style plane. To Flatlanders, it is a flat square, with boundaries all around. But to an external observer, the cube extends out of the plane in a direction that the Flatlanders cannot experience. Moreover, the cube and the square are not different entities. Rather, the square is merely one face of the cube, which can be conceived of as the square face extended upwards from the Flatland plane. Similarly, on the scenario we are imagining, the earthly career of a person, including their body, extends throughout time, and because we are temporal creatures we perceive only this temporal extension. But a person actually extends out of the temporal dimension altogether. This extension into atemporality is not something distinct from the body or its physical components. Rather, it *is* the body, including its physical components, extended atemporally.

This allows us to hold that the resurrected body is *genuinely* identical with the body that dies, in accordance with the composition principle (suitably reworded to include atemporal bodies). Moreover, we can avoid all of the problems that faced traditional theologians who held this principle. For example, consider the fact that different particles compose my body at different times. With temporal resurrection, we must identify *which* of these particles are needed. But with atemporal resurrection, there is no need. Every particle that has ever been a part of my body can itself be considered as a four-dimensional spacetime worm. The section of each worm that corresponds to the time when it was part of my body—but *only* that section—can extend orthogonally into the atemporal resurrection body. If a given particle spends some of its time as part of my body, and some of its time as part of another, there is no problem: these are different segments of the spacetime worm and can be extended into different atemporal resurrection bodies.

Atemporal resurrection, then, allows us to say that the body is really resurrected—and, moreover, it is easier to explain why it is *the same body* that is resurrected on this model than it is with temporal resurrection. It does not matter how many particles pass through my body, or how promiscuous those particles may be in moving from body to body, because they are not gathered up together again at the end of time. Rather, the temporal segments of these particles *that correspond to when they are part of my body* are extended atemporally into the resurrection body. What happens to those same particles' temporal segments that do not form part of my body makes no difference to me.[65]

Christ and resurrection

There is an apparent problem with the scenario I have been setting out. The New Testament consistently teaches that the resurrection of believers is similar in kind to the resurrection of Jesus. In 1 Corinthians 15, Paul insists upon the reality of Christ's resurrection (vv. 1–19), before talking about the future resurrection of believers (vv. 21–58). He links the two with the metaphor of "first fruits" (v. 20): Christ's resurrection is the beginning of

65. If the resurrection body contains all the particles that it contained in life (albeit only the temporal segments of those particles that correspond to when they were actually in the body), then it seems the resurrection body will be enormous. Moreover, those who lived longer lives will have bigger bodies than those who lived shorter lives. All of this raises worrying questions: will we be gigantic blobs of flesh? Will those particles be arranged in a form akin to earthly human bodies, or something quite different? Questions of this kind have been asked for as long as Christians believed in a resurrection at all, as Paul attests in 1 Corinthians 15:35. The account I have been developing is no more prone to such problems than any traditional account which seeks to maintain the composition principle. But it may have its own ways of overcoming them. I suggested in chapter 2 that an atemporal conception of heaven might be taken to imply a state that lacks both time and space as we understand it. If that is so, then the particles that compose the heavenly body might bear relations to each other that are structurally similar to spatial relations, but are nonetheless non-spatial. And if that is so then questions of the kind just mentioned may seem less appropriate: blobs, giants, and the like are physical objects quite unlike what would exist in space-less possible worlds, if such things are indeed possible. A conclusion of this kind would, I think, be compatible with Christian orthodoxy. As we shall discuss in chapter 5, the crucial element of the Christian doctrine of the resurrection of the body is not that the body should be qualitatively similar to the earthly body, but that the whole person be genuinely raised. And the account I am sketching is clear on that.

the general resurrection. What happened to Jesus will happen to everyone. Elsewhere, we are told that we are raised *with Christ* (Eph 2:60).

But how can this be squared with the scenario of atemporal resurrection? On that view, although resurrection can be thought of as lying in the personal future of the individual, it does not lie in the future from the point of view of anyone else's timeline. It is atemporal, a raising of the *entire* spacetime worm that is an individual person, extending it orthogonally to time. But this is not what happens to Jesus in the New Testament! From the viewpoint of the time of Jesus' ministry, his resurrection does not merely lie in the personal future of Jesus himself. It is in the future *simpliciter*. Jesus' resurrection is not a matter of the whole of Jesus' life being extended out of time. It is a matter of the earthly Jesus getting up and walking out of the tomb, and that is a temporal event. After his resurrection, Jesus exists not in some atemporal dimension but in the ordinary world, moving about and interacting with people in a wholly temporal way. It seems, then, that to believe in atemporal resurrection for believers is to decouple them from Christ's resurrection, a move that does violence to the logic of the New Testament. As David Wilkinson puts it:

> [T]he bodily resurrection is important for it locates the risen Jesus in time. . . . We therefore need to oppose any suggestion that the new creation is "timeless" and the subsequent undervaluing of the gift of time in this creation. Time is not a mistake or an imperfection in creation.[66]

One option for the atemporalist is simply to give up belief in the post-resurrection life of Jesus. Although he does not give details, Ian McFarland seems to adopt this course. He conceives of Jesus' resurrected life as occurring outside both space and time,[67] and writes accordingly:

> With his death and burial, Jesus' life is over. And to deny that the resurrection is a further episode in this life is to affirm that it is precisely in the earthly life of Jesus, bounded by birth in Bethlehem at its beginning and death in Jerusalem at its end, that God's life is revealed. The resurrection is not more of this life, but precisely the vindication of this life in its completeness.[68]

---

66. Wilkinson, *Christian Eschatology*, 105. Wilkinson sets up a false dichotomy here: to say that the resurrection life is atemporal is certainly not the same thing as to say that time is "a mistake or an imperfection."

67. McFarland, *Word Made Flesh*, 168.

68. McFarland, *Word Made Flesh*, 165.

This is not a "demythologizing" of the language of resurrection to make it into merely a kind of poetic way of talking about the importance of Jesus' life and his continuing influence, of the kind that was fashionable in the mid-to-late twentieth century. Rather, McFarland conceives of the resurrection as a real, objective event, but one that takes Jesus' life as a whole out of time. Consequently, he argues for the rather unusual position that although the post-resurrection appearances are not literally true, the story of the empty tomb is, for the reality of Jesus' resurrection means that his body simply vanished after his burial.[69] Other than this element, his account of Jesus' resurrection sounds a lot like the kind of resurrection I have been imagining for believers.

While this solution is (I think) conceptually coherent, it is hardly one that most Christians would be willing to countenance. Fortunately, it is possible to reconcile atemporality with a literal reading of the New Testament accounts of Jesus' temporal resurrection and subsequent appearances. To see this, forget about atemporal resurrections for a moment and think again in terms of a future, temporal resurrection. On such a view, there will come a point in the future of the universe that we know when heaven will come to earth and everyone will be raised from the dead. They will inhabit a new heaven and a new earth in which the reign of God will be absolute and universally acknowledged. And yet on this picture, *exactly the same problem* persists. Jesus' resurrection does *not* occur as part of a universal cosmic renewal. The resurrected Jesus exists not within a community of saints praising God in the new Jerusalem, but within a community of doubtful disciples in the old one.[70] He is almost like a time traveler: a man who belongs in a glorious future, displaced into a drab present. And after spending forty days in the old earth, he ascends and leaves it (Acts 1:9).[71] This is unlike everyone

69. McFarland, *Word Made Flesh*, 167–68. This reverses the more common view of a number of modern theologians that the tomb was not empty but the disciples had genuine experiences of the risen Christ. It seems to me that the logic of McFarland's position should require that Jesus' body vanish immediately upon his death, if his earthly existence is bounded by his birth and his death. McFarland seems willing to suppose that Jesus' dead body did exist for at least some time, but he does not explain this apparent inconsistency.

70. In a different context, David Wilkinson, *Christian Eschatology*, 94, also stresses this "discontinuity" between Jesus' resurrection and that of believers.

71. There is disagreement about how important to early Christianity belief in Christ's ascension was. N. T. Wright, *Surprised by Hope*, 109, argues that it was common, finding it taught by Paul (Rom 8:34) and John (20:17). William Loader, *Loose Ends*, 11–13, by contrast, considers it an innovation by Luke that reflects an understanding of salvation history quite different from Paul's or the other evangelists'. For a survey of different positions on this, see Zwiep, *Ascension*, 1–35. For my part I find Loader's arguments more convincing than Wright's. For example, Jesus' instruction to Mary not to touch

else, who will be resurrected and ascend immediately afterwards (1 Thess 4:16–17) and they will see heaven descending to earth (Rev 21:1–2). It seems, then, that there is a disconnect between Christ's (past) resurrection and the (future) general resurrection in the very fact that only the former has occurred in isolation, accompanied by no general resurrection and no renewal of the heavens and the earth.

All of this suggests that although Christ's resurrection is the model for the general resurrection, and his resurrected body is the template for all resurrected bodies, the circumstances of Christ's resurrection are supposed to be unique. Christians do not expect to rise from their graves and then walk around a familiar, untransformed earth, as Jesus did; and the New Testament does not tell them they will do so. On the contrary, they will rise as *part* of a dramatically transformed and renewed created order. The period between Jesus' resurrection and his ascension is something unique to him, a one-of-a-kind period in which he could demonstrate to his disciples the reality of his resurrection and instruct them for the future (Acts 1:2–3). On the atemporal view, we can say that although resurrection is a genuine event that transforms believers, it happens atemporally—though for Jesus, uniquely, it occurred temporally. This mirrors what believers in a temporal resurrection must say: that resurrection for believers occurs in the future as part of a universal cosmic renewal—though for Jesus, uniquely, it occurred in the past and in isolation. In both cases, it is Jesus' very role as the trailblazer and model for all humanity that makes his resurrection so unusual and distinctive, though others may expect to follow him, and their bodily transformation will be of the same kind, though occurring under different circumstances.

Conclusion

This chapter has set out the basis for our picture of an atemporal heaven. As I sketched out in the introduction, we will build up this picture throughout

---

him because he had not yet ascended, in John's Gospel, must be referring to an imminent event, not a much later Lucan-style ascension, given that he later *instructs* Thomas to touch him. However, it is easy to see why a belief in the ascension or something very similar must have arisen in Christianity, given the physical absence of the resurrected Christ after his final appearance to Paul (1 Cor 15: 8). Arie Zwiep, *Ascension*, 119–44 makes a convincing case for the view that the story of the ascension in Acts was Luke's invention, but it built upon a much older belief in *some* kind of ascension, probably originally thought to be part of the same event as Jesus' resurrection, "a single continuous movement from grave to glory" (p. 120).

the rest of the book in the form of a series of propositions about heaven. The first six are in place:

(1) Heaven is an atemporal state.

(2) The heavenly state is causally dependent upon the earthly state.

(3) The earthly state is whole-state-determining of the heavenly state.

(4) The heavenly state is bodily.

(5) The heavenly body is the same body as the earthly body.

(6) The heavenly body is composed of the same parts as the earthly body, respecting the composition principle.

If we accept all of these, we have a picture of an earthly existence that lasts for a certain period of time, and a heavenly existence which lasts for no period of time, in which the latter is directly causally dependent upon *the whole* of the former. Clearly, such a causal dependence would be different from mundane causality, but as we saw in chapter 2, this is coherent provided we adopt a relatively metaphysically neutral account of causality that sets no spatial or temporal conditions.

It is important to note that one can accept some of these claims without necessarily being committed to all of the others. I have argued that (2) allows us to make sense of (1). Appealing to the relation of causal dependence is what allows us to make sense of the claim that a given atemporal person is identical with a given temporal person. This is, I think, coherent if we assume perdurantism, which I have argued is itself entailed by the supposition of divine atemporality. But someone might argue that this entailment does not hold, and instead affirm divine atemporality and endurantism. Such a person might endorse (1) but reject (2), holding (for example) that identity across time (and beyond it) is basic.[72]

Again, I have argued that (3) has the benefit of avoiding the bottleneck problem. But one could hold (1) and (2) without endorsing it. Someone might prefer to think of the earthly state as final-state-determining, on the grounds that this respects the traditional future emphasis of eschatology. Such a person might look for a different solution to the bottleneck problem, such as abandoning the notion of criteria for identity over time. Or they might hold that it is not a problem after all (perhaps there are good reasons to think that a person's final earthly moments are of paramount significance, as the early modern spiritual writers thought). I think it would be harder

---

72. This would not entail having to reject all of the subsequent propositions, as it is not the case that each proposition is necessary to accept all subsequent ones. One could reject AH2 but accept AH4, for example.

for someone with this view to endorse (6), but perhaps that would also be acceptable: as we have seen, most contemporary defenders of resurrection are willing to abandon the composition principle.

In the next two chapters we shall consider what that atemporal existence might be like. In the process we shall add some more propositions to our conception of atemporal heaven, with the same proviso that one could reject some of them without having to abandon a fundamentally atemporal account.

5

Heavenly Activities

In the last three chapters, I have argued for the coherence of the view that heaven is atemporal. Along the way, we have seen some reasons for holding such a view: it avoids the most serious of the arguments against the desirability of heaven that we saw in chapter 1, and it also provides possible ways to avoid both the bottleneck problem and the issues surrounding the resurrection of the body that we saw in chapter 4.

But even if we grant that an atemporal heaven is coherent and successfully avoids these problems that dog temporal heaven, does it follow that we would actually *want* to go there? What would atemporal heaven be like? What would the blessed do there—if the concept of "doing" anything can even make sense in this context?

Changing and unchanging heaven

For many philosophers of religion—perhaps most, judging by recent publications on the topic—heaven is indeed a place where the blessed can expect to *do* all sorts of things. This is the concept of heaven that its proponents call "dynamic," in contrast to "static" accounts. Christopher Brown comments that this very language prejudices the case. The word "static" does not sound appealing.[1] Indeed, as Richard Bauckham observed forty years ago, in a

1. Brown, *Eternal Life*, 32n6. Brown's response to this is, in part, to argue that being *dynamic* does not entail having to *change*, and that a changeless God (and a changeless heaven) can still count as "dynamic" (p. 61). In my view, this is giving up too much terminological ground. Rather than trying to reclaim "dynamic" as a proper description of the static view, I would prefer to reject the "dynamic"/"static" terminology altogether and with it the need to present the "static" view as somehow dynamic after all.

different context, "static" is "always a pejorative word in modern theology."[2] Equally, we might observe that "dynamic" sounds inherently positive. Simply framing the discussion in these terms is thus to put the "static" view at a disadvantage. So why use this language? Why not call them, say, the "stable" and "unstable" views of heaven? Or, to use more ancient terminology, why not speak in terms of "being" and "becoming"? To try to avoid bias either way, I would prefer to use the more neutral terms "changing" and "unchanging."[3]

Eric Silverman, one of the most prominent defenders of a changing heaven, defines "dynamic" views as:

> conceptions of heaven that depict paradise as a place or state of existence where moral, aesthetic, epistemological, relational, and other changes or progress takes place.[4]

"Static" views, meanwhile, are:

> conceptions of heaven that portray paradise as a place or state of existence where there is no further moral, aesthetic, epistemological, relational, and other change or progress for the inhabitants of heaven.[5]

Christopher Brown points out that although Silverman talks as if these two descriptions exhaust all the possibilities, intermediate views are possible, according to which some kinds of change or development occur in heaven, but not others.[6] Indeed, I would go further and suggest that even Silverman's "static" category covers too wide a range of options. The passages he uses to illustrate this category (and its supposed limitations) all invoke images of sitting on clouds singing hymns. Silverman comments that, as a result of such images, "many in contemporary culture seem to believe that heaven would be boring, static, and pointless because nothing really happens. Without dynamic activity, change, and goals the heavenly existence would

---

2. Bauckham, "Suffering God," 8.

3. Another issue with the "static"/"dynamic" terminology is that it is ambiguous. As Antje Jackelén points out in *Time and Eternity*, 183–84, in a scientific context a "static" model is not one where time does not pass, but one where time always operates in the same way, while a "dynamic" model is one where time does not always operate in the same way. On this definition, the proponents of a "dynamic" heaven are actually defending a "static" conception.

4. Silverman, "Conceiving Heaven," 18.

5. Silverman, "Conceiving Heaven," 14.

6. Brown, *Eternal Life*, 32–33.

be unfulfilling and tedious."[7] Consequently, Silverman argues, "dynamic" conceptions are superior to "static" ones "for demonstrating that an eternal existence can be fulfilling and meaningful."[8]

This is a version of what, in chapter 1, I called the first category of arguments against heaven—those that are based upon a *particular account* of what goes on in heaven that appears to be undesirable. Silverman turns this from an argument against the coherence of heaven into an argument for a particular conception of heaven. But the plausibility of this argument depends upon assuming a particular *kind* of "static" existence. We can clearly distinguish between the following kinds of existence:

(1) "Unchanging"$_1$—an existence in which events occur, but no progress is ever made.

(2) "Unchanging"$_2$—an existence in which no events occur.

As an example of an unchanging$_1$ existence, consider a long-running sitcom such as *The Simpsons*, where events occur in every episode, but they never seem to have any permanent impact: every episode begins with every character in exactly the same situation they were in at the start of the previous episode, and nobody ages or develops.[9] But such a scenario is not unchanging$_2$—in an unchanging$_2$ scenario, nothing would happen *at all*.

Silverman's arguments are directed against a conception of heaven as unchanging$_1$. In the "cloud heaven," nothing significant may change, but events occur: one could hardly sing if time did not pass. Less hackneyed conceptions of heaven as unchanging$_1$ are available, and are not, on the face of it, undesirable. The fantasy versions of paradise described by Dunsany and Tolkien that we mentioned in chapter 4 are good examples: time passes and events occur in Elfland, but there is no permanent change there. For Silverman, the lack of any prospect of change is *in itself* abhorrent,[10] even if the situation is otherwise pleasant. I suspect that this is a case where one value is opposed to another, and there is no way of arguing for the "correctness" of one over the other: if Dunsany prefers an unchanging$_1$ paradise, who is to say he should not? My instinct is to side with him: for me at least, change is an inherently melancholy thing, for even a change that is for the better overall involves loss of some kind.

7. Silverman, "Conceiving Heaven," 15–16.

8. Silverman, "Conceiving Heaven," 24.

9. As time passes in the real world, some permanent changes are forced upon the fictional world, either because actors have become unavailable or died, or because the audience's sensibilities change—but these are the exception rather than the rule.

10. Silverman, "Conceiving Heaven," 26.

However, if an unchanging$_1$ world does seem abhorrent, I think this must arise from a fundamental mismatch between actions and consequences. Ordinarily, we think that a meaningful action is one that makes a difference. In an unchanging$_1$ world, we can perform actions, but they make no difference. The classic illustration of this is *Groundhog Day*, where Bill Murray's character, Phil, is trapped in a repeating cycle of events that he cannot influence. Sitting miserably in a bar, he has the following exchange with a bystander:

> Phil: What would you do if you were stuck in one place, and every day was exactly the same, and nothing you did mattered?
>
> Ralph: That about sums it up for me.

The lack of meaning that Phil finds in his fantastical situation is the same as the lack of meaning we may find in a mundane situation too: the ability to act without the possibility that our acts can make any difference. And in the film, Phil overcomes his misery when he realizes that he *can* make a difference: he can develop and improve his own character throughout the repeating cycles.

But none of this applies to unchanging$_2$ situations. In a world that is unchanging$_2$, there cannot be this problematic disconnect between our actions and their consequences, because there are no actions *at all*. The futility of endlessly repeating pointless activities that achieve nothing would never arise. So even if accept Silverman's criticisms of "static" conceptions of heaven in the sense of being unchanging$_1$, they do not apply to those that are unchanging$_2$. And, clearly, an atemporal heaven would be unchanging$_2$.

However, one might say that, although an unchanging$_2$ heaven avoids this criticism, it is still inferior to a changing heaven. This is because a changing heaven allows for *progress*, which is inherently desirable. Proponents of a changing heaven typically hold that the blessed are eternally progressing in the sense of developing their characters. This development may be in virtue, as Timothy Pawl and Kevin Timpe have argued,[11] or it may be in knowledge, as Keith Ward has suggested.[12] I suggest, though, that the changing heaven's currently fashionable status is connected to what Antje Jackelén has diagnosed as an increasing mistrust of eternity. In her examination of trends in hymn-writing, she notes that the concept of eternity appears less

---

11. Pawl and Timpe, "Paradise."

12. Ward, *Religion*, 309. In what follows I will focus on moral progression, but similar considerations can be applied to epistemological progression or other kinds.

often and is subjugated to that of time.[13] But, she thinks, this can lead to a distorted emphasis on temporality:

> This fixation can result in time's being forced to accomplish more than it actually can. It simply has to provide *everything.* . . . In a time that does not relate to eternity, speed can quickly become a value in itself. Acceleration is good; a delay—or even a standstill—is bad. . . . In this setting, boredom can no longer be experienced as a potential for creativity, but rather only as sheer misfortune. Change and instant gratification, on the other hand, signify happiness and good fortune.[14]

Although theologically motivated, Jackelén's gloomy analysis is a criticism of modern society in general rather than of any theological position. But it is hard to read these words and not think of the changing conception of heaven. Such a concept is indeed a privileging of *time* over *eternity*, for it seeks to recast eternity simply as more time. And, for the defenders of changing heaven, boredom is indeed something wholly negative. The supposed ability of this conception to answer the boredom argument is typically cited as one of its greatest strengths.

Karl Rahner offers a similar assessment:

> It seems to me that the conceptual models used to clarify what is meant by eternal are for the most part insufficient to deal with the radical break that takes place at death. Eternal—strangely described as continuing "beyond" and "after" death—is clothed too much with realities with which we are familiar. Eternal is thus imagined along the lines of continuing to live on, or as a meeting up with those who were close to us, or as friendship and peace, or as a banquet and a celebration. These and similar conceptions focus on the never-ending and ongoing character of eternal. Yet I fear that the radical incomprehensibility of what is really meant by eternal is in this way trivialized. . . . What is not properly perceived is the unspeakable enormity of the fact that the absolute divinity, God's very self, stoops down naked and bare into our narrow creatureliness.[15]

13. Jackelén, *Time and Eternity*, 56–57.

14. Jackelén, *Time and Eternity*, 58.

15. Rahner, "Experience," 325. Rahner's target here is not the changing conception of heaven specifically, but it is easy to see that conception as part of the more general movement to think of heaven as a kind of continuation of our earthly lives. A prominent example is Richard Swinburne's argument ("Life of Heaven") that the plausibility and attractiveness of the "dynamic" view of heaven is precisely its similarity to our familiar earthly existence.

In themselves, verdicts such as Jackelén's and Rahner's do not provide *arguments* against the conception of heaven as changing. They merely bemoan it. But serious arguments against it do exist. We can divide these into two groups.

Eternal progression: inherent problems

The first kind of objection to the notion of eternal progression seeks to show that it is *inherently* incoherent, or at least undesirable. The most well-established such objection argues that to be eternally developing is to be eternally undeveloped. This argument goes back at least to Kant, who wrote:

> Even assuming a person's moral-physical state here in life at its best—namely as a constant progression and approach to the highest good (marked out for him as a goal)—, he still (even with a consciousness of the unalterability of his disposition) cannot combine it with the prospect of *satisfaction* in an eternally enduring alteration of his state (the moral as well as the physical). For the state in which he now is will always remain an ill compared with a better one which he always stands ready to enter; and the representation of an infinite progression toward the final end is nevertheless at the same time a prospect of an infinite series of ills which, even though they may be outweighed by a greater good, do not allow for the possibility of contentment; for he can think that only by supposing that the *final end* will at sometime be *attained*.[16]

In *Groundhog Day*, after all, Phil escapes the repeating cycle *once he has become a better person*. Kant gives us the vision of a Groundhog Day that truly never ends, in which there is no escape from the futility.

Miroslav Volf responds to this argument by appealing to Gregory of Nyssa's claim that each new stage is so wonderful that the memory of the previous stages is forgotten. Apparently recognizing the obvious flaws with this answer, Volf goes on:

> If one is unpersuaded, one can argue plausibly that change need not be progressive/regressive, and movement need not be linear. The movement can also be cyclical (as in Nietzsche's notion of the "eternal return") or kaleidoscopic (as a child's play may be

---

16. "The End of All Things," 8:335, in Kant, *Religion and Rational Theology*, 227–28 (italics original).

described). In both of these later cases, change entails neither gain nor loss, and is compatible with contentment.[17]

I do not find this defense convincing. In the case of cyclical change, one can only say that there is no gain or loss if each cycle is the same as the one that came before it. So there is no real *change* at all in such a set-up. Things change from one moment to the next, but they always revert to their starting states, so no change is ever permanent. This inevitably raises the question: in what way is this supposed to be superior to a wholly changeless state?

Here is an alternative objection to Kant's argument. Suppose we accept Aristotle's distinction between "activity" (ἐνέργειᾰ) and "process"(κῑνησῐς): an "activity" is complete at any moment and can in theory be continued indefinitely. A "process," by contrast, aims at a goal, and finishes once the goal is attained.[18] We might distinguish between the activity of walking *simpliciter* and the process of walking *to a specific place*. Aristotle holds that activities are conducted for their own sake while processes are conducted for the sake of their goal, but this is clearly false. I can walk to a specific place for the purpose of exercise. If I do a jigsaw puzzle, it is because I enjoy doing puzzles, not because I want to have a completed puzzle.[19] And, it may be said, Kant makes the same error as Aristotle. He assumes that progression must be done *for the sake of* the final goal, and if the final goal cannot be achieved, the progression becomes pointless. But in fact, progression can be its own reward. The blessed in heaven progress not because they hope to attain some final state of perfection, but because the activity of improving is intrinsically worthwhile in itself.

Such a reply has some merit. Given a temporal view of heaven in which the blessed are constantly progressing, it does seem to me coherent to suppose that the goal of blessed, at any given moment, is simply their betterment *in that moment*. That is, I might seek to become (say) more charitable today than I was yesterday, without the need to have in view the final goal of becoming perfectly charitable.

Consequently, I think that the Kantian objection can be overcome. There is nothing *inherently* undesirable or incoherent about the notion of heaven as eternal progress. However, I propose a second class of objections to this notion of heaven, which I think are much more serious. Objections in this second class suggest that the concept of heaven as eternal progress

17. Volf, "Enter into Joy!," 269–70.

18. The distinction is made in Aristotle's *Nicomachean Ethics*, 10.3, 1173a, pp. 251–52. On this, see Bostock, "Pleasure and Activity."

19. Urmson, *Aristotle's Ethics*, 102–3.

is incompatible with key Christian beliefs.[20] In my view, the most powerful such objections focus on Christian beliefs about Christ. For any even remotely orthodox Christian, Christ is a *wholly morally perfect* human being. He is perfect not merely in his divinity, but in his humanity: his *human* will never assents to sin.[21] This doctrine presents two quite distinct problems for the proponent of eternal progression.[22]

20. The objections that Christopher Brown raises mostly fall into this category (*Eternal Life*, 43–54). In brief, they are: (1) weighty theological authorities reject the notion of moral progress in heaven; (2) moral progress in an everlasting heaven would outweigh moral progress made in one's earthly life, rendering it largely irrelevant; (3) moral progress is inconsistent with the traditional conception of the vision of God; and (4) heaven is supposed to be a state of rest that is quite unlike our earthly existence. Of these, I think that (3) and (4) are the most weighty. Peter Dillard, "Keeping the Vision," 406–7, gives another theologically based objection: if heaven is conceived in terms of eternal progress, it is very hard to give any non-arbitrary explanation why one should say that the blessed enjoy beatitude any more than the faithful on earth do. Brown and Dillard do not, however, offer any christologically based objections of the kind I develop here.

21. Some authors have recently argued that Christ's human perfection is compatible with his undergoing moral development, even as an adult and during his ministry (beyond his growing "in wisdom" as a child in Luke 2:52). Adam Pelser ("Temptation"), for example, notes that Christian tradition teaches mostly unanimously that Jesus exemplified moral perfection, but goes on to argue that if Jesus was truly tempted (as Christian tradition also holds) then, at least during his temptations, he must not have been perfectly virtuous after all (though he was sinless), because a perfectly virtuous person would be wholly immune to temptation. Eleonore Stump has argued for an interpretation of the story of the raising of Lazarus in which Jesus makes "a non-culpable mistake" (*Wandering in Darkness*, 336) by wrongly believing Mary would not be upset by his own delay in attending to her brother. Identifying this Mary with the Mary to whom the risen Jesus appears in John 20, Stump suggests that Jesus had learned from his earlier mistake: "Now he does not delay his coming, and so her weeping stops" (*Image*, 211). Here again, then, we have the suggestion of moral improvement on Jesus' part. (I am grateful to David Worsley for pointing out these arguments to me.) To my mind, the view of Jesus as experiencing moral improvement even throughout his ministry is hard to reconcile with the role he is supposed to play for Christians as perfect exemplar (on which, see below). But even if we accept it, both versions of this account suggest that Jesus does attain moral perfection by the end of his life: how, after all, could he have assented to his death for the sake of humanity if he had not? So even if we suppose that Christ developed morally, he still instantiated moral perfection, at the very least, by the time of his passion and death, and that is enough for the arguments I give in this section.

22. These objections assume a changing conception of heaven as one of constant *moral improvement* on the part of the blessed. This is how contemporary defenders of the changing heaven typically present it. Older versions more commonly focus on constant intellectual improvement. Heaven, on this view, is a place where the blessed are eternally learning new things about God. As John Vaughan put it over a century ago, "However perfectly the Blessed may know God's Divine perfections, there will always remain infinitely more to learn" (*Life Everlasting*, 73). The objections I give here could

Eternal progression: Christ's moral perfection

First, and in my view most seriously, there is what I shall call the *final end problem*. Let us define a state of *moral perfection* as follows:

Moral perfection: a state such that no morally superior state is possible.[23]

Here is my argument for the final end problem:

(1) If there is a final end to moral progression, eternal meaningful moral progression is not possible.

(2) If a state of moral perfection is possible, there is a final end to moral progression.

(3) If there has ever been a human being who existed in a state of moral perfection, a state of moral perfection is possible.

(4) There has been a human being who existed in a state of moral perfection.

(5) Therefore, eternal meaningful moral progression is not possible.

I take (4) to be unobjectionable within a Christian context, since it is axiomatic that Jesus existed in a state of moral perfection. I also take (2) to be unassailable. If it is possible to be morally perfect, which we are defining as a state that has no morally superior state, then that would indeed be the final

---

be reframed to address a heaven of intellectual improvement if they were coupled with the doctrine that Christ, in his perfect humanity, enjoys a state of knowledge in his human mind (not merely his divine omniscience) as perfect as is possible for human beings. However, although this is a traditional Christian belief (articulated by Aquinas at *ST*, III qq. 9–12), it is much less commonly defended today, and not (I think) by any defenders of a dynamic conception of heaven. One might also hold that the blessed have a capacity for understanding that is immeasurably greater than that of earthly humans, so they might learn new truths about God beyond even what Jesus could comprehend in his human mind during his earthly ministry. (I am grateful to Oliver Crisp for this last point.) Consequently, a conception of a changing heaven that revolves around intellectual, rather than moral, improvement may be more resilient against arguments of the kind I give here. It is, however, the moral kind of changing heaven that predominates among philosophers of religion today, which I think is vulnerable to these arguments.

23. By "possible" here I mean metaphysical possibility. A pencil, after all, cannot enter into a state that is morally superior to its current one, but that does not mean that it enjoys moral perfection, because the impossibility of its improvement is a contingent impossibility. (There is, presumably, a possible world in which pencils can undergo moral improvement, though that world is startlingly unlike the actual one.) There is, by contrast, no possible world containing a Jesus who is morally superior to the actual one. On the concept of moral perfection, see Graves, "God," 125–39. Graves also argues for an unimproveability element to the notion of moral perfection, though he does it in greater depth than I have here.

end of moral progress. Someone who exists in a state of moral perfection cannot, by definition, progress morally.

(1) seems to me to be intuitively true. A process that has a final end cannot be continued past that end. If it is, then that wasn't the final end after all. If I cycle with the goal of getting to Glastonbury, then once I have reached Glastonbury, that process is over (even if my main aim in making the trip was not to arrive at Glastonbury but to get some exercise). If I carry on cycling, then I was never really *cycling to Glastonbury*—I was just cycling *simpliciter*, and happened to stop off there. Similarly, my aim in doing a jigsaw puzzle is not to have a completed puzzle, but still, once I have it, the process of completing the puzzle is finished. The same applies to moral progression. If there is a final end to moral development, then once that end is reached, the moral development is finished, even if actually achieving that end was not the conscious goal of the person undergoing the development. Any further moral development past that point, if it is even possible, would not be meaningful. If it were meaningful, then the end would not have been reached.

There is a possible objection to (1). It could be the case that although moral progression has an end, namely the state of moral perfection, this end is not practically attainable. It could be that one approaches it asymptotically, meaning that the closer one gets to moral perfection, the smaller the steps one takes towards it. One would be eternally inching closer to moral perfection, but as the time passed approaches infinity, the degrees of improvement approach an infinitesimal.

Such a scenario may be theoretically possible, but it is deeply problematic. Suppose that, after a few million years in heaven, I have achieved a moral state that is *almost* perfection. Perhaps I perform a less than perfect act once a century.[24] Where do I go from this? After a few more million years, I perform a less than perfect act once every 101 years. A few million years after that, I act suboptimally once every 101 years and a month. And so on. There comes a point where calling it moral progress at all feels largely meaningless: the improvements are so incredibly slight, and so far spaced out, that they really make no difference.[25] So even if eternal moral progression is consistent with the existence of an end to moral progression, there could not be *meaningful* eternal moral progression.

---

24. I assume that, in heaven, morally wrong or sinful acts are impossible, but this would still be consistent with having the ability to choose between more and less good acts. On this, see Brown, *Eternal Life*, 47–48.

25. This is a moral version of the objection from diminishing returns I have made elsewhere to the notion of eternal progress in understanding God. See Hill, "Boredom," 147.

A possible reply to this would be to frame moral progression in terms not of *acting* better but of inner *attitudes*. Timothy Pawl and Kevin Timpe have argued that the eternal progress enjoyed by the saints is not a matter of *performing better actions*. Rather, even someone who already acts perfectly in every situation can still "gain new insights and new desires,"[26] allowing them to understand the benefits of acting in such a way and desiring to do so ever more deeply.[27] But the same consideration applies. If I spend millions of years increasing my understanding of (say) temperance and my desire to act temperately, there must come a point at which *either* I reach the state of perfect understanding and desire enjoyed by Christ *or* any further enhancement of my understanding and desire that still falls short of that perfect temperance is so marginal as to make no discernible difference. And this applies no matter how we characterize perfect virtue. (1), then, is indeed true.

(3) certainly seems like it should be true. Anything that is actually instantiated is *ipso facto* possible. So if there has been someone who instantiated moral perfection, moral perfection is possible. It might be objected that although such a state is possible in itself, it is not possible *for us*. Although Christ's human will is, in essence, identical to our own, it has the unique advantage of being hypostatically united to the divine Son. Consequently, the fact that Christ exists in a state of moral perfection does not indicate that it is possible for other humans to do so. To put it in terms drawn from Thomas Morris, moral perfection may be humanly possible and yet be impossible for those who are *merely* human.[28]

Although superficially attractive, this objection misses the mark. It may indeed be that Christ has a supernatural advantage in attaining perfection that other people lack. But the mere existence of a person who *cannot* improve morally, because he has already attained complete perfection, indicates that moral perfection cannot continue for ever. There is an end point *even* for someone hypostatically united to divinity. If it is impossible for human beings other than Christ to reach moral perfection, that merely indicates that *their* end point is more modest than Christlike perfection.

26. Pawl and Timpe, "Paradise," 99.

27. Elsewhere, Pawl and Timpe distinguish between two ways of being morally perfect. One consists of adhering to the Aristotelian mean, and has a limit of perfection: if you are adhering to the mean, you can't get closer to it. The second consists of how strongly one adheres to the mean, and this kind of perfection, "for all we know, doesn't admit of an upper limit. One can always cling more tightly to the mean" ("Incompatibilism," 418). But the same objection applies: if there is no upper limit to this kind of perfection, then it would be theoretically possible to exceed Jesus in it, which is theologically unacceptable.

28. Morris, *Logic*, 57–67.

In other words, appealing to the metaphysical distinction between Christ and other human beings does not eliminate the fact of an end point beyond which no further moral progression is possible. It merely moves that end point closer to us.

A more sophisticated version of this objection could appeal to the unity of Christ's personhood. Although Christ is supposed to have two natures, each with its own will, he is nevertheless a single person, and that person is identical with the person of the divine Son. Now the kind of moral perfection that is appropriate to a divine person might be different from the kind that is appropriate to a (merely) human person. Consequently, it could be the case that the kinds of virtues that the blessed instantiate are capable of infinite progression, without ever attaining the perfection enjoyed by Christ, simply because they are different virtues, or at least instantiated in a quite different way.[29]

Such a view seems to me to be theoretically coherent, but it faces two serious problems. The first is that the New Testament consistently portrays Jesus as instantiating *human* virtue, not some fundamentally different kind of divine virtue. Consider, for example, the instruction Jesus gives in John 15:12–13: "This is my commandment, that you love one another as I have loved you. No one has greater love than this, to lay down one's life for one's friends." The reference to dying for one's friends is obviously a foreshadowing of what will happen to Jesus: he instantiates the perfect love that he describes. But the principle is made a general one: this is what perfect love is *for everyone.* And Jesus explicitly instructs his disciples to love *just as* he himself has loved. It may well be that the instruction is impossible to carry out, because we, unlike Jesus, are imperfect. But Jesus' virtue, unattainable though it may be, is a perfect version of a virtue that we are instructed to cultivate. It is not a unique divine virtue that is different in kind from our own.

The second problem is that even if it were true that Christ, in his divine person, models a special divine virtue that is different in kind from our own, he still has a human nature with a human will that is inherently no different from our own. This human will, being perfect, must exhibit moral perfection of a distinctively human nature. Now it could be the case that it is, psychologically speaking, very different from our own. For example, Maximus the Confessor argued that, in humans, there is a difference between the "thelemic" will and the "gnomic" (or "prohairetic") will.[30] The thelemic

---

29. I am grateful to Andreas Bergman for this suggestion.

30. On Maximus, see Bathrellos, *Byzantine Christ*, 99–174. On the reception of Maximus' account by John of Damascus, see Blowers, "Gnomic Will."

will is the inherent impulse towards whatever is natural for us, while the gnomic will is the process of rational deliberation by which we decide what actions to perform. Maximus insisted that Christ's human nature must have had a thelemic will, but it did not have a gnomic will, because our need to deliberate about what to do is a sign of our fallenness. A perfect human would never have to deliberate at all, but would know perfectly what to do, and would do it unhesitatingly. So although Jesus had a human will, distinct from his divine will, it functioned very differently from our own.

Nevertheless, since it was a *human* will, its functioning was how our wills *should* function. If Maximus is correct then Jesus never had to deliberate about what to do, making his experience of life very unlike our own, but if our wills were perfect, that is how we would be, too. So if the blessed in heaven are in this state, their wills are perfect, and there is no further moral progression they can take. If, conversely, they are to progress for ever, then we are back to the same problem: either they must eventually exceed this perfect state, which is impossible, or they must approach it infinitesimally, which is not meaningfully different from simply being in it unchangingly.

Consequently, (3) stands as well. I conclude that the argument for the final end problem is successful in undermining the coherence of eternal moral progression in a Christian context.

The final end problem appeals merely to the existence of Christ as a morally perfect human being. It would work even if, *per impossibile*, the blessed in heaven were unaware of Christ's existence. A second problem, which we can call the *unreachable exemplar problem*, does appeal to their awareness of him.

Here is my argument for this problem:

(1) It is not possible to spend eternity meaningfully attempting something one knows one cannot achieve.

(2) If it is impossible for the blessed to achieve something, they know they cannot achieve it.

(3) If moral progression necessarily lasts for an infinite amount of time, then it is impossible to achieve moral perfection.

(4) For the blessed, moral progression consists of attempting to achieve Christ's moral state.

(5) Christ's moral state is moral perfection.

(6) Therefore, if moral progression necessarily lasts for an infinite amount of time, meaningful moral progression is impossible for the blessed.

As before, I think this argument is valid, so our focus is again on whether the premises are true.

Working backwards, we can once again take (5) to be axiomatic. Similarly, (4) is central to Christian belief and practice. Christ does not simply instantiate moral perfection—he models it. As the author to the Hebrews writes, "let us run with perseverance the race that is set before us, looking to Jesus the pioneer and perfecter of our faith."[31] This idea of Christ as the perfect model to imitate is central to much Christian spirituality. Thus, for example, Thomas à Kempis opened his fifteenth-century classic *The Imitation of Christ* like this:

> *He who follows me can never walk in darkness*, says the Lord.
>   By these words, Christ urges us to mould our lives and characters in the image of his, if we wish to be truly enlightened and freed from all blindness of heart. Let us therefore see that we endeavour beyond all else to meditate on the life of Jesus Christ.[32]

It seems wrong to suppose that this applies to Christians only in their earthly lives. If Christ is our model on earth, surely he would be in heaven too. So the situation I envisaged earlier, in which the blessed in heaven are focused on their moral improvement at any given moment but do not have a final goal in mind, is wrong. The blessed *would* have a final goal in mind, namely Christ. Their purpose in progressing morally is to achieve a state of moral perfection modeled on his.

One might object to this premise like this: It is true that, for a Christian, Christ is the exemplar of moral perfection. But it does not follow that the Christian is actually attempting to be as perfect as Christ. Rather, the Christian is simply attempting to be as morally good as she can, taking Christ as illustrative of what moral perfection would be like if it were possible to attain.

I do not think that such an objection is really coherent. If Christ has any normative function in the Christian's moral striving at all, then it must be that the Christian is attempting to replicate Christ's moral condition. That does not require that the Christian attempts to do precisely the things that Jesus did, of course. But she must at least be attempting to act as well, morally speaking, as Jesus did, to the best of her ability. If this is not the case then I cannot really attach any meaning to the notion that Christ functions as a moral exemplar at all. Even if the Christian is not explicitly thinking "I must try to be as good as Jesus was," if she is taking Jesus to be the model

31. Heb 12:1–2 NRSV.

32. Kempis, *Imitation*, I.1, p. 37. For more on the development of the theme of imitating Christ in Christian spirituality, see Constable, *Three Studies*, 143–248.

of perfect goodness, and if she is trying to be as good as possible, then she is attempting to imitate Jesus. To put it another way, any Christian would surely agree that, to the degree that you fall short of Christ's moral state, to that degree you still have progress to make. And that is simply another way of saying that all Christians seek to replicate Christ's moral state: he is the target at which they are aiming.

Premise (3) also appears to be true, and rests upon the same insight that grounds the first premise of the final end problem. If one were to achieve moral perfection, there could be no progression towards moral progression after that point. Now, this being so, the objection from Kant quoted earlier becomes much more forceful. Given eternal progression, the blessed would be progressing towards a state of perfection, but never reaching it, *while at the same time* having before their minds an example of the state to which they are progressing, but will never reach. Presumably they are aware that they will never reach it, as it would be peculiarly cruel of God to allow them to persevere under a misapprehension of their goal in heaven (and even if they were not aware to begin with, after a few aeons had passed they would probably work it out!). Premise (2), then, is surely true as well. Such a situation does indeed seem abhorrent, for it is an eternal exercise in futility: an unending struggle that yields ever-diminishing rewards, aimed at a goal that can never be reached, even though it is a theoretically possible goal.

That is not a heaven I would want to go to. But suppose we accept that, despite the foregoing arguments, such a heaven would not be actively unpleasant. Perhaps the unreachability of moral perfection would not bother the blessed. Perhaps the increasingly minuscule moral advances they make would be sufficiently satisfying. But I want to stress that *even then* we still have a problem, thanks to premise (1). This appeals to the inherent incoherence of endlessly attempting something one knows to be impossible. Certainly one can *try* something impossible, or at least wildly unlikely: I could attempt to save a penalty by Lionel Messi, or deadlift 500kg, or find a proof to Fermat's last theorem, all of which are possible in the sense that some people have managed them. But any such attempt by me will be a light-hearted one, done more as a joke than anything else, since I know *I* could never do any of those things. It would be quite a different matter for me to devote my entire life to trying to do them *while still knowing that I cannot do it*. Such an attempt would be a psychological impossibility. If I were really to devote my life to trying to prove Fermat's last theorem, it could only be because I believed that I was capable of doing it, however difficult or unlikely it might be. I could not make such an attempt in all seriousness if I did not believe that. But this is what the proponents of eternal moral progression envisage: not merely a lifetime, but an infinite period of attempting something known to be impossible.

One might object that this is only a contingent feature of our earthly psychology. Perhaps, in addition to the psychological transformation suggested above, the blessed will also be transformed such that they are psychologically capable of eternally attempting, quite happily, something they know to be impossible. But even if this is theoretically possible, I do not think that such a situation could be called *meaningful* striving. If the blessed were really like that, we would surely consider them to be, in some way, deluded, and we would consider their eternally prolonged efforts to be an exercise in futility, even if they did not realize it themselves. To put it another way: if God were to transform the blessed in this way, it would seem to be not an *improvement* on earthly psychology, but a *regression* to a less advanced state of awareness, because they would be unaware of the futility of their actions that we are able to recognize.[33]

An alternative possible objection is that the Christian life is all about attempting the impossible anyway. Christians seek to emulate Christ, in the knowledge that such emulation is impossible. Indeed, they are called to "[b]e perfect . . . as your heavenly Father is perfect,"[34] even though "[t]here

33. The notion that, in heaven, people would experience a transformation that seems on the face of it a regression is not a new one. G. K. Chesterton, dwelling on Matthew 19:14, famously argued for the need to imitate children in key spiritual respects, above all their ability to view the world with wonder. For Chesterton, much of our moral and aesthetic development as we leave childhood is really a deterioration, and to revert to a childlike state would be not to lose our faculties but to regain something. But I do not think that even Chesterton would have recognized the kind of transformation we are considering here in these terms: such a transformation would be a loss, not a gain.

34. Matt 5:48 NRSV. The apparently impossible goal set in this verse has long puzzled commentators. Pelagius and his vociferous disciple Caelestius appealed to it, among others, as evidence that perfection is indeed possible, on the grounds that it would be unjust for Jesus to issue commands that are impossible to obey—an implicit appeal to the "ought implies can" principle some fourteen centuries before Kant. The argument is found in Pelagius' *Letter to Demetrias* (Rees, *Pelagius*, II 35), and at greater length in the *First Breviate* of Caelestius (quoted in Augustine, *The Perfection of Human Righteousness*, chs. 2–3, in *Answer*, 289–92). A paraphrase also appears in Jerome, *Dialogue Against the Pelagians*, 1.14, in *Dogmatic and Polemical Works*, 248–49. Augustine's response is to admit that perfection is possible, but only with the grace of God, so Jesus' command is not unjust. Jerome's is to distinguish between lower and higher perfections: the former is obtainable by human efforts, while the latter requires both grace and an eschatological context to come to fruition. Modern commentators have recognized the Pelagian appeal to "ought implies can," but largely in passing (e.g., Matthews, "Immoral in a Dream," 51–52; Pigden, "Ought-Implies-Can"; Nelson, *Liberalism*, 9). As far as I know, there has been no in-depth scholarly examination of the Pelagian argument or its possible sources.

is no one who is righteous, not even one."[35] And yet not only are Christians psychologically capable of making this attempt, they are not (or should not be) discouraged by the impossibility of success. So the same could apply to heaven.

But such an objection overlooks the fact that although Christians believe that attaining perfection is impossible *in this life*, they do not suppose that it is *permanently* unobtainable. Paul, after all, wrote that "when the complete comes, the partial will come to an end."[36] "The complete" here is τὸ τέλειον, the same word translated as "perfect" in Jesus' injunction. Noticing this verbal link, Augustine interpreted the two verses in light of each other, writing:

> [L]et as many of us as run perfectly bear in mind that we are not yet perfect in order that we may become perfect in that place toward which we are running perfectly. Thus, *when that which is perfect has come, that which is partial will be destroyed* (1 Cor 13:10). That is, it will not be partial, but whole, because faith and hope will be replaced by the reality itself, not something which we believe and for which we hope, but something which we see and embrace.[37]

So for Augustine, the injunction to be perfect makes sense only when understood eschatologically. We strive for perfection in this life, and inevitably fall short, but we know that we *will* attain it in the next life. It is precisely this knowledge that gives us hope in this life and makes the effort meaningful.

The heaven of eternal moral progress, by contrast, lacks this feature. The blessed in such a heaven must strive endlessly to emulate Jesus without any hope of success. Indeed, if such a heaven awaits Christians then moral striving in this life is undermined, for Augustine's expectation of becoming "whole and complete" will never come to pass at all. Hope will never give way to that which is hoped for. On the contrary, how could such hope avoid turning to despair at the eternal failure to realize its goal? I conclude that the exemplar problem is indeed a serious obstacle to the notion of eternal heavenly moral progression, and more than this, shows that notion to undermine even the point of earthly moral progression.

As noted above, a "dynamic" conception of heaven might still be possible in the light of these objections. It would simply have to be conceived in a way that does not involve eternal moral progress. However, proponents of

35. Rom 3:10 NRSV.

36. 1 Cor 13:10 NRSV.

37. Augustine, *The Perfection of Human Righteousness*, ch. 8.19, in *Answer*, 297 (italics original).

a "dynamic" heaven typically *do* frame it in terms of moral progression. The reason is clear: if heaven is a place of change and improvement, what kind of change and improvement could be more important and significant than moral improvement? Well, perhaps one could appeal to *spiritual* improvement: the blessed will be eternally becoming more open to and appreciative of God. But then there is the same problem: either they must eventually surpass Jesus' spiritual state and relationship to God, or they must approach it asymptotically. The former is unacceptable, while the latter is effectively indistinguishable from an unchanging heaven anyway.

The beatific vision

If the blessed are not eternally progressing in virtue, what are they doing? One might think that if heaven is atemporal then they are not doing anything. In Matt 11:28 Jesus promises to give "rest" (ἀναπαύσω) to his hearers, while Heb 3:7—4:11 makes "rest" (κατάπαυσις) central to its eschatological vision.[38] Κατάπαυσις also appears in the Septuagint of Gen 2:2, to refer to God's rest on the seventh day, cited in Heb 4:4. This "rest" does not mean that God did nothing: ancient exegetes agreed that God is inherently active, so the divine rest simply involves different activities, such as contemplating creation.[39] Similarly, the "rest" for the faithful is, as H. A. Lombard puts it, "the pleasurable activity of complete and devoted service to God."[40] It also has connotations of inheritance and possession of the land, suggesting that to rest, in this context, means to adopt a certain relationship to the wider created order.[41] This is something we will see in more detail in the next chapter.

Whatever the intentions of the author to the Hebrews and other New Testament writers, this is certainly how the bulk of Christian tradition has

38. For details on the different uses of this term in ancient Jewish and Christian literature, see Attridge, *Hebrews*, 126–28; Laansma, "*I Will Give You Rest*"; Gleason, "Old Testament Background"; Wray, *Rest*, 25–32. For the huge range of interpretations of its use in Hebrews, see Lombard, "Katapausis"; Laansma, "*I Will Give You Rest*," 276–332. Attridge argues that the sheer variety of different uses and contexts makes it hard to establish precisely what the author to the Hebrews means by the term, beyond the fact that "the imagery of rest is best understood as a complex symbol for the whole soteriological process that Hebrews never fully articulates, but which involves both personal and corporate dimensions. It is the process of entry into God's presence, the heavenly homeland (11:16), the unshakeable kingdom (12:28), begun at baptism (10:22) and consummated as a whole eschatologically" (*Hebrews*, 128).

39. Lombard, "Katapausis," 65.

40. Lombard, "Katapausis," 66.

41. Buchanan, *Hebrews*, 64–65.

interpreted the theme of rest, both divine and eschatological.[42] Thomas Aquinas' God is engaged eternally in supremely pleasurable contemplation (of God).[43] And the activity of the blessed is contemplative in nature, for they enjoy the "beatific vision"—an intellectual contemplation of God. Christopher Brown stresses that for Aquinas, who developed this doctrine into its fullest form, the beatific vision is an *activity* on the part of the blessed. It is not something that they passively experience.[44]

The centrality of the beatific vision to Christian conceptions of heaven since at least Augustine is now widely recognized, so I will not try to reinvent the wheel by arguing for it here.[45] Aquinas calls it "the vision of the divine essence,"[46] implicitly presenting this as a metaphor for intellectual contemplation of God. He argues that this contemplation must go beyond simple recognition of God's existence, for that would be intellectually unsatisfying: rather, the intellect "will have its perfection through union with God as with that object, in which alone man's happiness consists."

It is important to recognize that despite the obvious Aristotelian heritage of Aquinas' formulation, the concept of the vision of God is grounded in a number of New Testament passages.[47] Most famously, Paul writes that "now we see in a mirror, dimly, but then we will see face to face."[48] In the Johannine literature, meanwhile, we find the idea of vision closely linked to union, or identification, with the divine. The author of 1 John writes that "when he is revealed, we will be like him, for we will see him as he is,"[49] while the book of Revelation expresses this more poetically in the claim that

42. I have argued elsewhere (Hill, "Defence of Inactivity") for the coherence of a conception of heaven as involving perfect *inactivity*. I still think that such a conception is both plausible and desirable—at least to me!—but for our current purposes I am happy to endorse the less extreme conception of heaven as involving perfect contemplative *activity*.

43. Aquinas, *ST*, I q. 18 aa. 3–4, vol. 1, pp. 253–58.

44. Brown, *Eternal Life*, 124.

45. Hans Boersma's study (*Seeing God*) is the most important recent work on this subject. Murphy, "Patristic Origins," also gives a helpful overview of the doctrine's origins and biblical sources, while Brown, *Eternal Life*, 89–194, and Nicolas, *Catholic Dogmatic Theology*, 297–308, give contemporary defenses of the doctrine.

46. Aquinas, *ST*, IIa q. 3 a. 8, vol. 6, pp. 49–51.

47. For more on the biblical sources for the doctrine, see Boersma, *Seeing God*, 3–4, esp. n. 3 and Murphy, "Patristic Origins," 59–60. Murphy mentions, but Boersma draws particular attention to (*Seeing God*, 129–30), the importance of the story of the Transfiguration in influencing the concept of the beatific vision.

48. 1 Cor 13:12 NRSV.

49. 1 John 3:2 NRSV.

"they will see his face, and his name will be on their foreheads."[50] The vision of God is thus a *transformative* phenomenon: the blessed do not simply gaze at God but become united to God. This is a theme we will consider in more detail in the next chapter.

The beatific vision involves not merely union with God but a close relationship to the created universe as well. According to Aquinas, God knows all things other than God *in* God, through contemplation of the divine ideas.[51] It would therefore follow that even if God is the sole object of contemplation for the blessed, there is at least the possibility of their knowing objects other than God through the divine ideas, like viewing an object in a mirror, to use Aquinas' analogy. However, there is an infinite number of such ideas, given that there is an infinite number of possible objects. If heaven were temporal, then one might imagine the blessed contemplating first one object in God, and then another. Such a scenario would face the obstacle that we saw in chapter 1 when discussing the notion of God's understanding functioning as memory for the blessed: that of access. Given an infinite range of possible objects of contemplation, how could a person choose which to contemplate? That would require understanding of all those objects at once, which would be impossible for a finite mind. One might get around this by supposing that *God* decides what objects—or, more precisely, which aspects of God—a person in heaven contemplates at any given moment.

If, however, heaven is atemporal, then the blessed cannot contemplate different objects at different times. Whatever divine ideas they contemplate, if any, they contemplate *those* and those alone eternally. They cannot contemplate the infinity of possible objects, for the reasons just given. So what *do* they contemplate? A plausible answer could be that they can contemplate the *actual* world, which although vast, is finite in scope. In so doing they are really contemplating God's will, since any actual being other than God exists only because God wills it to do so. Accordingly, Aquinas also holds that, although God is the primary object of the beatific vision, the blessed also contemplate God's creation. They understand all created things, for a desire to understand creation is a natural desire for human beings, and in the beatific vision all such desires are met. It does not follow, though, that they know everything about every *individual* created thing, such as every thought that every person has ever had. And it also does not follow that they have knowledge of merely *possible* things, for to do that they would have

50. Rev 22:4 NRSV.

51. Aquinas, *ST*, I q. 14 a. 5, vol. 1, pp. 189–90.

to comprehend God's power, which is impossible.[52] So the blessed do not experience omniscience, but they do experience what we might call *maxiscience*: knowledge as great as a created being can have.

As we shall see in the next chapter, this is closely related to the divine love, and we can understand this contemplative activity as sharing in the divine love. As such, the *activity* of the blessed would be the activity of God, to whom the blessed are united. Before we look at this more closely, however, I want to consider how all of this relates to the importance of the body.

The beatific vision and the body

A common criticism of the conception of heaven as based on the beatific vision is that it does not do justice to the Christian doctrine of resurrection. There are two main forms of this criticism.

The first focuses on the traditional two-stage Christian eschatology. As I briefly described in the introduction, Christians traditionally believe that when a person dies their soul immediately goes to heaven (barring complications such as purgatory) and enjoys the beatific vision there. Later, at the end of time, they are reunited with their body, enter the resurrection life, and resume their enjoyment of the beatific vision. John Morreall points out the problem with this:

> [I]f the blessed in heaven are perfectly happy right now in their condition as souls, it is hard to see what purpose the resurrection would serve. There are only three possibilities: either the resurrection would make the blessed less happy than they were as pure souls, or it would make them more happy, or it would have no effect on their happiness.[53]

---

52. Brown, *Eternal Life*, 161–64.

53. Morreall, "Perfect Happiness," 30. Caroline Bynum, *Resurrection*, 252, and Joshua Mugg, "Can I Survive?," give similar arguments, while James Turner, *Resurrection*, 20–73 goes into more depth. For Turner, belief in the intermediate state between death and resurrection undermines Paul's argument in 1 Corinthians 15 that if Christ was not raised then those who have died have perished. This is because, if there is an intermediate state of bliss, then the dead Christ would have been in such a state, and so too would those who have died in the faith, even without any resurrection. In my view Turner's arguments decisively undermine the concept of the intermediate state, though this is not essential to my argument, as I outline in the conclusion to this book. (Thomas Aquinas appeals to similar reasoning to argue that the intermediate state cannot be the final state of the soul: see his commentary on 1 Corinthians 15:17–19, in *Selected Philosophical Writings*, 192.)

Morreall argues that all three possibilities are unacceptable. God would not *decrease* the happiness of the blessed by restoring their bodies to them; having bodies cannot make them *more* happy, because that would mean that either they do not enjoy the beatific vision now or the beatific vision is insufficient for perfect happiness; and if they are indifferent to being embodied then resurrection is pointless.

We can characterize the problem as arising from a desire to hold two apparently inconsistent claims:

(1) The beatific vision is sufficient for perfect happiness.

(2) It is better to enjoy the beatific vision with a body than without one.

We can see Thomas Aquinas wrestling with how to reconcile these two claims, as he offered different solutions at different points in his career. In his commentary on Lombard's *Sentences*, he emphasizes the second, suggesting that the happiness of the saints increases in both intensity and extent when they are reunited to their bodies.[54] But when he later came to write the *Summa Theologiae*, he had apparently decided that the first claim was more important, stressing that the beatific vision is sufficient for perfect happiness. At the same time, he still insisted that being reunited with the body does add to the soul's happiness in a way:

> The desire of the separated soul is entirely at rest, as regards the thing desired; since, to wit, it has that which suffices its appetite is not wholly at rest, as regards the desirer, since it does not possess that good in every way that it would wish to possess it. Consequently, after the body has been resumed, happiness increases not in intensity (*intensive*), but in extent (*extensive*).[55]

What can it mean to say that happiness increases "in extent" but not "in intensity"? Brandon Dahm makes a distinction between "desires from lack" and "desires from fulfilment." The former is a desire for something that one lacks, while the latter is a desire to share something that one has. In the case of the beatific vision, he suggests, the disembodied soul has no desires from lack, because they are perfectly met by the beatific vision. Nevertheless, it desires to share this happiness with the body, a desire that can be met only

---

54. Aquinas, *ST*, Supp. q. 93 a. 1, vol. 21, pp. 98–101; see Brown, *Eternal Life*, 204–12. The supplement to the *Summa* was compiled after Aquinas' death from his *Sentences* commentary. Accordingly, Aquinas is here following the lead of Lombard, who insists that "without any hesitation" one must hold that the saints have greater joy after the resurrection than they do before (*Sentences*, IV 283.2, p, 270).

55. Aquinas, *ST*, IIa q. 4 a. 5 ad 5, vol. 6, pp. 62–63. See Brown, *Eternal Life*, 212–27.

after the resurrection.[56] Consequently, the saints enjoy perfect happiness before the resurrection, but the resurrection still extends their happiness.

In my view, this move is not successful, for two reasons. The first is that it depends upon being able to separate *desire* from *lack*. But it is surely a conceptual truth that desire is for something that one does not yet have, or at least that one believes one does not yet have. Even if I desire to continue to enjoy good health, when I am already healthy, this is still something I do not yet have, for it is one thing to have good health right now and another to continue to have it in the future. In the case we are considering, the soul desires the body to share in its happiness precisely because the body does *not* share its happiness. This is clearly a lack.

The second problem is that the notion of the soul "sharing" its happiness with the body is incoherent. The example that Dahm gives is of a new father rushing out to share the news of his child's birth with other people. The father's happiness would be just as intense even if there were nobody to share it with, but being able to share it increases the "extent" of the happiness. But in this example, the father is sharing his happiness *with other people* who are capable of experiencing happiness. In the case of the resurrection, the body is not an additional person with whom the soul shares the joy of the beatific vision. If a body is not a person, it cannot experience anything itself. There is only one experiencer, both before and after resurrection. And to speak of extending the "extent" of an experience when there is only one person experiencing it throughout the whole process is incoherent. We can speak only in terms of that single person experiencing more things, or experiencing them in a different way.

Peter Dillard defends Aquinas' account by appealing to his parallel account of punishment. For Aquinas, a murderer's hand is not guilty *in itself* of the murder, because it did not will it. But the hand is part of the whole person, who did, and the hand therefore justly shares in the punishment of the whole person.[57] Dillard proposes a thought experiment in which a prisoner grows extra fingers during his sentence: although these fingers did not participate in the original crime, they justly share in the punishment because they are part of the person who committed it. There has therefore been an extension in the punishment. Similarly, there could be an extension in reward for a person who acquires new body parts, or a new body, after receiving it. To give an example not used by Dillard, suppose a mad scientist grafts an additional limb onto me, so perfectly that it functions exactly like my normal ones. I can now experience tactile sensations in that

56. Dahm, "Distinguishing Desire," in Brown, *Eternal Life*, 230–31.

57. Aquinas, *ST*, IIa q. 81 a. 1, vol. 7, p. 405, in Dillard, "Keeping the Vision," 408–9.

limb in addition to those in my normal limbs. And suppose that I enjoy the sensation of relaxing in a Jacuzzi, both before and after the operation. In the post-operative Jacuzzi, the *extent* of my sensation is greater in the sense that I have more limbs in which to feel it. And something like this is what Aquinas is suggesting. But if feeling the Jacuzzi in more limbs means that I enjoy it more, then the intensity of the experience is greater after all, which Aquinas wants to deny. If, however, I do not enjoy it more, then increasing the extent is pointless. I feel it in more places, but the quality of the experience is unimproved. The fundamental problem is that body parts do not feel sensations—*people* feel sensations *in* their body parts. Similarly, body parts are not punished, contrary to what Aquinas thinks. *People* are punished, perhaps *through* their body parts. And if persons are not identical with their bodies—as they must not be, if there is a state between death and resurrection at all—*bodies* do not experience beatitude. *People* experience beatitude—again, perhaps *through* their bodies.

If this is so, then Aquinas' distinction between "in intensity" and "in extent" is incoherent, at least as applied to happiness. I can certainly feel happy *about more or fewer things*, so my happiness can be greater or less in extent in that sense, but my happiness varies in its intensity accordingly. If I am happier about more things, I am happier. Similarly, if the addition of a body makes the happiness of the saints greater in extent, it makes them happier. It follows that they were not perfectly happy before.

In my view, then, the two claims (1) and (2) above are indeed inconsistent, and Morreall is correct in his argument that this poses a serious problem for the traditional two-stage doctrine of heaven. Well then, why not abandon the notion of souls enjoying the beatific vision before the resurrection? Morreall argues that this is problematic for two reasons. First, that would introduce a temporal gap into a person's timeline which would disrupt their identity over that gap. Second, it is important to Christianity that the saints be in heaven *right now*.[58]

But the atemporal conception of heaven avoids both of these problems. We have already seen how it allows us to say that the heavenly person is the same person as the earthly one. And although (say) "St Gregory is now in heaven" would never be true, "St Gregory is in heaven" would always be true. We shall see more in the next chapter about how the blessed in heaven might relate to people on earth. So atemporalism gives us a way to abandon the traditional two-stage eschatology whilst avoiding the problems that Morreall identifies with doing so. In so doing, it escapes the problem he identifies with the doctrine of resurrection and the beatific vision.

58. Morreall, "Perfect Happiness," 31–32.

But there is a second problem associated with resurrection and the beatific vision, which is that the body does not seem very important to it. Christina Van Dyke criticizes Thomas Aquinas' concept of the beatific vision along these lines:

> Ultimately, Aquinas's account of the beatific vision appears to render our bodies nothing more than glorious hood ornaments. They will not be integrally involved in our contemplation of God's essence, and they will be not carrying out any of the other activities in which human beings participate in this life, either. Our perfected bodies will be signs of the completion of human nature and the corresponding glory of God, but they serve no deeper purpose.[59]

For Van Dyke, the problem arises from a combination of Aquinas' highly intellectualist account of the beatific vision, in which even the epistemological role that the body plays in our earthly life is superseded, with his insistence on a hylomorphic anthropology, in which human persons are identical not with souls but with body-soul composites.[60] These two commitments pull in opposite directions.

There are two responses we can make to this criticism. First, it is worth considering why the doctrine of the resurrection of the body was so important to early Christians. It was not because they envisaged the resurrection life as characterized by "bodily" activities. It was because they thought that, without the body, human persons are incomplete. Tertullian expressed this view with his typical forcefulness: "[E]ven now, admitting the salvation of the soul alone, are you not assigning that salvation to man reduced to half? What is belief in the resurrection, unless believing it entire? . . . God is not raising the dead, if he does not raise them up entire. . . ."[61] This point has remained central to Christian tradition. Thus we find Karl Rahner writing: "'Body' means the whole man in his proper embodied reality. 'Resurrection' means, therefore, the termination and perfection of the *whole* man before God, which gives him 'eternal life.'"[62]

This view is fundamentally at odds with the Platonic concept of human beings as identical with souls. When this Platonic outlook has influenced Christianity, tension has inevitably arisen with the emphasis on bodily resurrection. Thus we find Aquinas insisting that the soul is incomplete

---

59. Van Dyke, "Shiny Happy People," 290.
60. Van Dyke, "Shiny Happy People," 289.
61. Tertullian, *Resurrection*, ch. 57, pp. 168–71.
62. Rahner, *Theological Investigations II*, 203.

without the body, and yet at the same time arguing that the soul can experience the beatific vision without the body.

The response, then, is obvious: repudiate the Platonic view more consistently than Aquinas did, and hold that human beings need their bodies to exist at all.[63] Whether one holds animalism (the view that we are identical with our bodies) or constitutionalism (the view that we are constituted by our bodies) makes little difference for our purposes. Indeed, this view would be consistent with a form of substance dualism that identifies the human being with the combination of body and soul such that the soul cannot do anything without the body. Now we can say that the body is absolutely necessary for the beatific vision, not because of any distinctively somatic elements to that vision, but because without it, human beings could not exist in heaven at all. Once again, our rejection of any interim state for the soul in between death and resurrection fits well with this, as we no longer need to account for any bodiless existence.

I think that this is a sufficient response to the criticism. However, it feels somewhat unsatisfying. The body may be necessary for the beatific vision to occur, but it does not seem to be contributing much towards it. An objection of this kind depends on a view that I shall call *functional dualism*. Functional dualism in turn depends upon two definitions:

> *Non-somatic processes*: processes that do not involve the body, apart from the central nervous system.

> *Somatic processes*: processes that involve the body beyond the central nervous system.

Functional dualism can then be defined like this:

> FD: mental processes are non-somatic.

63. Morreall considers this response ("Perfect Happiness," 34), and rejects it on the grounds that it is essential to Christian eschatology that the soul is the bearer of personal identity and is capable of existing without the body. But while such a view has been widely held throughout Christian history I see no reason to think it is *essential* to Christian doctrine. It is not found in either the Bible or the conciliar creeds, and of course plenty of Christian theologians and philosophers alike reject it. On biblical conceptions of the soul, see Schüle, "'Soul' and 'Spirit'"; and for Karl Barth's complex account, see Viazovski, *Image and Hope*, 188–214. Among contemporary Christian philosophers of religion who reject it we may count Kevin Corcoran, *Rethinking*; Nancey Murphy, *Bodies and Souls*; Trenton Merricks, "Word Made Flesh"; Lynne Rudder Baker, "Persons"; William Jaworski, "Hylomorphism." For non-soul-based Christian anthropology from a range of authors in the light of contemporary science, see Brown, Murphy, and Malony, *Whatever Happened*. For an overview of the contemporary range of views on this topic from an author who does favor souls that can exist without the body, see Cooper, *Body*, xvi–xxviii.

The definition is metaphysically neutral: it is compatible with substance dualism, animalism, and everything in between. A substance dualist need not be a functional dualist, though in practice I think all them are. A functional dualist who is an animalist will hold that all mental activities require bodily processes, but will distinguish between different kinds of bodily processes. This is *functional* dualism, then, because it conceives of human activities as divided into two distinct classes. We may also note that there are degrees of functional dualism. Someone may hold that some, most, or even all mental activities are non-somatic.

Thomas Aquinas was a functional dualist. Following Aristotle, he held that the intellect is immaterial, because the fact that it can understand all material objects shows that it is in potency with respect to them, and therefore itself immaterial.[64] Moreover, it differs from sensation in being associated with no bodily organ.[65] We can see, then, why the objection we are considering is a serious problem for Aquinas: his thought contains an irreconcilable tension between (a) his functional dualism, (b) his conception of the beatific vision as fundamentally intellectual and non-somatic, and (c) his insistence on the importance of the resurrected body.[66]

For some critics, the concept of the beatific vision is problematic not because of any functional dualism on the part of the believer in the beatific vision but because of their *own* assumption of functional dualism. John Morreall, again, is a good example. He asks what the bodies of the blessed would do in heaven, focusing his attention on two possible functions: perception and movement. After arguing that neither sensory perception nor bodily movement could contribute to the beatific vision, he concludes:

> [I]f persons in heaven do not have such essential features of embodiment as perception and activity, and if their embodiment does nothing to contribute to their happiness, then what good does it do them to have bodies at all? What purpose could be served by the resurrection if the body has no role in the beatific vision?[67]

64. Aquinas, *Commentary on* De Anima, 7.131–59, p. 345.

65. Aquinas, *Commentary on* De Anima, 7.194–221, pp. 346–47.

66. Joseph Trabbic, "Human Body," argues that for Aquinas, the body is essential to perfect happiness because without the body a human being is incomplete. This is despite the fact that, for Trabbic, Aquinas *also* holds that "the intellect can achieve its perfection in the vision of God in complete separation from the body" (p. 562). Clearly, this reflects precisely this tension between Aquinas' desire to give the body a role in the beatific vision and his functional dualism.

67. Morreall, "Perfect Happiness," 34.

Morreall assumes that because the beatific vision is non-sensory, it does not involve the body. In other words, he makes an implicit appeal to functional dualism. We can make the appeal explicit if we articulate the argument like this:

(1) An adequate concept of heaven must take the body seriously.

(2) A concept of heaven that involves no somatic processes does not take the body seriously.

(3) The beatific vision involves no somatic processes.

(4) Therefore, a concept of heaven based on the beatific vision is inadequate.

As we have seen, (2) is dubious. If we hold that having a body is necessary for a human person to exist—perhaps that human persons are identical with their bodies—isn't this taking the body seriously, even if it performs no somatic processes? But for the sake of argument let us grant this, along with (1). The argument then revolves around (3). (3) assumes a form of functional dualism according to which at least one mental activity—the contemplation of the beatific vision—is non-somatic.

But functional dualism, even in its mildest form, is almost certainly false. *All* of our mental activities are in fact somatic.[68] For example, the close links between emotion and physical sensation have long been recognized, although the details of how they relate to each other have been controversial. In the 1880s, William James and Carl Lange independently proposed that emotions are caused by, or may even simply *be*, the awareness of physical reactions in the visceral organs. This theory came under heavy fire in the 1920s by Walter Cannon, who argued that we lack sufficient sensitivity in the visceral organs, and also reported a series of experiments

68. Recognition of this has led to the movement known as "embodied cognition," which challenges traditional cognitive science in its methodologies and conclusions. This has led to some dramatic claims about what it shows. For some researchers, such as Varela, Thompson, and Rosch, *Embodied Mind*, 172, the embodied nature of cognition entails a radical non-realism about the external world, which has no intrinsic properties at all. For some philosophers, such as George Lakoff, "Embodied Mind," the insights of embodied cognition promise a complete Copernican revolution in philosophy, undermining not merely common philosophical positions but the very kinds of philosophical questions that are meaningful, in areas as diverse as philosophy of mathematics, ethics, and religion. For other commentators, such as Lawrence Shapiro, *Embodied Cognition*, such claims are too extravagant. I share Shapiro's hesitation about the embodied cognition movement, but what I want to stress here is that one does not need to endorse that movement whole-heartedly to recognize the importance of the body to our mental processes. Cognition is, to a large extent, embodied, even if "embodied cognition" sometimes makes claims that go beyond that fact.

on animals showing that emotional reactions depended on the presence of the thalamus.[69] More recently, the two-stage model of emotion associated with Stanley Schachter and Jerome Singer distinguishes between the physiological reaction and the cognitive categorization of the reaction. On this view, many different emotions have identical physiological bases, but we interpret them differently depending on the circumstances.[70] Despite the differences, though, all of these theories recognize a very close relationship between emotion and physiological response, to the extent that exerting control over one's physical movement can influence emotion (for example, smiling can not only elevate one's mood[71] but make one more likely to find things funny).[72] And indeed recent research has indicated that the same regions of the brain are responsible for awareness of bodily states and for emotional responses.[73]

The role of the body goes beyond emotion. There is evidence, for example, that our self-consciousness depends upon awareness of our bodies. Signals from throughout the body, but particularly the torso, allow the brain to construct a model of the self. Even our awareness of the passage of time may be based upon our heartbeats and other bodily rhythms.[74] Reasoning and decision-making are also closely connected to movement. A number of experiments have shown, for example, that moving one's arms in different directions influences decisions: people can recognize negative words more quickly if they are making a pushing movement, and they recognize positive ones more quickly if they are making a pulling movement.[75] Similarly, lifting objects to a higher position makes it easier to describe positive experiences, while putting them in a lower position makes it easier to describe negative ones.[76]

---

69. Cannon, "James-Lange Theory." Cannon was an outspoken supporter of vivisection, and his paper makes uneasy reading today, though his description of a postoperative cat as "the complete picture of intense fury" (p. 116) suggests the satisfying possibility that he and his colleagues did not escape unscathed themselves.

70. Sinclair et al., "Construct Accessibility." For a modified version of this theory see Cohen, "Two-Stage Model."

71. Strack et al., "Inhibiting and Facilitating."

72. Markman and Brendl, "Constraining Theories," 6.

73. Critchley et al., "Neural Systems."

74. Park and Blanke, "Inner and Outer Body."

75. Markman and Brendl, "Constraining Theories." Markman and Brendl argue that the effect depends not just on the direction of physical movement but on the location of the *perceived* self, which can also vary.

76. Casasanto and Dijkstra, "Motor Action."

The implication of all this is that the beatific vision, as a mental activity, *would* involve somatic processes. Let us suppose, then, with Thomas Aquinas, that the beatific vision is the intellectual contemplation of God, but contrary to Thomas, we can say that this contemplation is a somatic state that involves the whole body. Hans Boersma tentatively endorses the suggestion of Gregory Palamas that, in the resurrection, the bodily senses are transformed so that the saints can literally *see* God.[77] For Boersma, this is coherent only if combined with the idealist metaphysics found in Gregory of Nyssa and Jonathan Edwards.[78] But Boersma does not explain why idealism leads to such a view, or justify his claim that "[a] materialist metaphysic renders a Palamite transformation of both the senses and the intellect—or, for that matter, any transformation from kernel to grain (cf. 1 Cor 15:37)—unintelligible."[79] The idea is that, since for Gregory the body consists solely of intelligible properties, it would be coherent for him to suppose that the transformation of the mind at the eschaton could be reflected in the body, since the body is wholly dependent upon the mind.[80] But one could just as easily reverse the process: if the mind depends upon the body, rather than vice versa, then the eschatological transformation of the body is what drives the transformation of the mind. Such a view seems to me closer to the emphasis in 1 Corinthians 15 and elsewhere in the New Testament: it is the resurrection of the *body* that is paramount. And it is *God* who transforms the body: the notion that bodily transformation is parasitic upon mental transformation is alien to the New Testament. Our artificial distinctions between the intellectual, the emotional, and the bodily break down in the face of an all-encompassing state which involves the whole person—and which could be conceived atemporally. Such a state would, clearly, be transformational.

Conclusion

In the previous chapter I identified six propositions about atemporal heaven. We can now add to this list:

> (7) In heaven, the blessed enjoy the beatific vision, an unchanging contemplation of God.

---

77. Boersma, *Seeing God*, 422–24.
78. Boersma, *Seeing God*, 424–28.
79. Boersma, *Seeing God*, 425.
80. Boersma, *Seeing God*, 427–28.

(8) The beatific vision involves maxiscience: the sharing of divine knowledge to the greatest extent possible for finite creatures.

(9) The beatific vision is somatic, involving and transforming the whole body.

(10) There is no non-bodily intermediate state.

As before, these propositions are to some degree independent. As we have seen, (9) strongly implies (10), but one could hold (7), and perhaps (8), without being committed to (9) or (10) (and indeed this is the position of Thomas Aquinas). Nevertheless, (9) in particular seems to me to capture an important element of Christian thinking about the resurrection life as being fundamentally transformative. We shall consider some of the features of this transformation in the final chapter.

6

Heavenly Transformation

I n the previous chapter, I suggested that the concept of the beatific vision is closely connected to that of union with God. Through their contemplation of God and of the divine ideas, the blessed share in the divine activity, which is directed towards the world. In this chapter I want to consider how this might function in more detail, before looking at what it might mean for individual and cosmic transformation.

Becoming divine

Theosis, or divinization, has attracted increasing theological attention since the last couple of decades of the twentieth century.[1] It is particularly associated with Orthodox theology, but there is now widespread recognition that it is important in other traditions too, including both Catholic and Protestant theology.[2] It is the doctrine that the ultimate destiny of the blessed

1. For a brief summary of some key studies, see Meconi, "Consummation." For more in-depth studies, see Finlan and Kharmalov, *Theosis*, and Kharmalov, *Theosis*, as well as the works cited in note 2 below.

2. Two recent papers, taken together, turn received wisdom on this topic on its head. Mark McInroy, "How Deification Became Eastern," argues that the notion that *theosis* is largely absent in western theologians is a nineteenth-century innovation, while Paul Gavrilyuk, "Deification Rediscovered," argues that the notion that it is a distinctive and central element of eastern theology is even more recent. Carl Mosser, "Orthodox-Reformed Dialogue," argues that ecumenical dialogue between eastern and western churches has been a major driver in the overturning of these misconceptions. On the history of the doctrine throughout Christianity, see the papers in Christensen and Wittung, *Partakers*. On the Orthodox tradition in particular, see Meyendorff, *Byzantine Theology*, and Russell, *Deification*. On Latin patristic notions of *theosis*, see

is, in some sense, to become divine. Or, as Pseudo-Dionysius defines it, "Divinization consists of being as much as possible like and in union with God."[3]

The doctrine has a long history. Biblically, it is rooted above all in 2 Pet 1:4, and its promise that human beings can become "participants in the divine nature" (NRSV). New Testament scholars disagree about how to interpret this verse, but the one point that most do agree is that the verse does not teach *theosis* as traditionally understood.[4] However, later Christian theology—which is our concern here—interprets it both eschatologically and ontologically, especially in conjunction with other verses, such as Paul's claim that Christians "are being transformed into the same image"

---

the papers in Ortiz, *Deification*. Studies on *theosis* in the thought of other non-eastern theologians include, among others: Augustine (Williams, *Ground of Union*; Meconi, *The One Christ*); Thomas Aquinas (Townsend, "Deification in Aquinas"); Nicholas of Cusa (Hudson, *Becoming God*); Martin Luther (Braaten and Jenson, *Union with Christ*; Marquardt, "Luther and Theosis"); John Calvin (Billings, "United to God"); Jonathan Edwards (McClymond, "Salvation as Divinization"; Strobel, *Jonathan Edwards's Theology*, 192–207); Karl Barth (Neder, *Participation*, 90–91); Thomas F. Torrance (Habets, *Theosis*).

3. *Ecclesiastical Hierarchy*, 1.3, in Pseudo-Dionysius, *Complete Works*, 198.

4. Twentieth-century exegetes tended to interpret this verse as fundamentally pagan. Ernst Käsemann called it an expression of mysticism, representing "a relapse of Christianity into Hellenistic dualism" (*Essays*, 180), indistinguishable from Gnosticism. Similarly, though less pejoratively, J. N. D. Kelly likened it to "Greek mystical philosophy" (*Epistles*, 303). For Richard Bauckham, *Jude, 2 Peter*, 179–84, the author of 2 Peter is following in the footsteps of other Hellenized Jewish literature such as 4 Macc 18:3, and Bauckham notes (p. 184)—against Käsemann—that the verse seems uncontroversial in the original context of the letter. More recent commentators emphasize the Jewish background to the verse. Albert Wolters, "Partners," sees the reference to the "divine nature" (θεία φύσις) simply as a circumlocution for God, with whom Christians are in a covenantal relationship. Scott Hafemann rejects both views, seeing the verse as an expression of traditional Christian eschatology, concluding that it "neither signals a dualistic departure from early Christian eschatology nor does it provide support for the later Christian doctrine of *theosis*" ("Divine Nature," 99). Andrew Mbuvi, *Jude and 2 Peter*, 76, argues for an ethical interpretation. Jörg Frey agrees, commenting that the author "does not imagine a physical 'theosis' of believers, but the final attainment of salvation and 'eternal life' with Christ by those who are not 'carried away' (2 Pet 3:17) but are 'found blameless' at the Last Judgment (2 Pet 3:14)" ("Second Peter," 43–46). James Starr comes closer to the traditional Christian interpretation of the verse, arguing that it refers to the acquisition by Christians of the divine properties of immortality and moral perfection—but still concludes starkly that "2 Peter 1:4 does not speak of the Christ believer's divinization or *theosis*" (*Sharers*, 232). Finally, Stephen Finlan, "Second Peter's Notion," represents a contrary voice: he incorporates many of the aforementioned elements into his exegesis of the verse, but assumes throughout (rather than showing) that it should still be understood in the traditional way as "divinization."

(2 Cor 3:18 NRSV)[5] and can "become the righteousness of God" (2 Cor 5:21 NRSV).[6] For Stephen Finlan and Vladimir Kharmalov, "*[t]heōsis* is central to the theology of Paul throughout," a statement that is exegetically dubious but thoroughly in accordance with traditional Christian reception of these texts.[7] In later patristic theology, at least from Athanasius onwards, the concept of *theosis* takes on more explicit significance,[8] finding perhaps its fullest expression in Maximus the Confessor and in the Orthodox theological tradition influenced by him.[9]

Let us, then, grant the importance of *theosis* for the Christian conception of heaven. How could this work? To put it another way, what could be the truth conditions for "Human beings have become divine"? There are, to my mind, two obvious answers, neither of which seems viable.

The first possibility is that human beings may acquire the properties that are essential to divinity—whatever these may be, precisely. For example, if they are omnipotence, omniscience, and moral perfection, then human beings might become omnipotent, omniscient, and morally perfect, and in virtue of exemplifying these properties they would be divine.

But this seems worrying on a number of counts. First, these divinized humans would be indistinguishable—as far as their nature goes—from the Father, the Son, and the Holy Spirit. The Trinity would effectively be swamped by vast numbers of new members.[10] If there are divinized human

5. Margaret Thrall, *2 Corinthians 1–7*, 285–86, offers the usual interpretation of this verse as referring to both the present and the future glorification of believers. However, Paul Duff, "From Glory to Glory," argues that it has no eschatological dimension, instead referring to past and present glorification. Michael Cover (*Lifting*, 258–95) does not weigh in on this element, but notes that, compared to other uses of Moses as a type for spiritual transformation (most notably Philo in *Allegorical Interpretation of Genesis 2 and 3*, III.100–1, in *Creation*, 368–71), Paul is restrained in his language, suggesting only that believers will see the "image" (εἰκών) of God—an ironic "underachievement" (p. 295).

6. Here again there is no scholarly consensus on how to interpret this verse. Most scholars hold that it means that sinners are "given a righteous status before God" (Thrall, *2 Corinthians 1–7*, 443). Timothy Keene, "Missional Reading," following a suggestion by N. T. Wright, instead interprets it missiologically: Paul is exhorting his readers to imitate him (Paul himself) in conducting mission work. Morna Hooker similarly regards the verse as focusing on action: "If God's righteousness is a restorative power, bringing life and reconciliation, then those who 'become righteousness' will be the means of manifesting that power in the world. . . . What Christ is to us—righteousness, wisdom, sanctification, redemption—Christians must now be to the world" ("Righteousness of God," 374–75).

7. Finlan and Kharmalov, introduction to *Theosis*, 4.

8. Finch, "Athanasius."

9. Vishnevskaya, "Divinization."

10. The Father, the Son, and the Holy Spirit are, according to orthodox

beings distinct from the existing members of the Trinity, but equally divine as them, then they would be proper objects of worship and prayer. But while some Christian traditions do practice praying to the saints, they are never prayed to *as divine*.[11] And all of Christian tradition balks sharply at the notion of worshipping the saints alongside the Holy Trinity.

The second possibility may therefore seem preferable. This is to suppose that human beings can be absorbed into God in some way, losing their distinctive identity, rather as a river flows into the sea. This would be similar to the relation between Atman (the self) and Brahman (the highest universal reality) according to some Hindu traditions.[12] On this view, we become divine not by acquiring the properties of divinity in our own right, but by simply joining with the God who already exemplifies those properties. Or to put it differently, divinization should be conceived not as divine-property-acquisition but as divine-person-union.

But there are problems with this, too. First, if we take the doctrine of the Trinity seriously, difficult questions arise. *Which* divine person do the blessed unite with? Presumably it cannot be all of them, because that could only happen if there were no true distinction between the persons, and that is the modalist heresy. Biblical passages can be found suggesting that believers aspire to imitate or unite with the Father,[13] the Son,[14] *and* the Holy Spirit.[15]

Second, God is—classically—supposed to be perfectly simple.[16] I find it very hard to conceive of a perfectly simple being coming to incorporate a preexisting, complex being. If, at the end of this process, the perfectly simple being is still perfectly simple, then this seems to me no different from a situation in which the complex being has just ceased to exist and the simple being remains unchanged. If, on the other hand, the perfectly simple being

Trinitarianism, distinguishable by their mutual relations: the Father is unoriginated, but the Son and Spirit are not, for example. But they are one *in nature*. Similarly, the divinized humans might be distinguishable from the existing divine persons (none would be either unoriginated, begotten of the Father, or proceeding from the Father), but their *nature* would be identical with that of the existing divine persons.

11. This is a vast subject, but two useful overviews are Scott, *Miracle Cures*, and Bartlett, *Why Can the Dead*.

12. Some theologians, such as Sara Grant, *Alternative Theology*, perceive in this teaching a close affinity not to the doctrine of *theosis* but to the Thomist doctrine that the essence of God is existence itself. On this, see Soars, *World and God*, esp. 69–96.

13. Matt 5:48.

14. Rom 8:29; 1 Cor 15:49; Phil 3:21; 1 John 3:2.

15. John 3:6; 14:17.

16. On the meaning and contemporary reception of the doctrine of divine simplicity, see Barrett, *Divine Simplicity*, 3–34.

has become complex, then God has changed and indeed lost one of the key divine properties, which is also deeply problematic. Proponents of this kind of *theosis* must, then, hold that God is complex, a view that raises well-known problems.[17]

Third, the future life is supposed to be embodied, as we saw in the previous chapter. This does not seem to be compatible with absorption into an incorporeal God.[18] Fourth, and relatedly, both the Bible and later Christian theological tradition represent the blessed as distinct from God. They are in the presence of God, they perceive God, they may even in a sense be divine, but they are not simply identical with the Father, or with the Son, or with the

17. For example, if God is complex, then God has parts, in which case God's parts would seem to be ontologically prior to God.

18. This objection could of course be avoided by supposing that God is corporeal. This is ruled out by the broadly classical conception of God that I am presupposing. However, many ancient Christians as well as Jews believed God to be corporeal. Such a conception is presupposed by a literal reading of much of the Bible, which never explicitly teaches divine incorporeality. There is substantial literature on divine corporeality in the Hebrew Bible: see, among others, Moore, "Gigantic God"; Hamori, "When Gods Were Men"; Sommer, Bodies of God; Knafl, Forming God; Wagner, God's Body; Stavrakopoulou, God. On the New Testament, see Wilson, Embodied God. On ancient views about divine physicality in general, see Markschies, God's Body. On evidence for early Christian belief in a physical God, see Paulsen, "Early Christian Belief"; Griffin and Paulsen, "Augustine." The classic text on this topic is John 4:24, with its claim that "God is spirit (πνεῦμα)" (NRSV). For some modern commentators (e.g., Keener, Gospel of John, 618–19) this does mean that God is incorporeal, but for others (e.g., Bultmann, Gospel of John, 191; Barrett, St John, 238–39; Carson, John, 225–26) it refers not to God's metaphysical status but to what God is like: invisible, powerful, life-giving, etc. Paradoxically by modern assumptions, at least some ancient Christians cited this verse in *support* of the claim that God is physical, as πνεῦμα was taken in the sense of "breath" and therefore understood in a corporeal sense. Tertullian does so when asserting God's physicality (*Against Praxeas*, ch. 7, p. 138; see Stead, "Divine Substance"). Origen testifies that this was a common interpretation and devotes some effort to arguing that it is incorrect (*On First Principles*, I.4, p. 9). In the late fourth century, the first Origenist controversy was, to a large extent, waged over whether or not God should be conceived as incorporeal, with Theophilus of Alexandria calling a council in 400 that condemned the doctrine of divine incorporeality. On this controversy, see Clark, Origenist Controversy; Golitzin, "Demons Suggest" and "Vision of God"; Harding, "Origenist Crises"; Lundhaug, "Body of God"; Luckritz Marquis, Death of the Desert. Today, the Church of Jesus Christ of Latter-day Saints also teaches the corporeality of the Father and the Son, though not the Holy Spirit (*Doctrine of Covenants*, 130.22, in *Doctrine*, 265). So the idea of a corporeal God is not as contrary to Christian tradition as one might initially suppose. For a philosophical analysis of the claim that God is physical, see Wainwright, "God's Body," and for a theological defense, see Halton, Human-Shaped God. As Wainwright points out ("God's Body," 473), belief in divine physicality seems to be incompatible with belief in divine simplicity, so adopting this solution to the current problem would also mean avoiding the second problem mentioned above—at least for a theologian willing to endorse a radically non-classical conception of God.

Holy Spirit. To cite Revelation again, they inhabit the heavenly Jerusalem, worshipping God. They do not worship themselves.

So both of the relatively straightforward understandings of what *theosis* might be are untenable, at least from the perspective of orthodox Christianity. Indeed, they share a more fundamental problem, which is that they transgress the distinction between Creator and creature. In Christian theology, God is fundamentally different from all creation. God does not merely possess properties that other things do not. God is a different order of reality altogether. There is, in Aquinas' terminology, no distinction between God's essence and God's existence.[19] God is what makes the existence of anything possible. The gulf between divinity and non-divinity is not simply vast, it is *fundamentally uncrossable*. But both of the ways of conceiving *theosis* contradict this.

It seems, then, as though a viable doctrine of *theosis* is impossible. On the one hand, it needs to take seriously the biblical claim that human beings can expect to share the divine nature, as well as the longstanding conviction of Christian theologians that this prospect is the central hope of Christianity. But on the other hand, it needs to respect the fundamental difference between Creator and creature, and take into account the traditional accounts of the resurrection life as embodied, communal, and *focused* on God without being *identical with* God. These appear to be incompatible conditions upon the doctrine.

But this paradox may suggest a third way of understanding *theosis*. There is another doctrine in Christianity that concerns the union of divinity with humanity in apparently paradoxical terms: the incarnation. Compositionalist models of incarnation conceive of Christ as a composite of divinity and humanity.[20] God the Son assumes (or unites with) a human body and soul,[21] in such a way that they are truly *God's* body and soul, but without actually *becoming* a body and soul or otherwise becoming confused with them. This, according to its proponents, is sufficient for God the Son to be genuinely a human being, but the two natures remain distinct. What if we were to understand *theosis* in these terms? Perhaps human beings can look forward to entering a hypostatic union with God just as Jesus did, in virtue

19. Aquinas, *ST*, I q. 3 a. 4, vol. 1, pp. 35–36.

20. For examples of this approach in contemporary analytic theology, see among others Leftow, "Timeless God"; Senor, "Compositional Account"; Le Poidevin, "Identity"; Crisp, "Compositional Christology"; and Flint, "Should Concretists Part?"

21. I use the language of "soul" neutrally here, without meaning to presuppose any form of dualism. "Body and soul" refers simply to the whole of what, in most people, constitutes the entire person, whether that be a body alone or a body plus some other component.

of which they would be divine just as Jesus is.[22] This would have the virtue of doing justice to the biblical texts that portray Jesus as a forerunner of all human beings.

However, this also will not do. There are two reasons for this. The first is that orthodoxy requires that the blessed do not become exactly like Christ. The twelfth and thirteenth anathemas of the Second Council of Constantinople, in 553, condemn this notion.[23] Second, this proposed way of understanding theosis differs from the doctrine of incarnation in one crucial respect: with incarnation, God the Son is united to a human body and soul which did not exist before entering into this relation with the Son. Rather, they came into existence already united hypostatically to the Son (i.e., having the Son for their metaphysical basis). This is necessary because if Christ's body and soul had existed before being united to the Son, they would have constituted a human person in their own right, exactly like every other human being. And if that had been so, then after union with the Son, either they would have continued to constitute a person in their own right or they would not. But neither of these options is permissible: the first would be the Nestorian heresy, while the second would be to suppose that a person had gone out of existence, that is, effectively to suppose that having the Son incarnate in him killed Jesus.[24]

But with *theosis*, the human person being deified clearly does exist before the deification occurs. It would seem, then, that after deification, either that person must continue to exist as a distinct person from God (in which case they are not really divine at all), or they cease to exist as a person at all (which is obviously not acceptable). It follows, then, that incarnation does not offer a suitable model for *theosis*.

Theosis, love, and knowledge

Instead, I propose that a viable solution is to suggest a modification of the first way of understanding *theosis*, the acquisition of properties. Suppose that rather than acquiring all of the divine properties, the blessed acquire

22. This assumes that multiple incarnations are possible, something that has proven controversial in the literature. On this, see Le Poidevin, "Multiple Incarnations."

23. The condemnation (found in Price, *Acts*, II 286) was aimed at the "Isochrists," a group of extreme Origenists known primarily from Cyril of Scythopolis' *Life of Sabas*, ch. 83–90, in *Lives*, 196–209, and who were said to have believed that human souls became exactly "like Christ" after death. On the identity of this group, see Price, *Acts*, II 270–80. On Cyril and his sources, see Binns, *Ascetics and Ambassadors*, 56–76.

24. Thomas Aquinas makes effectively this point at *ST*, III q. 4 a. 2, vol. 15, p. 76; also q. 6 a. 3, vol. 15, p. 101, where he argues that Christ's soul could not have existed before the union, on similar grounds. See also Leftow, "Timeless God," 280.

only one property above all, namely the divine love. As is well known, discourse about divine "properties" does not reflect the way that biblical authors talk about God. Katherine Sonderegger puts it eloquently:

> How often have we shielded ourselves from this Terrible One by dense and technical accounts of problem cases, of scholastic distinctions that serve only the thirst of the schools, of meta-physical systems that can lead the faithful only farther and farther away from the Loving God who is zealous in all His Ways! ... [W]e arrange Divine Predicates like so much furniture in an empty warehouse. How dull and heavy and wearisome, it seems, that we must carry all these threadbare things around! But such things should not be! To speak of God, to name the Divine Per-fections, should be honey in the comb, the river of delight, the freshness and strong elixir of love.[25]

Sonderegger has in mind biblical passages such as the famous statement from 1 John 4:8 that "God is love" (NRSV).[26] No biblical text claims that God *is* knowledge, or power, or necessary existence, or any other divine attribute. But here, God is identified with love. As Sonderegger indicates, a doctrine of God that takes this seriously will make love God's primary feature, and understand any other divine features solely in its light.

Here, it seems, is a possible key to the doctrine of *theosis*. It also strikes me as significant that the author of 1 John links *love* closely with *knowledge*: knowing God and loving others are closely associated throughout this passage. We see something similar in 2 Pet 1:3–4, where participating in the divine nature follows the *knowledge* of God. Accordingly, Thomas Aquinas elaborates on this passage:

> [A]s man in his intellective power participates in the Divine knowledge through the virtue of faith, and in his power of will participates in the Divine love through the virtue of charity, so also in the nature of the soul does he participate in the Divine Nature, after the manner of a likeness, through a certain regen-eration or re-creation.[27]

Here, then, is a possible way of thinking of love: as bound up with knowl-edge.[28] I think it is an empirically observable fact that the more one learns

25. Sonderegger, *Systematic Theology*, 472.

26. On this verse, see Brown, *Epistles*, 549–53. Brown stresses (p. 550) that the au-thor intends to contrast God's love with the world's hatred.

27. Aquinas, *ST*, IIa q. 110 a. 4, vol. 8, p. 354.

28. Aquinas says more about the relation between love and knowledge at *ST*, IIa q. 27 a. 2, vol. 6, p. 321, where he argues that knowledge is a part-cause of love because

about something, the more one tends to like it. A rock might not interest me very much. But if I were, somehow, to learn about its chemical composition, about its immense history, about the structure of its crystals, about the arrangement of its molecules, I would not only find it fascinating but find a kind of beauty in the rock. More broadly, we could apply this to the whole natural world. The better we understand it, the more beautiful we find it, and to find something beautiful is to love it.

That, of course, is not the same thing as loving a *person*. But one can think of inter-personal love as closely connected to knowledge of a different kind. In his important study of the concept of God's love, Jordan Wessling builds on J. D. Velleman's analysis of (human) love as based on *perception of value*.[29] Velleman writes:

> In my view, appreciation for someone's value as a person is not distinct from loving him: it is the evaluative core of love. I do not mean that love is a value judgment to the effect that the beloved has final value as an end in himself. Love is rather an appreciative response to the perception of that value. And I mean "perception" literally: the people we love are the ones whom we succeed in perceiving as persons, within some of the human organisms milling about us.[30]

Wessling comments:

> There is something deeply right about viewing love as a kind of appreciative response to a person's dignity. For it is nearly inconceivable to suppose that someone can genuinely love another while also maintaining that the person he loves is not perceived (in the specified sense) as extraordinarily valuable, worthy of rich appreciation, and utterly irreplaceable.[31]

---

one has to recognize the goodness of something in order to love it. On this, see Sherwin, *Knowledge and Love*, esp. 1–17, 147–203.

29. This is therefore a version of the *value-appraisal* theory of love, as opposed to the *value-bestowing* theory, according to which the lover does not simply recognize value in the beloved but creates that value through the act of loving. Irving Singer is probably the most prominent defender of a theory of this kind, though Singer seeks to incorporate elements of appraisal into his theory (*Nature of Love*, 369–437). In my view it is correct to think that there is more to love than appraisal, as to love is (or can be) a choice, but I would see this as going *beyond* appraisal rather than being a substitute or basis for it. Troy Jollimore (*Love's Vision*) offers an account of love roughly along these lines. For our purposes, it is enough to suppose, very plausibly, that an appraisal of value is a necessary element to love, without needing to suppose that it is sufficient. I return to the notion of love as act below.

30. Velleman, "Beyond Price," 199.

31. Wessling, *Love Divine*, 46.

For Wessling, *perception* is not the same thing as *belief.* Love involves "a kind of experience of a particular individual," which "concretizes the lover's response to dignity."[32] He goes on to flesh out this account of love as realized in caring about the welfare of the beloved and desiring to be united to them—which, in turn, he argues, characterize the love of God for creation.

Wessling's understanding of "perception" as distinct from, though related to, "belief" is reminiscent of the standard distinction between propositional knowledge and knowledge by acquaintance.[33] If my love for, say, rocks depends upon propositional knowledge *about* rocks, my love for a person must depend upon *personal familiarity* with that person. I cannot really be said to love a person I do not know. One might think, conversely, that there are some people whom one likes *less* as one knows them better. But I am optimistic enough to think that this can go only so far. Suppose I meet someone about whom I am neutral. After a short acquaintance, I find this person obnoxious. Greater knowledge has led to less love. But if I could come to know that person *really* well, I would understand what makes her act the way she does. I would understand her innermost drives and desires, the fears and misunderstandings that cause her to act reprehensibly. Through understanding her in this way, I might still disapprove of her behavior, but I would empathize entirely with her as a person. I would, plausibly, love her as a result of this greater knowledge. I would, in Wessling's terminology, have come to *perceive* her as supremely valuable.

Similarly, God is supposed to know everything and love everything. Yet some things—and some people—appear supremely unlovable. Is it not a contradiction to say that God knows the most heinous sinner perfectly and yet also loves them perfectly? It seems to me that a conception of love as closely bound up with knowledge is the only way to resolve this paradox. Even the worst human being is fundamentally lovable deep down. To God's perfect understanding, even the worst person imaginable is lovable: God loves them not *despite* understanding them so well, but *because* of it. If we think of divine omniscience as involving knowledge by acquaintance rather than propositional knowledge alone, we might say that the claim that God knows everything does not mean (merely) that God is aware of the truth-value of every meaningful proposition. It means, rather, that God is familiar with every *thing* that exists. God's knowledge is of objects rather than of facts. And it is through acquaintance that we come to love people. Consider,

32. Wessling, *Love Divine,* 46.

33. Eleonore Stump, *Wandering in Darkness,* 39–63, refers to these as "Franciscan" and "Dominican" knowledge respectively, developing a narratological distinction between them to argue for the importance of "Franciscan knowledge" alongside the more familiar (to analytic philosophers) Dominican variety.

for example, the love of a carer for a child. She does not love the child in virtue of learning various facts about her. She loves the child in virtue of spending time with her and becoming personally acquainted with her—it is through *presence* that love emerges. But God's presence is supposed to be universal. God is what sustains creation—God is existence itself, and therefore intimately connected to creation at every level. God does not simply know everything about me: God is present within me and intimately familiar with me on a personal level. And this, plausibly, is why God is love.[34]

A possible objection to this view is that it rests upon the assumption, associated especially with Socrates, that virtue is essentially a kind of knowledge, and that nobody ever chooses what they believe to be wrong.[35] Such an objection itself presupposes that this intellectualist view is false, which could be open to question—but in either case, it is not the basis for the position I am suggesting here. Rather, my position is motivated by the Christian assumption of the fundamental goodness of creation. Through God's omniscience, God *recognizes* the fundamental goodness of the world, which God's will has *caused* to be good. So it is in virtue of the fact that God understands everything perfectly that God loves everything perfectly, because a lack of love stems from a lack of *perception* of the thing or person as valuable.

If this is so, we can return to the conception of the beatific vision outlined in the previous chapter, and particularly the idea that the blessed might enjoy maxiscience, as much knowledge as a created being can have. To the extent that the blessed's knowledge of God includes understanding what God understands, however limited, to that extent the blessed would share God's love. In this scenario, the blessed remain distinct from God. But in the beatific vision, they share some of God's understanding—or, better, familiarity—with created things. Remaining creaturely, they cannot share God's understanding fully, but we can imagine that their understanding of any given object, or person, vastly exceeds any knowledge available to those on earth. They would, accordingly, have immense love for anything they contemplate through the vision of God in this way. In this way, the blessed

---

34. Martin Luther famously claimed that "the love of God does not find, but creates, that which is pleasing to it" (*Works*, 31:57), which he argued made it precisely the opposite of human love, which is based solely upon appraisal. The approach I am adopting here blurs the boundaries by suggesting that both kinds of love involve both appraisal and action. However, in God's case, God does not passively review created objects and love them on the basis of this review, because God is the creator of all things. It would be more accurate to think of God creating, knowing, and loving each thing in a single act, which is perhaps a little closer to Luther's view.

35. On this view in Socrates and Plato, see, for example, Dorter, "Virtue"; Brickhouse and Smith, *Socratic Moral Psychology*, esp. 63–131.

could participate in the most characteristic property of divinity while remaining quite distinct from God. Even lacking other divine properties, they could legitimately be called divine because they share the *most* divine feature of God, outward-looking love.

An objection to this sort of account of *theosis* is that if the blessed acquire only some divine properties, then they do not really count as divine. For example, if omnipotence is essential to divinity, and the blessed do not acquire it, then they are not divine. Indeed, on this reading, they have not even acquired omniscience or love to the same degree as God's.

A possible response to this would be to appeal to the Thomist account of analogy.[36] According to this view, words that are used of God and creatures alike are not used univocally—they mean somewhat different things. But they are not used equivocally either—they do not mean *completely* different things. They are, rather, used analogically. We might say that just as the knowledge that human beings have is not the same kind of thing as God's knowledge, so too the divinity that the blessed have is not the same kind of thing as the divinity of the Godhead.

The standard criticism of the doctrine of analogy is that put by Duns Scotus: if language is used analogically, it must be reducible to univocal language, or it is ultimately equivocal.[37] For example, if a courageous person is described as "a lion," there must be some property (namely courage) that the person and the lion really share for that description to be appropriate at all. Similarly, if "knowledge" means something different for God and human beings, there must be some property that humans and God really share to make it appropriate to use the same word at all. And this property must, at least in theory, be able to be spoken of univocally.

In my view, this is a powerful rebuttal to the notion of irreducible analogy. But it need not be fatal to our view of *theosis*. Suppose we accept the Scotist claim that the divine properties are similar to creaturely properties, but infinite in extent, such that the words used to refer to divine and creaturely properties are used univocally. Then the knowledge that the blessed derive from the beatific vision, and the love that accompanies it, could be qualitatively exactly similar to the knowledge and love that characterize

36. The doctrine is found in Aquinas, *ST*, I q. 13, esp. aa. 5–6, 9–10, vol. 1, pp. 158–64, 170–75. Though today associated with Aquinas, this was the usual view of medieval theologians. Two useful accounts that not only articulate Aquinas' theory but place it in its historical context are Rocca, *Speaking*, 7–195, and Long, "Thomas Aquinas." For a philosophical assessment, see Davies, "Aquinas."

37. As with much of his work, Scotus formulated this as a criticism of Henry of Ghent rather than of Thomas Aquinas. On his doctrine of univocity, see Mann, "Duns Scotus"; D'Ettore, *Analogy*, 18–32; Pini, "Before Univocity." On Scotus' own context and his influence, see Smith, "Analogy after Duns Scotus."

God. They would simply be more limited in scope. But on the basis of this exact qualitative similarity of knowledge and love, we could *analogically* say that the blessed are divine. In other words, this theory of knowledge and love provides us with a way to use the language of *divinity itself* analogically, even if we take the Scotist view that analogical language must be grounded in univocity.

This also helps to avoid another problem, that of the co-instantiability of divine and creaturely properties. If, as Thomists believe, "knowledge" refers to something different in the two cases of God and human beings, then this is because the divine knowledge is part and parcel of the fundamentally different nature of God compared to creaturely things. God is not a substance in the usual sense that has properties in the usual sense. God's knowledge is not simply a property that is unfamiliar to us—it is something qualitatively different from a "property" at all. How, then, could a creature instantiate it alongside non-divine properties?

On the Scotist view of divine properties, however, it is much more plausible to suppose that a creature could instantiate some divine properties but not others, because the divine properties are not fundamentally different in kind from creaturely ones. A creature could, perhaps, have infinitely extended knowledge without being infinite in other respects.

So we have a scenario where the maxiscience enjoyed by the blessed—through their sharing of God's knowledge in the beatific vision—forms the basis for their sharing in the divine love for creation, since this love is bound up with (personal) knowledge of creation. So far, this has not touched on our main theme of time and atemporality: the blessed could love in this way whether they are temporal or atemporal. But there is one way in which I think that an atemporal account fares better than a temporal one. I think that any plausible theory of love must take account not merely of the role of appraisal but of the *activity* of the lover. That is, to love is not merely to observe; it is to act. This is why love is not fickle: the true lover does not love the beloved just until someone better comes along. Troy Jollimore, for example, argues:

> [L]oving someone is a way of opening one's eyes to her (and of being committed to this way of seeing) in a way that involves both appreciating the properties she bears as an object and identifying with her as a subject. . . . A reasonable lover knows that other people are, in a fundamental moral sense, as significant as her beloved. . . . But in the case of her beloved, she does more than simply acknowledge his valuable characteristics: she appreciates them. The lover takes the features of her beloved to which she is responding to be real and genuinely valuable, independent

of her own attitudes; she does not create these values but notices and appreciates them. Contra the typical antirationalist position, it is not value but generous attention that is bestowed upon the beloved.[38]

This identification and appreciation is an *action* on the part of the lover. If this is correct, and if human love reflects divine love, then God's love for creation also involves divine activity. And if *that* is so, then the love of the blessed that they share with God must also involve activity. Just as God identifies with and appreciates each creature, the blessed act upon their knowledge of those creatures through the beatific vision in the same way, through identification and appreciation. But if God is atemporal then this is an atemporal activity. If the blessed are temporal, then they can imitate that activity, but they cannot really *join* with it, because temporal and atemporal activities are so different. But if they are atemporal, they could be meaningfully said to join with the divine loving activity towards creation. And this would give us a further way of understanding *theosis*, as it involves not merely resembling God in key respects but acting *with* God in a unified act of love.

Atemporality and divinity

For some writers, atemporality is an intrinsically divine property. In other words, to be embedded within time is *part* of what it is to be a creature. If this is so, then the notion that the blessed are atemporal is problematic. But why should atemporality be exclusive to God alone? Often, this claim goes unsubstantiated. John Cooper, for example, asks:

> [W]hy should we think that we humans share [divine] timelessness when we die? Isn't that attributing a divine property to a mere creature? Aren't we essentially temporal beings, dead or alive?[39]

But the questions remain rhetorical. Again, Robin Le Poidevin writes: "The suggestion that being temporal is a merely contingent feature of humanity, albeit a typical one, does not have much to recommend it."[40] But Le Poidevin gives no reason to recommend the opposite view either.[41]

38. Jollimore, *Love's Vision*, 123–24.

39. Cooper, *Body*, 194.

40. Le Poidevin, *And Was Made Man*, 24.

41. See also Brown, *Eternal Life*, 26, who motivates a similar claim by appealing to everyday experience, but without explaining why the fact that our everyday experience is temporal and changeable means that these are *necessary* features of human existence.

John Wm. Houghton gives a reason for withholding atemporality from creatures, namely that it "cannot be a property of a free creature, which is by definition subject to change, i.e., the change involved in making a choice."[42] He appeals to Aquinas' claim that angels are changeable in their choices, meaning that they cannot be truly eternal.[43] But temporality cannot be a condition for *all* kinds of freedom, or Aquinas' God could not be both free and atemporal. Creatures' temporality is required not by their freedom, or even their capacity for choice, but by their inconstancy—that is, their tendency to *change* their choices. And why suppose that this must be a feature of the kind of freedom enjoyed by the blessed?

Paul Griffiths argues that divine atemporality is derived from divine simplicity: temporality is a form of complexity, since to be temporal is to be "partly here and partly there."[44] Although he does not say so, this presupposes four-dimensionalism. An endurantist could hold that since a temporal object exists in its entirety at any given moment at which it exists, temporality in itself does not require complexity. Griffiths goes on:

> All creatures, all *realia* other than the LORD, exactly are complex (not simple) in these ways. It is definitional of creaturehood to be like that, because to be complex is also to be contingent, to be capable of not being as you are at the moment, and to be capable of not being at all.[45]

But it is not true that complexity entails contingency. A proposition can be complex and yet necessary, as many mathematical propositions are. Neither is it clear that creatureliness requires complexity in *every* way in which God is simple. One could imagine a possible world in which all created substances are perfectly simple. Indeed, Leibniz thought, at least in his later works, that this describes the actual world.[46] And as we have seen in chapter 2, something could be complex without being temporal. Griffiths' argument, then, is really an assertion, and one that need not be true.

Similarly, R. Keith Loftin and R. T. Mullins state:

> [T]he temporality of creation is a good thing, and . . . God is going to redeem the temporality of creation. God did not make temporal life only to scrap it in the eschaton. God made temporal life because it has value and makes several of His purposes

---

42. Houghton, "Review," 283.

43. Aquinas, *ST*, I q. 10 a. 5, vol. 1, p. 107.

44. Griffiths, *Decreation*, 71.

45. Griffiths, *Decreation*, 71.

46. On Leibniz's views on the simplicity of all substances, see Garber, *Leibniz*, 55–98, and Hillman, "Substantial Simplicity."

for creation possible. This is in stark contrast to claims that God
is going to bring about a timeless eschatological state of affairs.
We think that such a thing is not only impossible, but that it is
unbiblical.[47]

This passage suggests an argument of this sort:

(1) If God values some created object, God values all the properties
with which God created that object.

(2) Any property that God values will be present in the resurrection life.

(3) God values temporal objects.

(4) Therefore temporality will be present in the resurrection life.

Even if we grant (1), we will surely hesitate to grant (2). As we will consider
shortly, there are biblical passages teaching that the nature of created species
will be changed at the eschaton. If God created wolves and lions as carnivores, and if God therefore values their carnivory, God nonetheless does
not preserve it in the resurrection life. One might object, perhaps, that God
did not create these animals as carnivores, since carnivory appeared not as a
direct creation by God but as a result of the natural process of evolution. But
that simply pushes the problem one step back: God created a natural world
in which creatures evolve by natural selection, but evolution by natural selection will not be a feature of the new heavens and the new earth either,
since there will be no reproduction there.[48] So either God does not value the
property of created beings that they reproduce and evolve by natural selection (rendering (1) false) or God does value this property but nevertheless
does not instantiate it in the resurrection life (rendering (2) false).

So it is consistent to hold that God values all temporal creatures, and
seeks to redeem them, without having to hold that this requires that their
temporality be preserved. Loftin's and Mullins' argument effectively rests
upon the assumption that temporality is *essential* to created beings, and that
God could not eradicate their temporality without destroying them. But I
see no reason to think that this assumption is true.

At the same time, all created objects that we are aware of *are* temporal.
So we can hold that atemporality is a *distinctively* divine property without needing it to be an *exclusively* divine property. Nothing in creation is
atemporal in its nature, but God has the ability to raise temporal things to
an atemporal state. If this is so, then the atemporality of the blessed would
be a form of sharing in the divine life, which would allow them to share

47. Loftin and Mullins, "Physicalism," 102.
48. That, at least, is strongly implied by Matt 22:30.

in the divine knowledge and love in the way we have been considering.[49] But one could hold this without needing to suppose that the blessed have been granted a property which is *definitionally* exclusive to God alone. For example, Edward Epsen argues that divine eternity, defined as atemporality, should be understood only in the context of Trinitarianism: it is because God is three persons, and each person gives himself wholly to the other two, that there is no temporal succession in God. Thus, eternity is a corollary of perfect community. And he appeals to the work of Maximus the Confessor and Dumitru Staniloae to suggest that *theosis* is in part a matter of human beings being graciously allowed to participate in this community, and consequently in eternity:

> With respect to eternity, then, the orthodox theological tradition teaches two things: one, that God really is eternal through the interpersonal communion of the Trinity; and two, that because he is eternal, we too can be eternal because it is an outcome of the glory to which we [are] called, the purpose for which time and every other feature of the created world was made. Time is thus part of the means of theosis. Even though time is a mark of a spiritually impoverished reality, it is not a bad thing, not an evil. It is the condition of the ability of the human mind to concentrate its energies in the present. But as such, time points to the condition that is its undoing, namely the full pouring out of the mind's energies into the uncreated energies of God, the supreme goodness and beauty that alone can satisfy our restlessness.[50]

49. William Charlton, "Heaven," 556, envisages an atemporal heavenly existence along these lines, but does not develop the idea. Arthur Peacocke similarly seems to hint at such a thing when he states that human hope is subject to God's purposes, which "must *ex hypothesi*, because they are *God's*, finally achieve their fulfillment beyond space and time within the very being of God himself" (*Creation*, 353, italics original).

50. Epsen, "Eternity Is a Present," 426. Part of Epsen's argument is that time itself "is constituted by, or exists in virtue of, the distention of the mind, the fact that the human power of attention is so weak and limited that it cannot help longing for what it does not yet have and missing what it has had but lost" (p. 425). This does not seem to me coherent: if the mind has lost something, or will acquire something, then it is temporal anyway, whether it yearns for these things or not. And if the account *is* nevertheless coherent then it is surely false, because it would entail that the passage of time requires the existence of human minds. But we know that many millions of years passed before human beings ever existed.

The heavenly self and the earthly self

I have argued that the doctrine of divine atemporality entails a tenseless ontology of time and four-dimensionalism. What does *transformation* look like, given such a picture? If heaven is temporal, then the temporal part of a person that comes after the moment of resurrection is glorified, perhaps enjoying a *theosis* similar to what we have just been discussing. But such a view is unsatisfying. What about the portion of their life that comes *before* resurrection? Given a tenseless ontology of time, that section of their life exists, in a sense, even after it is over. What if much of it was terrible, or sinful? Is it sufficient to say that the later temporal parts of that person are redeemed, if the earlier are not?[51]

R. T. Mullins and R. Keith Loftin have developed an argument of this sort against perdurantism.[52] Suppose perdurantism is true. Then the Peter who denies Christ is a temporal slice of the whole four-dimensional Peter. And this Peter is not subsequently redeemed. Only the later temporal parts of Peter are redeemed. But it is essential to Christianity that the *whole* person be redeemed. Perdurantism, therefore, is incompatible with Christianity.

One might respond to this argument by pointing out that it misrepresents perdurantism. Even the most extreme stage theorist would probably reject the notion that Peter-at-t_1 and Peter-at-t_2 are distinct persons, and a more moderate perdurantist would certainly reject it. They are, rather, temporal parts of a single four-dimensional person, and they are not persons in their own right.[53] This is why perdurantism is compatible with common notions of justice: we can justly punish someone at time t_2 for a crime committed at time t_1, because although two distinct temporal parts of that

---

51. Mullins, "Personal Identity," also develops a related argument, framed in terms of Jesus' promises in the beatitudes that, e.g., those who mourn now will be comforted. For Mullins, any four-dimensionalist view of time entails that those who mourn in the past are eternally mourning, and are not genuinely identical with those who are comforted in the future. He argues that this also shows four-dimensionalism to be simply incompatible with Christianity.

52. Loftin and Mullins, "Physicalism," 108–10.

53. Precisely *why* they are not persons in their own right is not always clear. An obvious move is to appeal to the principle that a person cannot have other persons as proper parts. I have argued elsewhere (Hill, "Compositionalism") that that principle is mistaken. But the alternative solution I suggest there to mereological puzzles could be easily adapted here: what prevents Peter-at-t_1 from being a person is not the mere fact that he is a proper part of Peter-as-a-whole, but the fact that those (spatial) parts of Peter-at-t_1 that would seem to qualify him as a person—whatever precisely those may be—overlap with the parts that qualify Peter-as-a-whole as one. And different persons cannot share the same person-making parts.

person are involved, only one *person* is involved. Similarly, then, it is not Peter-at-*t2* that is redeemed, it is Peter-as-a-whole.

But such a response would not be adequate. Consider the analogy with spatial parts. No orthodox Christian would be willing to countenance the idea that only some spatial parts of a person are saved. Indeed, the fact that the *whole person* is to be saved is what underlies the traditional emphasis on the resurrection of the body, as we saw in the last chapter. So the notion that some temporal parts of Peter do not share in his redemption is indeed very problematic.

If heaven is atemporal, though, we have a way to address this problem. We can begin by noting that if the blessed enjoy maxiscience, they would have unsurpassed knowledge *of their own earthly lives*. If they are atemporal, this would not simply be memory of their lives, but a sharing in God's direct and intimate familiarity with them. Joseph Bracken raises such a possibility:

> At the moment of death one sees one's past life as a completed reality in and through recognition of the pattern of one's life that has been woven into the complex structure of the kingdom of God. . . . [E]very moment in the duration or time-span of an individual's life would be part of the divine "now" or present moment of the divine life.[54]

But we can go further than this. Let us call the person who lives on earth *E*, and that same person existing atemporally in heaven *H*. *E* and *H* are the same person, so these terms pick out distinct stages on that person's "timeline" (with the proviso, of course, that *H* is not really on a "timeline" at all). As we saw in chapters 3 and 4, the picture depends to a large degree upon the notion that *H* causally depends upon *E*. This is both existential dependence (*H* would not exist if *E* did not) and qualitative dependence (*H* has [some of] the features it has *because E* has [some of] the features *it* has). This mirrors the relation between (say) me-at-*t1* and me-at-*t2*: me-at-*t2* exists *and* has certain features in virtue of the fact that me-at-*t1* exists and has certain features. It is because of this that we can say both that *E* and *H* are the same person, and that *E* is prior to *H*, even though they are not related temporally.

But the fact that *H* is atemporal raises the intriguing possibility of relations between *E* and *H* that are not possible between earlier and later versions of the same person. Consider the fact that we can distinguish between different psychological states within *E* (evidently) and within *H* (as I argued in chapter 2). We could describe this as follows: *E* has a temporal sequence of psychological states, beginning at her birth (or thereabouts) and ending

54. Bracken, *World*, 230.

at her death. *H* has an atemporal sequence of psychological states, all of which are logically posterior to the whole sequence in *E*. In this scenario, the two sequences are quite distinct from each other, with one wholly following on from the other.

But the situation could be more complex than this. Consider three (temporally) successive psychological states of *E*: *a*, *b*, and *c*. And consider three (atemporally) successive states of *H*: *x*, *y*, and *z*. It could be that *x* depends upon (is caused by?) *c*, *y* depends upon *a* and *x*, and *z* depends upon *b*. We have a complex network of overlapping dependencies. Nothing in *E* depends on anything in *H*—that would destroy the notion that *H* (atemporally) comes after *E*—but *H* has a very intimate relation with *E*, interlocking with it in a complex way. In such a situation, rather than talking about two sequences—one temporal and one atemporal—it might be more reasonable to talk about a *single* sequence, which has some temporal elements and some atemporal elements. This is a sequence of psychological elements of a greater whole, composed of *E* and *H*.

On this picture, the thoughts and experiences that I think of as *mine* are really just part of a greater whole, which includes all of those thoughts and experiences but also includes many more, atemporal ones. But who is having those thoughts and experiences? Why should I think it is *me*? Well, because *H* is not a different person from *E*. *H* just *is E*, translated to an atemporal state in the way we have been considering. We might draw a parallel, again, with time travel. Brian Leftow describes a situation in which a single time traveler makes multiple leaps to the same place and time, resulting in three versions of her all appearing on a stage together. In such a situation, Leftow suggests, we have a single individual appearing in three "personae," which offers a model for the Trinity.[55] In such a case, each "persona" could interact with the others as if they were different people, even though they are not. Similarly, the temporal *E* and the atemporal *H* could relate to each other in ways similar to how any temporal person might relate to any atemporal person (such as God), even though they are the same person.

We might draw another parallel to the distinction between the conscious and subconscious minds. All the thoughts and experiences I am conscious of are really just a part—perhaps a relatively small part—of what is going on in my mind as a whole. There are many subconscious processes going on, to the extent that one might think of the subconscious mind as more truly *me* than the conscious mind is. Yet even though I am not consciously aware of my subconscious mind, I do not doubt that it is really *me*. I do not worry that my conscious mind is just a part of some other person.

55. Leftow, "Latin Trinity," 308.

This is partly because I recognize that my subconscious mind is different in important respects from my conscious mind—it is not conscious, for one thing—and partly because I understand that this is just how minds work. We all have a subconscious mind, whether we recognize it or not.

Similarly, on the conception of heaven we are developing, H is different in important respects from E. It is atemporal, and although its experiences can be sequentially ordered, it is not a temporal sequence, and its order might be very different from the order of the temporal sequence on which it draws and with which it is mingled. $E + H$ is greater than E alone, just as my whole earthly mind is a greater mind than my consciousness alone, but it is not the mind of some other person. It is simply that there is more to a person than just E, even though E herself might not realize it. And accordingly, we can now suppose that $E + H$ has all of the experiences that E does, and has them *as her own*, precisely because of these relations. It is just like the person who is the combination of my conscious and subconscious minds, who has all the experiences that my conscious mind does (as well as others), and has them *as his own*—because *they are his*—because that person is me. It is simply that there is more to me than I am normally consciously aware of.

Mike Higton offers a striking eschatological metaphor that our conception reflects:

> [O]ne could think of each person as a text about Christ that at present is garbled and corrupted, and can only be read in snatches and with caution, but which in the eschaton will be edited into full legibility.[56]

Higton expresses this temporally: it *will* be the case that each person *will* be emended in this way. For the atemporalist, the full "text" is read not with a future perspective but with an eternal one. Once the atemporal elements are "edited into" the person, the temporal elements take on a new meaning as part of that greater whole.

We might wonder what the sequence of psychological states of $E + H$ would be like. We could imagine that $E + H$ has a sequence of thoughts that includes the thoughts of E alone but transforms them. This could be a result of H's maxiscience: H may have memories of being E, but this understanding of E would be dwarfed by what H knows through the beatific vision. Perhaps, with the atemporal perspective of H, $E + H$ perceives everything that E does but reinterpreted in light of the love of God. For example, where E dwells bitterly on the success of a rival, $E + H$ incorporates that thought

---

56. Higton, *Christian Doctrine*, 220.

into a larger and vastly more understanding meditation on how that other person's success manifests the love of God. To reiterate: this would not simply be a case of H looking "back" upon her earthly life and adopting a new attitude towards it. Rather, the very psychological states that E experiences *during* her life would themselves become *parts* of psychological states experienced by $E + H$.

This seems to me to capture something important. A common criticism of the concept of heaven is that it devalues earthly human life, by making it into little more than an annoying preamble to the really important stuff. But on this conception of heaven, nothing could be further from the truth. Heaven is not earth, but it is utterly bound up with it. My heavenly self is, in a sense, my earthly self transformed. If we adopt the view of the earthly life as whole-state-determining, as I argued in chapter 4, then who I am in heaven is determined not solely by who I am on my deathbed, but by who I am throughout my life. That means that who I am at each moment of my life matters eternally. Parents sometimes mourn the loss of their small children as those children grow up and change beyond recognition. This is a reflection of the fact that we value who people *used* to be as well as who they are now. The atemporal conception of heaven captures this. Toddler-me is part of the whole $E + H$ just as much as adult-me is.

But what if I have changed greatly throughout my life? What if I have changed my mind about things over the years? All of those incomplete, partial viewpoints could be integrated into a single, coherent attitude in my heavenly self. What if I have been a great sinner? My sinful actions would also determine the nature of my heavenly self, but not by making my heavenly self sinful. Perhaps when E intends harm, $E + H$ perceives the matter as God perceives it—a case of a limited, hurting creature lashing out—and incorporates that pain into self-love and empathy for those others who are hurt by it. Julian of Norwich wrote that, in heaven, sins will become honorable scars.[57] If a Christian can believe—as many have done—that human evil is simply part of a divine plan that we cannot understand, it seems to me just as plausible, if not more so, to suppose that an individual's wrongdoing can be incorporated into their heavenly identity in such a transformative way. In this way, we can see how the transformation of resurrection can bring about a transformation of the entirety of a person's life—not by changing the past, but by incorporating it into a larger picture.

To switch metaphors again, think of the traditional Japanese art form of *kintsugi*, in which broken ceramics are repaired using lacquer mixed with

---

57. *A Revelation of Love*, ch. 39, in Julian of Norwich, *Writings*, 241. On this, see Adams, *Horrendous Evils*, 121–24.

gold, silver, or platinum dust. Rather than trying to hide the cracks and make the piece look as good as new, the repairer instead draws attention to the cracks, but in a way that transforms them and makes them beautiful. The result is a piece whose history of breakage and repair is visibly encoded on its surface, in a way that enhances its aesthetic appeal. Similarly, we might say, $E + H$ contains all of the negative elements of E's life. But they are given new meaning in the greater context of $E + H$, compared to that of E alone. As such, these imperfections are not rubbed out but embraced and transformed into something positive.

This, then, gives us an answer to the problem of Peter's redemption. Loftin's and Mullins' argument assumes (rightly) that for Peter to be truly redeemed, every temporal part of him must be redeemed, and also (wrongly) that the redemption of any given temporal part must involve an *intrinsic* change in that part. Since intrinsic change in past temporal parts is impossible, we have a problem. But the scenario I have been suggesting is one of *extrinsic* change. The past slices of Peter are redeemed not by being transformed in themselves—by acquiring new monadic properties—but by being caught up in a wider context that reinterprets them.

So far, I have assumed that all the causal relations between E and H go one way, to ensure that H is genuinely posterior to E. But one might modify the account we have given here so that H determines aspects of E as well as vice versa. If we did that, then not only would H be (intimately and deeply) aware of E, but E might also be (dimly) aware of H as well. Here again time travel is perhaps a useful illustration. If old-me travels back in time and meets young-me, young-me is aware of the meeting and may learn something about old-me (though hopefully not enough to generate any temporal paradoxes). Old-me also has awareness of the meeting, just as young-me does, but on top of this is also privy to a huge amount of information about young-me, since he *remembers* being young-me. So the mutual understanding between the two selves is not symmetrical.[58] Similarly, if E has awareness or knowledge of H, it could be greatly inferior in both scope and kind to H's awareness and understanding of E. This would, perhaps, be sufficient for us to retain the crucial claim that E is (non-temporally) prior to H and that the state of H is still something that E can, in a sense, anticipate experiencing.

If all this is coherent, as I think it is, then it would provide a way of holding that there is an aspect of the human person that is eternal and heavenly, even though we are (largely) unaware of it.[59] It is not a *soul*, as it is the

58. Jorge Luis Borges envisages such a meeting, with this epistemological asymmetry between the two selves, in two stories: "The Other" and "August 25, 1983" (in Borges, *Book of Sand*, 3–11, 99–104).

59. It is tempting to suggest that this could be the "spirit" referred to by Paul in

whole self transformed. Rather, it is an aspect of the person that, as Aaron Garrett puts it, is eternal, not immortal.[60] The idea is reminiscent of Meister Eckhart's insistence that the highest part of us exists in the atemporal realm with God, even while we serve others in the temporal realm.[61]

We have generated something of a paradox. If heaven is atemporal, then heaven is extremely unlike our earthly life. A temporal heaven, by contrast, is more familiar. One might think, then, that to conceive of heaven as atemporal is to push it further away from earth: it is an escapist doctrine, one that idealizes an unearthly state. And yet our discussion in this chapter has taken it in the opposite direction. We have arrived at a picture of heaven where the blessed are deeply concerned with earthly things—where our earthly lives actually form a component of our heavenly selves. On the temporal conception, by contrast, heaven comes after earth, and so the blessed have simply moved on, and their earthly lives are significant only as the brief premise to the infinite story that follows. So the atemporalist can say, in a way in which the temporalist cannot, that what we do here on earth *matters*, though it may not make sense until we can view it from the perspective of eternity.

Cosmic resurrection and the reign of the saints

Christianity has a tradition of viewing salvation in purely human terms, illustrated starkly by John of Damascus' rhetorical question, "If there is no resurrection, then how do we differ from brute beasts?"[62] For John, it is a basic premise that the nonhuman animals will not be resurrected, because God cares only about human beings. At the other extreme we find Thomas Berry, who devoted much of his career to calling for a greater appreciation for—and protection of—the natural world by Christians and other religious traditions. For Berry, like John, there is no prospect of redemption for the natural world—but this is not because it is unimportant, but because it

---

passages such as 1 Thess 5:23 and 1 Cor 2:11–12. Christian tradition interprets these passages as referring to a *component* of the human being that transcends the earthly life, and such a view coheres well with the scenario I am suggesting. Some recent exegetes agree with this analysis: Fee, *Corinthians*, 119n183, for example, identifies πνεῦμα in 1 Cor 2:11 with νοῦς. However, most exegetes today tend to interpret these passages as referring not to a component of the human person but to the whole person, conceived in a certain way. On this, see Wright, *Paul*, 490; Fitzmyer, *First Corinthians*, 180; Ellis, *1 Corinthians*, 123.

60. Garrett, "This Tablet," 141–42.

61. See Putt, "Letting Go," 172–73.

62. *On the Orthodox Faith*, 4.27, in John of Damascus, *Writings*, 401.

simply does not need it. On the contrary, the natural world is the arena and vehicle for human salvation: "the ultimate sacred community could be the universe itself."[63]

But the New Testament teaches something in between these two extremes. Human salvation is indeed intimately connected with the world around us, but that world also stands in need of transformation. The future resurrection of human beings is just part of a cosmic regeneration.[64] Thus Paul tells the Romans that the world is "groaning in labor pains" for its imminent renewal,[65] and the Corinthians that ultimately God will be "all in all."[66] As David Wilkinson complains, traditional Christian theology rarely has much to say about this, preferring to focus on the hope for the future of the individual, or of humanity as a whole, or at most for life on earth, effectively ignoring that the universe is far vaster than all of these things.[67]

Certainly recent years have seen a great deal of theological attention paid to the nonhuman living world. If this has led to a lack of interest in the universe beyond earth's biosphere, this is perhaps hardly surprising given the pressing ethical and theological questions that the living world presents. The question of how Christian theology should respond to the environmental crisis has been scrutinized at length since Lynn White's brief but epochal 1967 paper argued that Christianity is to blame for much of it.[68] More fundamentally, though, increasing awareness of the moral importance of the nonhuman world has led to a recognition that it poses an acute form of the problem of evil. If nonhuman animals have moral value, what are we to say about a natural world that is full of predation, parasitism, and other forms of suffering? The problem is especially difficult given that this suffering predates the existence of human beings, so it cannot be blamed on human sin disrupting a perfect world; and besides, death and predation have been an essential element of the process of evolution by natural selection which makes the natural world, including human beings, possible in the first place.[69]

63. Berry, *Christian Future*, 39. On Berry's eschatology, see McLaughlin, *Preservation*, 103–24.

64. On this in the New Testament, see Wright, *Surprised by Hope*, 93–108. On biblical imagery of this cosmological hope, see Wilkinson, *Christian Eschatology*, 53–87.

65. Rom 8:22 NRSV.

66. 1 Cor 15:28 NRSV.

67. Wilkinson, *Christian Eschatology*, 23–52, 90, 103–4.

68. White, "Historic Roots." On White's influence and the shape of the debate that he began, see Jenkins, "After Lynn White."

69. Some theologians have sought to answer this by saying that an evolutionary process of this kind is the *only* possible way that God could have created intelligent

Biblical images of the renewal of the world are largely anthropocen-
tric. There is little indication that the cosmos will be transformed for its
own sake, rather than merely as improved scenery for human actors. For
example, Isa 11:6–8 is traditionally taken to describe a transformation of the
natural world into a state of peace. However, it really describes a *domestica-
tion* of the elements of the natural world that are dangerous to humans.[70]
If this is so, then the passage does not reflect any awareness that violence
in the natural world is bad *for animals*, only that it is desirable for dangers
to humans to be eradicated. If we follow Christian tradition in interpreting this passage as a description of the renewed earth,[71] it tells us only that
at the eschaton the nature of species such as wolves and lions will change:
thenceforth, any wolves and lions that exist will be herbivores. It gives us no
reason to suppose that the individual wolves and lions that lived and died
before the eschaton will be resurrected with this changed nature, let alone
that any of the individual animals they killed will be resurrected too. Like
Tennyson's Nature, God on this view is "So careful of the type. . . . So careless
of the single life."[72]

But if we take nonhuman animals seriously as having moral significance, we must go further. Wolves and lions do not exist solely as hazards to
humans and their domestic animals: the suffering of any individual animal
matters for its own sake. Theologians such as Christopher Southgate have,
accordingly, called for an eschatology that allows for the redemption not
simply of the universe as a whole but for each individual creature that has
ever lived in it. Only such a radically universal redemption, they hold, can
make sense of the immensity of suffering that has gone on for hundreds of
millions of years.[73] Jürgen Moltmann gives a different reason for the same

---

beings like ourselves, and this outcome is worth the cost. Authors who adopt this "only
way" line include Nancey Murphy, "Science," and Christopher Southgate, *Groaning*,
90–91. However, I agree with Mats Wahlberg's analysis ("Evolution") that such an argument requires surrendering divine omnipotence and is therefore unsuccessful. But
even if one accepts the "only way" argument, that is still not much consolation for those
creatures that must suffer in order for us to evolve. Accordingly, while Christopher
Southgate endorses the "only way" theodicy, he *also* argues that there must be eschatological redemption for all the suffering creatures. And if one rejects the "only way"
argument then this need is all the more pressing, since it seems that God allows for
great creaturely suffering without any necessity for it.

70. Van Ee, "Wolf and Lamb."

71. Such an interpretation has its roots in the New Testament: in Rom 15:12, Paul
applies Isa 11:10 to Christ, suggesting an eschatological interpretation of the whole
passage. Indeed, for some interpreters, the text was originally intended to have such a
meaning; see Witherington, *Isaiah*, 111.

72. Tennyson, "In Memoriam," 55.7–8, in *Selected Edition*, 397.

73. Southgate, *Groaning*, 82–90.

hope: for him, it is the only way to make sense both of God's purpose and of the fact that human beings are inherently related to the rest of creation:

> [I]f "history" is no more than the field of human interaction, the result is an eschatology forgetful of nature, or even hostile towards it. If God's future, as the future of the Creator, has to do with the whole creation, then wherever eschatology is narrowed down to merely one sector of that creation, whether it be the individual sphere or the historical one, that contraction has a destructive effect on the other sectors, because it deprives them of hope. . . . But true hope must be universal, because its healing future embraces every individual and the whole universe. If we were to surrender hope for as much as one single creature, for us God would not be God.[74]

How can we accommodate cosmic redemption on an atemporal understanding of heaven? For some commentators, the attempt is inherently mistaken. David Wilkinson argues that a fundamentally temporal universe requires a temporal transformation, for the very fact of resurrection is itself temporal.[75] Antje Jackelén, by contrast, sees close links between the valuing of eternity—conceived as non-temporal in some way—and the hope of cosmic redemption. She argues that in past centuries, time was regarded as merely the prelude to eternity, whereas today time is given intrinsic value. This makes possible a new way of understanding the value of eternity:

> Eternity lends hope to time. . . . If eternity is no longer merely a question of the future for Christian souls, but rather must also include the liberation of all of creation, of the entire universe, then a new perspective arises. All simple before-and-after schemes must be eliminated. . . . The time-eternity relation thereby appears richer. Eternity is more than simply that which comes after time. It can also be conceived of as something that affects time and lends it a new quality.[76]

Perhaps unsurprisingly, I share this view. If we take seriously the traditional Christian commitment to the composition principle, as I have argued we should, it is very hard to see how there could be a *future* redemption for all of the billions of individual creatures that have lived and died over the course of deep time. The problem is the same as the traditional puzzle of the cannibal, but on a grander scale. Think of a child's lump of clay, which is one

74. Moltmann, *Coming of God*, 132.

75. Wilkinson, *Christian Eschatology*, 105, 131.

76. Jackelén, *Time and Eternity*, 57.

day formed into one model, then the next day squashed and formed into another, and so on day after day. There is enough clay for one model at a time, but the child will be disappointed if she wants to reconstitute all of them at once. Similarly, the earth has enough organic matter for a vast succession of life forms to use it in turn, but not enough for them all to share it at once—as they would have to do if all are to be raised together at the end of time.

The solution is to apply the idea of atemporal resurrection, which I have outlined in terms of individual humans, to the cosmos as a whole. I suggested earlier that, for any particle P that is temporarily part of my body, that temporal part of P during which it is a part of my body could be extended out of time to be a part of my atemporal, resurrected body. We can expand this to say that all of the *other* temporal parts of P are also extended out of time as well, as parts of the atemporal, resurrected body of whatever creatures they are part of. More generally, every particle of the universe could be extended out of time, forming one immense atemporal cosmos, composed of innumerable resurrected bodies of all the creatures that have ever lived. On such a conception, we do not have to worry about how to share out a limited number of particles among them all, because even if a single particle has been part of billions of individuals over the course of its existence, they each lay claim to a *different* temporal part of it. Every animal—and indeed every object, biological or otherwise—that has ever existed can be raised atemporally without any ontological conflicts or overlaps.[77]

As N. T. Wright puts it:

> Heaven, in the Bible, is not a future destiny but the other, hidden, dimension of our ordinary life—God's dimension, if you like. God made heaven and earth; at the last he will remake both and join them together forever.[78]

---

77. To my knowledge, contemporary theologians and philosophers of religion have had little to say about the eschatological fate of the non-living part of the universe, even though it must constitute an overwhelmingly vast majority of the universe as a whole. But the idea that even non-living things are involved in the cosmic renewal has biblical warrant: Revelation 21–22 describes not only a catalogue of precious stones but a river in the heavenly city. Eastern Orthodox spirituality arguably recognizes this more clearly than western theology. John Chryssavgis, for example, writes that "[t]he world in its entirety comprises an integral part of the liturgy. God is praised by trees and birds, glorified by the stars and moon (Ps. 18:12), worshiped by sea and sand" ("A New Heaven," 158). If that is so, then the moon and the sand would seem to have as much right to resurrection as the trees and birds—for to suppose that God cares only about living things is just as partial, in its way, as to suppose that God cares only about humans. (I am grateful to Andy Macqueen for this point.)

78. Wright, *Surprised by Hope*, 19.

In Rev 21:1–2, a "new" (καινός) heaven and earth appear. Καινός refers to the quality of the thing in question: it is "new" in the sense of fresh, or
renewed, rather than in the sense of replacing a previous thing.[79] To return
to Jürgen Moltmann, he argues that this union of heaven and earth indicates
a radical change to the nature of time itself:

> The mystery of God . . . is the completion of history and cre-
> ation, its perfecting into the kingdom of glory in which God
> himself "indwells" his creation. If God himself appears *in* his
> creation, then his eternity appears *in* the time of creation, and
> his omnipresence *in* creation's space. Consequently temporal
> creation will be transformed into eternal creation, and spatial
> creation into omnipresent creation. If the eternally living God
> is going to "swallow up death for ever" (Isa. 23.8) through his
> real presence, then what in time is "corruptible" will perish too
> (II Esd. 7.31). Consequently "time shall be no more"; it will be
> gathered up, fulfilled and transformed through the eternity of
> the new creation.[80]

We can combine this insight with the account we have sketched of the vision
of God. For the blessed—and indeed for the renewed creation as a whole—
God is experienced in a direct, unmediated way. But for this to happen, the
blessed—and creation as a whole—must participate in the divine life, which
means the divine atemporality. To use an inadequate analogy, standing on
a boat and watching a whale surface is an awe-inspiring experience—but
one cannot really perceive the whale directly unless one gets into the water
and shares its native environment. Similarly, to experience God face-to-
face, rather than in a mirror, requires sharing God's mode of being. And as
Revelation makes clear, this is not a matter of the individual being taken up
into the heaven where God dwells—it is a matter of God transforming earth
such that it becomes heaven.

---

79. Beale and Campbell, *Revelation*, 361. Aune, *Revelation*, 1115–17, provides a useful discussion of the theme of cosmic renewal in ancient Jewish literature.

80. Moltmann, *Coming of God*, 280 (italics original). Moltmann's own account of
what this means is not entirely consistent. He goes on to characterize creaturely timelessness as "relative eternity," which is derivative of God's "absolute eternity," but he also
describes it as "aeonic time" (p. 282), defines eternity as "the simultaneity of past and
future" (p. 290), and states that eternity "has nothing to do with timelessness" (p. 291)
It is hard to see how all of this constitutes a coherent account. Moltmann is, I think,
struggling to find a way to articulate the idea that the renewed creation participates
in the divine eternity (and therefore there is an end to time as we know it), while also
holding that this participation does not involve an eternity that is qualitatively identical
to God's eternity.

Charles Gutenson, similarly, considers the possibility that God might bring people, at the point of death, into God's own life, to share the divine eternity—understanding this as direct experience of the whole of time, so something similar to what I have called subjective atemporality. He writes:

> [I]t would quite possibly mean experiencing time as God does through the dissolution of the fragmentariness of human existence and an awakening to an experience of life in undivided wholeness. When one dies, perhaps it is not merely the totality of that life, but the whole of history which appears to that person in undivided wholeness.[81]

This suggestion allows us to make sense of the notion that the saints *reign* over heaven and earth. I suggested earlier that if the blessed are atemporal then they can share in God's atemporal actions. This is closely connected to their sharing in the divine knowledge. As I have argued, they could share in God's understanding of creation—not merely the (atemporal) renewed creation, but the (temporal) unrenewed creation, too. It would be coherent to suppose that God could allow them to participate in the divine actions towards this creation. God, of course, does not need any assistance; it would be like a parent letting a small child "help" with a task, with the aim of letting the child feel involved rather than with the aim of making the task easier. And so it could be that the blessed are graciously allowed to hear and respond to prayers. As Peter Lombard writes:

> It is not inconceivable that the souls of the saints, who *in the hidden face* of God rejoice in the illumination of the true light, in their contemplation of it perceive what is done elsewhere, insofar as it pertains to them for joy, and to us for assistance. For just as our petitions are known to the angels in the Word of God which they contemplate, so also they are known to the saints who are with God.[82]

The role of the blessed in petitioning on behalf of the living was extremely important to later medieval spirituality. Pope John XXII faced formidable opposition to his claim that the blessed do not enjoy the full beatific vision before the general resurrection precisely because this threatened the practice of praying to them. He retracted this view just before his death in 1334, and his successor, Benedict XII, issued the statement quoted in the

---

81. Gutenson, "Time," 122.

82. *Sentences*, IV, 264.2, p. 248 (italics original). Lombard goes on to support this idea by citing several texts where Augustine talks about angels offering prayers to God, and arguing that if this is true of angels it should also be true of the souls of the blessed. It is striking that he has no authorities to cite in direct support of this latter idea.

introduction securing the full beatific vision for the blessed.[83] As we saw there, he couched this in explicitly temporal language: the blessed *right now* are experiencing the beatific vision. But if the reason for using this temporal language is to ensure that the blessed are able to hear the prayers of the faithful and to intercede on their behalf with God, and if (as I have argued here) the blessed could fulfill this role in an atemporal state, there is no reason to prefer the temporalist view over the atemporalist one.

Conclusion

We now have the rest of our propositions about heaven:

(11) The whole created order, including all individual living creatures that have ever existed, is raised.

(12) Descriptions of the eschatological consummation of the universe should be read as referring to its atemporal raising, rather than a future event.

(13) Through their sharing of God's knowledge, the blessed share in God's love for creation.

(14) They also share in the divine activity towards creation.

(15) This can incorporate the earthly life into the heavenly life in a way that reinterprets and transforms it.

(16) Consequently, the blessed can be said to reign together with God.

(17) Consequently, they can be said to share in the divine nature.

In the conclusion to the book, we shall consider these along with the other propositions we have collected.

83. On this controversy, see Trottmann, *La Vision Béatifique*, "Benedict XII"; Bynum, *Resurrection*, 279–317.

Conclusion

The end of the story can only be told in metaphors, since it takes place in the kingdom of heaven, where time does not exist.

—JORGE LUIS BORGES, "The Theologians"[1]

It is time to sum up the picture that we have been developing. I have suggested a conception of heaven with a number of different components:

(1) Heaven is an atemporal state.

(2) The heavenly state is causally dependent upon the earthly state.

(3) The earthly state is whole-state-determining of the heavenly state.

(4) The heavenly state is bodily.

(5) The heavenly body is the same body as the earthly body.

(6) The heavenly body is composed of the same parts as the earthly body, respecting the composition principle.

(7) In heaven, the blessed enjoy the beatific vision, an unchanging contemplation of God.

(8) The beatific vision involves maxiscience: the sharing of divine knowledge to the greatest extent possible for finite creatures.

(9) The beatific vision is somatic, involving and transforming the whole body.

(10) There is no non-bodily intermediate state.

(11) The whole created order, including all individual living creatures that have ever existed, is raised.

1. Borges, *The Aleph*, 34.

(12) Descriptions of the eschatological consummation of the universe should be read as referring to its atemporal raising, rather than a future event.

(13) Through their sharing of God's knowledge, the blessed share in God's love for creation.

(14) They also share in the divine activity towards creation.

(15) This can incorporate the earthly life into the heavenly life in a way that reinterprets and transforms it.

(16) Consequently, the blessed can be said to reign together with God.

(17) Consequently, they can be said to share in the divine nature.

As I have already indicated, this is a modular proposal, not an all-or-nothing package. I have argued that these ideas, taken together, constitute a coherent understanding of heaven, but one could accept some elements without necessarily being committed to them all. Different options are available depending on the strength of different commitments one might have. In particular, the full package includes (12), which specifies that eschatological language about the future should not be taken literally. (12) is implied by (3): if the individual's heavenly self is directly causally dependent upon each moment of her earthly life, rather than just the final one, then it is reasonable to think that the same thing applies to the universe as a whole. And if temporal existence is whole-state-determining, then any future end point of the universe is no more significant than any other. It would make less sense to combine this with belief in a literal future eschaton, because any such eschaton would not be the point at which the universe is renewed. Rather, the universe is being renewed throughout its history, with every moment in time having a direct bearing on its atemporal state. And as I have argued, taking this view allows one to avoid the bottleneck problem and also to make sense of how the transformed cosmos could contain every individual creature that has ever existed, allowing for a truly universal restoration and redemption.

But if one rejects (3), one could reject (12) as well. If the temporal existence is final-state-determining, then the *end* of life is what leads into atemporal existence. If this is so then one can retain a traditionally future-oriented eschatology, at both the individual and cosmic level. That is, if the final state of the universe is the threshold at which it passes into an atemporal state, then one could picture this happening at a literal point in future time when the universe ends. And for some, retaining this view might well be worth the difficulty of finding alternative answers to the bottleneck problem and the need for redemption of all nonhuman life.[2]

Again, I have argued that dropping the notion of an intermediate state for the soul in between death and resurrection greatly helps in providing a role for the body in the beatific vision.[3] But that is not directly related to the question whether heaven is atemporal. One *could* hold that when a person dies, their soul continues to exist (temporally). On such a view, the "life" of the soul would be a temporal extension of their earthly life. And it could still be the case that their ultimate destination is atemporal. It would simply be that the spacetime worm that is translated out of time, and into the atemporal state, would include temporal parts that postdate the person's death. This would be a rather strange picture, but I do not think there is anything incoherent about it, and it would allow one to combine belief in an atemporal *final* post-mortem state with belief that the saints are literally right now in "heaven" (understood as a temporary, temporal state), as well as with the belief that there is an immaterial element to the human person, which for some recent philosophical theologians remains important. It would also allow for a belief in purgatory, understood as a temporal condition that comes after death.[4]

2. John Cooper, for example, insists: "Future eschatology is part of the biblical view of reality and ought not too easily be jettisoned in favor of some other worldview" (*Body*, 193). As I indicated in the introduction, the question whether any particular view is indeed taught in the Bible (let alone the more fundamental question whether, if it is, Christians must adhere to it) is not part of my remit. My point here is that someone who does agree with Cooper on this issue can still be an atemporalist about heaven by modifying the picture I have suggested.

3. On this, see ch. 5. As I mention there, James Turner, *Resurrection*, 20–73, subjects the doctrine of an intermediate state to very severe criticisms.

4. Whether an atemporal purgatory could be possible is not a question I have space here to consider. It certainly seems an unpromising suggestion, but if I am right to argue that it is coherent to suppose that one's heavenly life comes "after" one's earthly one, in some sense, despite being atemporal, it might also be coherent to suppose that purgatory is an atemporal state that comes "after" one's earthly life and also "before" one's heavenly life in a similarly non-temporal way. But I am not sure what advantage there would be to thinking of purgatory in such a way, even supposing it to be coherent. Purgatory is supposed to bring about changes to those in it, but if it were atemporal they could not experience any change while in purgatory. One would have to say instead that their heavenly selves would differ from their earthly selves in ways caused by their purgatorial selves, even though neither the purgatorial nor the heavenly selves would themselves undergo change.

Heaven and literal language

Different understandings of eschatology are sometimes divided into two groups: *unrealized* and *realized*. On the former understanding, the eschaton is literally a future event. On the latter, the eschatological material in the Bible should be understood as referring, in mythological terms, to our current earthly reality. On this view, there is no future eschaton, and to hope for one is to misunderstand the genre of eschatological writing.[5] For many theologians, a balanced understanding of eschatology must include elements of both. The kingdom of God is here now, and yet is also still to come. Christians are being transformed right now, and yet their resurrection still lies in the future.

I have argued for a conception of heaven that does not literally lie in the future, on either the individual or cosmic scale. But I want to stress that it is not, for all that, a purely realized eschatology. If heaven is atemporal then it is a state that literally exists (though it does not exist at any time) and is quite distinct from our mundane earthly existence. It is not a colorful way of talking about that earthly existence. I argued in the last chapter that this conception of heaven allows us to conceive of a transformation of our earthly lives as they are caught up into the heavenly life and reinterpreted. But this is not a flowery way of saying that heaven just *is* our earthly life understood in a new way. On the contrary, on this view, it is *because* heaven is a metaphysical reality and the blessed are really transformed into it that their earthly lives can be reinterpreted in this way.

However, if one accepts the full set of propositions listed above, there are some elements to traditional eschatological belief that are not to be taken literally, because they are couched in temporal language. As we have seen, this is implicit in (3) and explicit in (12). Anyone who adopts these claims must take the future-oriented language of the creedal statements we saw in the introduction non-literally.

But I think this is not a major hurdle to overcome. For one thing, the language in the conciliar creeds is remarkably restrained. Think again of the statement from the Nicene Creed:

5. Realized eschatology is associated particularly with Rudolf Bultmann and C. H. Dodd, who argued that Jesus taught the full presence of the kingdom of God in his work, and the early Christians believed that the eschaton had already occurred and had only to be completed. See e.g., Dodd, *Parables*, where the term "realized eschatology" itself originates; and Bultmann (*Theology, Presence*). On Dodd, see Baird, *History*, 35–57. For an in-depth analysis and criticism of Dodd in particular, see Sullivan, *Rethinking Realized Eschatology*. For a more recent theological defense of realized eschatology, see Tanner, "Eschatology," and for a philosophical appraisal, see Burley, "Dislocating the Eschaton?"

[Jesus Christ] went up into the heavens and is seated at the Father's right hand; he is coming again with glory to judge the living and the dead; his kingdom will have no end. . . . We look forward to a resurrection of the dead and life in the age to come.[6]

The phrase "is coming" translates ἐρχόμενον, a participle that does not specify tense. "Look forward" is προσδοκῶμεν, which in this context is taken from 2 Pet 3:13 but does not itself specify when the looked-for thing occurs. Only "the age to come"—μέλλοντος αἰῶνος, not a biblical phrase—is specifically future.

And yet Christian tradition actually requires us to read some of the tensed language in this creed non-literally. Consider what it says about the incarnation:

[Jesus Christ] came down from the heavens, and was incarnate from the Holy Spirit and the Virgin Mary and became man . . .

The series of aorist verbs here (κατελθόντα, σαρκωθέντα, ἐνανθρωπήσαντα) indicates a discrete past event. This is hard to square with the dominant traditional understanding of the incarnation, which in contemporary terminology is "concretist."[7] On this model, two elements are involved in the incarnate Christ: the divine Son, and a human body and soul (his "human nature").[8] In the incarnation, the divine Son "assumes" or acquires the human body and soul, and in virtue of this assumption, the divine Son can genuinely be called human. In such a model, the traditional language of Christ's "divine nature" and "human nature" is taken to refer to these two components: the "divine nature" is strictly identical with the divine Son, and the "human nature" simply is the human body and soul which is united to the Son.

It is important to note that models of this kind are designed, among other things, to insulate the Son from Jesus. This may seem an odd claim given that holders of such models want to say that Jesus *is* the Son. But the "is" here does not express strict identity. Rather, it expresses the claim that

6. Tanner, *Decrees*, I 24.

7. Models of this kind are defended by Alfred Freddoso, "Logic, Ontology"; Eleonore Stump, "Aquinas' Metaphysics"; Brian Leftow, "Timeless God"; Oliver Crisp, *Divinity*; Andrew Loke, "Solving a Paradox"; Thomas Flint, "Should Concretists Part?," 79–87; Katherin Rogers, "Incarnation." Such models were standard among medieval theologians, who disagreed mainly about what the relations were between the component parts of the composite Christ; see Cross, *Metaphysics*, 29–136.

8. I use the traditional language of "body and soul" here to emphasize that the human part of Christ has everything that a normal human would have. This is so whether or not we take "soul" literally to mean some non-physical component. Concretism is neutral regarding questions of this sort.

there is only one person in Christ—the Son—and any personal properties that we attribute to Jesus should, strictly speaking, be applied to the Son. Consider, for example, the careful qualifications that Cyril of Alexandria makes when articulating his understanding of the incarnation:

> We do not say that the nature of the Word was changed and became flesh, nor that he was transformed into a perfect man of soul and body. We say, rather, that the Word, in an ineffable and incomprehensible manner, ineffably united to himself flesh animated with a rational soul, and thus became man and was called the Son of Man. . . . So it is we say that he both suffered and rose again; not meaning that the Word of God suffered in his own nature either the scourging, or the piercing of the nails, or the other wounds, for the divinity is impassible because it is incorporeal. But in so far as that which had become his own body suffered, then he himself is said to suffer these things for our sake, because the Impassible One was in the suffering body.[9]

Cyril is treading a difficult tightrope: on the one hand he wants to stress (against his interpretation of Nestorius) that it is really the Son who experiences everything that Jesus experiences; but on the other he is equally keen to stress that those experiences are located in the human body and soul, and that the divine Son remains distinct from them. The primary motivation is a desire to preserve divine impassibility. For Cyril, as for most classical theologians, it is an unquestionable premise that God cannot change. He therefore has to find a way to say that God becomes human that does not require that God be changed into a human, and that allows God to be Jesus in a way that does not entail that God undergo the changes that Jesus experienced in his life. The idea of the Son *acquiring* a human nature, which can undergo these changes for him, makes this possible.

So on this view, the Son does not *become* Jesus at all, strictly speaking. Jesus is not the Son at a certain point of time, as (say) Octavian is Caesar Augustus at an earlier time. Jesus could not literally have memories of his heavenly life, because his heavenly life is not in his personal past (this of course does not rule out his having knowledge about his heavenly life or even immediate experience of it thanks to his union with the Son). Consequently, any talk of the Son's "becoming" human has to be non-literal to some degree.

Any believer in the doctrine of incarnation as it is traditionally understood, then, *must* take the statement of the Nicene Creed about the Son "coming down from heaven" and being "made man" non-literally. Not only

---

9. Cyril, *Second Letter to Nestorius*, chs. 3, 5, in Russell, *Cyril of Alexandria*, 263–64.

must the language of spatial descent be understood metaphorically, but so too must the very notion of the incarnation involving "becoming" or "making" at all. For on a traditional understanding of incarnation, the Son does not change in any way: from the eternal viewpoint of the Son, the incarnation is eternal. Only from our temporal viewpoint is the incarnation something that begins at a particular moment in time. Yet traditional models of the incarnation are not criticized for denying key elements of the creed, because they capture what is important about those elements. If, then, it is acceptable to interpret the creed's temporal language about the incarnation non-literally, it is surely equally acceptable for a believer in heavenly atemporality to interpret other phrases in exactly the same way.

John Mbiti, time, and the New Testament

I have been arguing that traditional futurist eschatological language can be taken non-literally without collapsing into realized eschatology. There is one more point I want to make about this kind of language, which is that it does not necessarily have a straightforward literal meaning to start with. It is easy to assume that biblical eschatological language presupposes a conception of time like our own. James Alison, for example, writes in this context that "our whole conception of time is of something which has an end."[10] For Alison, the "extraordinary element" introduced by Jesus' life and teaching "is the possibility of a mode of time which has no end."[11] But in saying this, Alison assumes that Jesus and the biblical authors are working with, and modifying, the same conception of time that we bring to the text today.

John Mbiti has powerfully challenged these assumptions.[12] He observes that westerners typically read the Bible on the assumption of what he calls a "three-dimensional linear" concept of time, according to which history is conceived as a line, divided into the past, present, and future.[13] Under this interpretative framework, eschatological material in the New Testament is naturally understood to be referring to events in the future (perhaps the distant future). But Mbiti argues that, although the linear view of time can be found within the New Testament, it is not the only notion of

10. Alison, Living, 109–10.

11. Alison, Living, 110.

12. On Mbiti's eschatology, see also Engdahl, African Church Fathers, 155–87, and Ndunjo and Kagema, "Assessment."

13. Although he does not cite McTaggart, Mbiti has in mind something like both McTaggart's "A series" and "B series" (McTaggart, "Unreality of Time"). Despite their differences, both series conceive of time in a linear way, with events ordered by their temporal relations. Africans, according to Mbiti, do not think of time like this at all.

time to be found there, and it is a mistake to read the whole text within its interpretative framework. He writes:

> The Church exists between two eschatological termini: the Cross and the Parousia. Between these points, it lives simulta-neously as though it is travelling (in history) and has arrived (in the Parousia of Christ). This paradox defies a three-dimensional linear concept of Time. The Church is in the rhythm of realizing Christ's Lordship and reconciliation (Rom. 5: 10), of justifica-tion by faith (Rom. 5: 1) and transformation "into His likeness from one degree of glory to another" (II Cor. 3: 18).[14]

This might sound like a version of realized eschatology. But the striking thing about Mbiti's analysis is that he considers, and rejects, such a read-ing.[15] Rather than a realized eschatology, which collapses talk of the "king-dom of God" or the parousia of Christ into present experience, Mbiti wants to maintain a distinction between the two foci of present experience on the one hand and the eschaton on the other. His purpose is to recast this New Testament teaching, as he understands it, in terms of an African under-standing of time. Mbiti's most well-known (or, perhaps, notorious) theory is that Africans have a distinctive understanding of time that is wholly at odds with the western linear view. On Mbiti's interpretation, Africans have no concept of the future other than imminent events that are of immediate concern now (and also cyclical events such as the changing of the seasons). Particular events in the distant future are literally inconceivable, and there are no tenses in African languages capable of expressing them.[16] Western-ers' attempts to preach about the distant future event of the parousia have therefore failed, since Africans lack the conceptual categories needed to un-derstand it. Mbiti therefore proposes a Christian eschatology that rejects the linear assumption that eschatological language describes particular events

---

14. Mbiti, *New Testament Eschatology*, 45–46.

15. Mibiti, *New Testament Eschatology*, 34–38.

16. Mbiti originally argued that Africans hold this view in his classic work of philo-sophical anthropology *African Religions and Philosophy*, 15–28. Commentators since then have been divided on whether Mbiti's analysis of African thought is accurate; and if it is accurate, whether it really applies to all Africans or only some groups. Broadly supportive scholars include Booth, "Time and Change"; Reichardt, "Time"; Onyeocha, "Problematic." Opponents include Ayoade, "Time"; Okè, "African Ontology"; Kazeem, "Time in Yoruba Culture." A more neutral analysis can be found in Kalumba, "New Analysis." For our purposes, whether Mbiti was right to attribute the "non-linear" un-derstanding of time to Africans is not relevant. What matters is that he sought to recast Christian eschatology into terms that respected such an understanding of time, in a way that has some similarities to our discussion.

in the distant future, but which nevertheless retains a distinction between those events and the present.

Mbiti's analysis of the African understanding of time—as he understood it—was primarily epistemological and linguistic in focus. He offered not a metaphysics of time but an analysis of how people think and speak about it. As a result, his eschatology suffers from a lack of clarity. What, precisely, does it mean to say that the church "lives simultaneously as though it is travelling (in history) and has arrived"? Mbiti's emphasis throughout is on Christ as the focus of the two termini: it is in Christ that the present reality and the eschatological reality come together, and consequently it is through Christ that individuals can experience both together. Strikingly, this applies not merely to cosmic eschatology but to individual eschatology:

> It is in this relationship [between humanity and God] that for Man eternal life finds expression in the fellowship between him and God, between the recipient and the Giver.... [S]ince this is an eschatological reality, the fellowship of which we may experience here and now, it fills us with the prospects of full appropriation in another dimension of Time and of existence.[17]

The metaphysics of atemporality that I have sketched offers one way of providing conceptual space for something like Mbiti's proposals. As I have argued, our picture is certainly not one of realized eschatology, in the sense of reinterpreting eschatological material (including talk of life after death) as really talk of our experience in this life. On the contrary, it assumes a genuine reality beyond this temporal experience. But like Mbiti, we can combine this assumption with a denial that such talk is of the *future*. It is, instead, of an atemporal reality.

As such, the atemporal conception creates a meaningful way to make sense of the "eschatological tension" of the New Testament that lies between the "now" and the "not yet."[18] As we saw in chapter 4, the believer in atemporal heaven can legitimately *look forward to* their heavenly existence. On the cosmic scale, the whole of creation can, figuratively speaking, look forward to its renewal and re-creation as the new heavens and the new earth. Yet all of this has real bearing on the present, too. If we think of the earthly existence of individuals and of the cosmos as a whole as whole-state-determining, then each moment of our existence is directly causally connected to our heavenly existence. And as we saw in chapter 6, we can think of our

17. Mbiti, *New Testament Eschatology*, 144.

18. The term "eschatological tension" goes back to Oscar Cullmann, *Salvation*, 202. On Cullmann, see Playoust, "Oscar Cullmann"; Moltmann, *Coming of God*, 10–13; Baird, *History*, 476–88.

earthly lives as a component of a greater existence that is composed of both earthly and heavenly lives and makes sense of both. Our current existence, then, is part of this greater whole, but only in our heavenly existence can we perceive it: as Jürgen Moltmann puts it, "[t]he eschatological moment has two sides."[19] Thus the believer in an atemporal heaven can say that we "have received a spirit of adoption" and yet "wait for adoption,"[20] and that we "have redemption" and yet await the "day of redemption,"[21] for "we have a building from God, a house not made with hands, eternal in the heavens."[22]

19. Moltmann, *Coming of God*, 295.

20. Rom 8:15, 23 NRSV.

21. Eph 1:7, 4:30 NRSV.

22. 2 Cor 5:1 NRSV. For the range of interpretations of this verse, see Thrall, *2 Corinthians 1–7*, 363–67. Victor Furnish argues (*2 Corinthians*, 288–95) that it should be read in the context of the whole passage 2 Cor 4:16—5:5, which is a series of contrasts between the earthly and the heavenly focused on the nature of Paul's own ministry. If this is so, then Paul's purpose here is not to describe the metaphysical make-up of human beings, or the nature of the resurrection body, but to refer to "the realm of the unseen and eternal to which believers are oriented even as they exist in the present realm of the visible and the transitory" (p. 294); the believer experiences a "paradoxical double existence" (Young and Ford, *Meaning and Truth*, 132). Indeed, Wilhelm Bousset argued that in this passage, Paul conceives of the heavenly body as "already present with God in heaven" rather than as a future state, with the startling corollary that Paul therefore believes not that the earthly body will be resurrected and transformed but that God will replace our earthly bodies with already-existing heavenly ones (*Kyrios Christos*, 104). Some modern scholars share Bousset's view that the heavenly body "already seems to exist" (Oropeza, *Second Corinthians*, 307n352—though Oropeza interprets the verse as speaking literally of a building, rather than of a body). If Paul did indeed think of the heavenly body as already existing now, then it would not be far off the picture I have been suggesting: we would need only to replace the *currently existing heavenly body* with an *atemporally existing heavenly body*, which would allow us to identify it with the earthly body, atemporally resurrected, and avoid the notion of swapping bodies. Unfortunately from my point of view, Bousset's interpretation has not proved popular among more recent scholars. Margaret Thrall pronounces curtly that it "may be discarded" (*2 Corinthians 1–7*, 370), though without giving any reasons. Others regard the present tense of "we have" (ἔχομεν) as indicating not the present existence of the heavenly body but only the present certainty of what will be given in the future (Furnish, *2 Corinthians*, 265). But even if that is so, the model of heaven that I have suggested does provide one possible metaphysical underpinning for the disjunction that Paul presents between the earthly and heavenly bodies, with the reality of the latter coloring the experience of living in the former.

Bibliography

Abrams, Daniel. "The Boundaries of Divine Ontology: The Inclusion and Exclusion of Metatron in the Godhead." *HTR* 87 (1994) 291–321.

Adams, Marilyn McCord. *Horrendous Evils and the Goodness of God.* Ithaca, NY: Cornell University Press, 1999.

Alison, James. *Living in the End Times: The Last Things Re-imagined.* London: SPCK, 1997.

Andersen, Holly. "The Development of the 'Specious Present' and James's Views on Temporal Experience." In *Subjective Time: The Philosophy, Psychology, and Neuroscience of Temporality*, edited by Valtteri Arstila and Dan Lloyd, 25–42. Cambridge, MA: MIT Press, 2014.

Andrew of Caesarea. *Commentary on the Apocalypse.* Translated by Eugenia Scarvellis Constantinou. Washington, DC: Catholic University of America Press, 2011.

Aquinas, Thomas. *Aristotle On Interpretation: Commentary by St. Thomas and Cajetan.* Translated by Jean T. Oesterle. Milwaukee, WI: Marquette University Press, 1962.

———. *A Commentary on Aristotle's De Anima.* Translated by Robert Pasnau. New Haven, CT: Yale University Press, 1999.

———. *On Love and Charity: Readings from the Commentary on the Sentences of Peter Lombard.* Translated by Peter A. Kwasniewski, Thomas Bolin, and Joseph Bolin. Washington, DC: Catholic University of America Press, 2008.

———. *The Power of God.* Translated by Richard J. Regan. Oxford: Oxford University Press, 2012.

———. *Selected Philosophical Writings.* Translated by Timothy McDermott. Oxford: Oxford University Press, 1993.

———. *Summa Theologica.* Translated by Fathers of the English Dominican Province. London: Burns, Oates, & Washbourne, 1920–24.

Aristotle. *Nicomachean Ethics.* Translated by David Ross. Oxford: Oxford University Press, 1980.

Athenagoras. *Legatio and De Resurrectione.* Edited by William R. Schoedel. Oxford: Clarendon, 1972.

Atkinson, David William. "The English Ars Morendi: Its Protestant Transformation." *RR* 6 (1982) 1–10.

Attridge, Harold. *Hebrews: A Commentary on the Epistle to the Hebrews.* Minneapolis, MN: Fortress, 1989.

Augustine. *Answer to the Pelagians*. Translated by Roland Teske. Hyde Park, NY: New City, 1997.

———. *Tractates on the Gospel of John 28–54*. Translated by John W. Rettig. Washington, DC: Catholic University of America Press, 1993.

Aune, David. *Word Biblical Commentary: Revelation 17–22*. Nashville, TN: Thomas Nelson, 1998.

Ayoade, John. "Time in Yoruba Thought." In *African Philosophy: An Introduction*, edited by Richard Wright, 93–111. Lanham MD: University Press of America, 1984.

Baird, William. *History of New Testament Research*. Vol. 3, *From C. H. Dodd to Hans Dieter Betz*. Minneapolis, MN: Fortress, 2013.

Baker, Lynn Rudder. "Persons and the Metaphysics of Resurrection." *RS* 43 (2007) 333–48.

Barker, Stephen. "Expressivism about Reference and Quantification over the Non-Existent without Meinongian Metaphysics." *Erk* 80 (2015) 215–34.

Barrett, C. K. *The Gospel according to St John*. 2nd ed. London: SPCK, 1978.

Barrett, Jordan. *Divine Simplicity: A Biblical and Trinitarian Account*. Minneapolis, MN: Augsburg Fortress, 2017.

Bartlett, Frederic. *Remembering: A Study in Experimental and Social Psychology*. 1932. Reprint, Cambridge: Cambridge University Press, 1995.

Bartlett, Robert. *Why Can the Dead Do Such Great Things? Saints and Worshippers from the Martyrs to the Reformation*. Princeton, NJ: Princeton University Press, 2013.

Bathrellos, Demetrios. *The Byzantine Christ: Person, Nature, and Will in the Christology of Saint Maximus the Confessor*. Oxford: Oxford University Press, 2004.

Bauckham, Richard. *Jude, 2 Peter*. Word Biblical Commentary. Waco, TX: Word, 1983.

———. "'Only the Suffering God Can Help': Divine Passibility in Modern Theology." *Them* 9 (1984) 6–12.

Beagle, Peter S. *The Last Unicorn*. 40th anniversary ed. New York: Penguin, 2008.

Beale, G. K., and David Campbell. *Revelation: A Shorter Commentary*. Grand Rapids: Eerdmans, 2015.

Bede. *Commentary on Revelation*. Translated by Faith Wallis. Liverpool: Liverpool University Press, 2013.

Benedict XVI. *Jesus of Nazareth: From the Baptism in the Jordan to the Transfiguration*. New York: Doubleday, 2007.

Berder, Michel. "'Du Temps, Il N'y En Aura Plus!' Observations Sur la Signification de χρόνος en Ap 10,6." In *Fins et Commencements: Renvois et Interactions*, edited by Maxime Allard, Emmanuel Durand, and Marie de Lovinfosse, 319–21. Louvain: Peeters, 2018.

Berkovitz, Joseph. "Aspects of Quantum Non-Locality I: Superluminal Signalling, Action-at-a-Distance, Non-Separability and Holism." *SHPMP* 29 (1998) 183–222.

Berry, Thomas. *The Christian Future and the Fate of Earth*. Maryknoll, NY: Orbis, 2009.

Billings, J. Todd. "United to God through Christ: Assessing Calvin on the Question of Deification." *HTR* 98 (2005) 315–34.

Binns, John. *Ascetics and Ambassadors of Christ: The Monasteries of Palestine 31–631*. Oxford: Oxford University Press, 1996.

Blowers, Paul. "Maximus the Confessor and John of Damascus on Gnomic Will (γνώμη) in Christ: Clarity and Ambiguity." *USQR* 63 (2012) 44–50.

Boersma, Hans. *Seeing God: The Beatific Vision in Christian Tradition*. Grand Rapids: Eerdmans, 2018.

Boethius. *The Consolation of Philosophy.* Translated by David R. Slavitt. Cambridge: Harvard University Press, 2008.

Bohm, David. *Quantum Theory.* Englewood Cliffs, NJ: Prentice-Hall, 1951.

Booth, Newell. "Time and Change in African Traditional Thought." *JRA* 7 (1975) 81–91.

Borges, Jorge Luis. *The Aleph.* London: Penguin, 1988.

———. *The Book of Sand and Shakespeare's Memory.* London: Penguin, 2001.

Bostock, David. "Pleasure and Activity in Aristotle's Ethics." *Phron* 33 (1988) 251–72.

Bourne, Craig. *A Future for Presentism.* Oxford: Oxford University Press, 2006.

Bousset, Wilhelm. *Kyrios Christos: A History of the Belief in Christ from the Beginnings of Christianity to Irenaeus.* 1913. Reprint, New York: Abingdon, 1970.

Braaten, Carl, and Robert Jenson, eds. *Union with Christ: The New Finnish Interpretation of Luther.* Grand Rapids: Eerdmans, 1998.

Bracken, Joseph. *The World in the Trinity: Open-Ended Systems in Science and Religion.* Minneapolis, MN: Fortress, 2014.

Brake, Andrew. *Visions of the Lamb of God: A Commentary on the Book of Revelation.* Eugene, OR: Wipf & Stock, 2019.

Bray, Gerald, ed. *Documents of the English Reformation.* Cambridge: James Clarke, 2019.

Brickhouse, Thomas, and Nicholas Smith. *Socratic Moral Psychology.* Cambridge: Cambridge University Press, 2010.

Briggs, R. A., and Graeme Forbes. "The Growing-Block: Just One Thing after Another?" *PhS* 174 (2017) 927–43.

Brogaard, Berit. "Presentist Four-Dimensionalism." *Mon* 83 (2000) 341–56.

Brown, Christopher. *Eternal Life and Human Happiness in Heaven: Philosophical Problems, Thomistic Solutions.* Washington, DC: Catholic University of America Press, 2021.

Brown, Raymond. *The Epistles of John.* Garden City, NY: Doubleday, 1982.

Brown, Warren, Nancey Murphy, and H. Newton Malony, eds. *Whatever Happened to the Soul? Scientific and Theological Portraits of Human Nature.* Minneapolis, MN: Fortress, 1998.

Brueckner, Anthony, and John Martin Fischer. "Why Is Death Bad?" *PhS* 50 (1986) 213–21.

Buchanan, George Wesley. *To the Hebrews.* Garden City, NY: Doubleday, 1972.

Bultmann, Rudolf. *The Gospel of John: A Commentary.* Oxford: Blackwell, 1971.

———. *The Presence of Eternity: History and Eschatology.* New York: Harper, 1957.

———. *Theology of the New Testament.* Vol. 2. London: SCM, 1955.

Burley, Mikel. "Dislocating the Eschaton? Appraising Realized Eschatology." *Sophia* 56 (2017) 435–52.

Burrell, David. "Creation, Metaphysics, and Ethics." *FP* 18 (2001) 204–22.

Byerly, T. Ryan, and Eric Silverman, eds. *Paradise Understood: New Philosophical Essays about Heaven.* Oxford: Oxford University Press, 2017.

Bynum, Caroline Walker. *The Resurrection of the Body in Western Christianity, 200–1336.* New York: Columbia University Press, 1995.

Cannon, Walter. "The James-Lange Theory of Emotions: A Critical Examination and an Alternative Theory." *AJPs* 39 (1927) 106–24.

Carson, D. A. *The Gospel according to John.* Grand Rapids: Eerdmans, 1991.

Carter, Jason. "St. Augustine on Time, Time Numbers, and Enduring Objects." *Viv* 49 (2011) 301–23.

Casasanto, Daniel, and Katinka Dijkstra. "Motor Action and Emotional Memory." *Cog* 115 (2010) 179–85.

Casati, Roberto, and Giuliano Torrengo. "The Not So Incredible Shrinking Future." *Ana* 71 (2011) 240–44.

The Catholic Church. *Catechism of the Catholic Church.* London: Chapman, 1994.

Chakravartty, Anjan. "Causal Realism: Events and Processes." *Erk* 63 (2005) 7–31.

Chalmers, David. *The Character of Consciousness.* Oxford: Oxford University Press, 2010.

Charlton, William. "Heaven." *NB* 97 (2016) 547–59.

Chiang, Ted. *Stories of Your Life and Others.* London: Macmillan, 2015.

Christensen, Michael, and Jeffery Wittung, eds. *Partakers of the Divine Nature: The History and Development of Deification in the Christian Traditions.* Grand Rapids: Baker Academic, 2007.

Chryssavgis, John. "A New Heaven and a New Earth: Orthodox Christian Insights from Theology, Spirituality, and the Sacraments." In *Toward an Ecology of Transfiguration,* edited by John Chryssavgis and Bruce V. Foltz, 152–62. New York: Fordham University Press, 2013.

The Church of Jesus Christ of Latter-day Saints. *The Doctrine and Covenants of the Church of Jesus Christ of Latter-day Saints.* Salt Lake City, UT: The Church of Jesus Christ of Latter-day Saints, 2013.

Clark, Elizabeth. *The Origenist Controversy: The Cultural Construction of an Early Christian Debate.* Princeton, NJ: Princeton University Press, 1994.

Coburn, Robert. "Professor Malcolm on God." *AJPh* 41 (1963) 143–62.

Cohen, Marc. "The Two-Stage Model of Emotion and the Interpretive Structure of the Mind." *JMB* 29 (2008) 291–319.

Constable, Giles. *Three Studies in Medieval Religious and Social Thought.* Cambridge: Cambridge University Press, 1995.

Cook, Robert. "God, Time and Freedom." *RS* 23 (1987) 81–94.

Cooper, John. *Body, Soul and Life Everlasting.* Grand Rapids: Eerdmans, 2000.

Corcoran, Kevin. *Rethinking Human Nature: A Christian Materialist Alternative to the Soul.* Grand Rapids: Baker Academic, 2006.

Cover, Michael. *Lifting the Veil: 2 Corinthians 3:7–18 in Light of Jewish Homiletic and Commentary Traditions.* Boston: de Gruyter, 2015.

Craig, William Lane. "Divine Timelessness and Personhood." *IJPR* 43 (1998) 109–24.

———. "The Tensed Vs. the Tenseless Theory of Time: A Watershed for the Conception of Divine Eternity." In *Questions of Time and Tense,* edited by Robin Le Poidevin, 221–50. Oxford: Clarendon, 1998.

Crisp, Oliver. "Compositional Christology without Nestorianism." In *Metaphysics of the Incarnation,* edited by Anna Marmodoro and Jonathan Hill, 45–66. Oxford: Oxford University Press, 2011.

———. *Deviant Calvinism: Broadening Reformed Theology.* Minneapolis, MN: Fortress, 2014.

———. *Divinity and Humanity.* Cambridge: Cambridge University Press, 2007.

Critchley, Hugo, Stefan Wiens, Pia Rotshtein, Arne Öhman, and Raymond Dolan. "Neural Systems Supporting Interoceptive Awareness." *NN* (2004) 189–95.

Cross, Richard. *The Metaphysics of the Incarnation*. Oxford: Oxford University Press, 2002.

Cullmann, Oscar. *Salvation in History*. London: SCM, 1962.

Cyril of Scythopolis. *Lives of the Monks of Palestine*. Translated by R. M. Price. Kalamzaoo, MI: Cistercian, 1991.

Dahm, Brandon. "Distinguishing Desire and Parts of Happiness: A Response to Germain Grisez." *ACPQ* 89 (2015) 97–114.

Daley, Brian. "A Hope for Worms: Early Christian Hope." In *Resurrection: Theological and Scientific Assessments*, edited by Ted Peters, Robert J. Russell, and Michael Welker, 136–64. Grand Rapids: Eerdmans, 2002.

Davies, Brian. "Aquinas, God, and Being." *Mon* 80 (1997) 500–20.

Davis, Cruz. "Paradise . . . Lost? Against Locational Accounts of Heaven." In *Heaven and Philosophy*, edited by Simon Cushing, 77–99. Lanham, MD: Rowman and Littlefield, 2017.

De Florio, Ciro, and Aldo Frigerio. "In Defense of the Timeless Solution to the Problem of Human Free Will and Divine Foreknowledge." *IJPR* 78 (2015) 5–28.

Della Rocca, Michael. "Primitive Persistence and the Impasse between Three-Dimensionalism and Four-Dimensionalism." *JP* 108 (2011) 591–616.

Demske, James. *Being, Man, and Death: A Key to Heidegger*. Lexington, KY: University Press of Kentucky, 1970.

D'Ettore, Domenic. *Analogy After Aquinas: Logical Problems, Thomistic Answers*. Washington, DC: Catholic University of America Press, 2019.

Dillard, Peter. "Keeping the Vision: Aquinas and the Problem of Disembodied Beatitude." *NB* 93 (2012) 397–411.

Dipert, Randall. "Peirce, Frege, the Logic of Relations, and Church's Theorem." *HPL* 5 (1984) 49–66.

Dodd, C. H. *The Parables of the Kingdom*. London: Nisbet, 1936.

Dorter, Kenneth. "Virtue, Knowledge, and Wisdom: Bypassing Self-Control." *RM* 51 (1997) 313–43.

Dowe, Phil. *Physical Causation*. Cambridge: Cambridge University Press, 2000.

Duff, Paul. "Transformed 'from Glory to Glory': Paul's Appeal to the Experience of His Readers in 2 Corinthians 3:18." *JBL* 127 (2008) 759–80.

Dunsany, Lord. *The King of Elfland's Daughter*. New York: Putnam, 1924.

———. *Time and the Gods*. London: Gollancz, 2000.

Dupuis, Jacques, ed. *The Christian Faith in the Doctrinal Documents of the Catholic Church*. New York: Alba, 1996.

Eckhart, Meister. *Sermons*. Translated by Claud Field. London: Allenson, 1932.

Ellis, E. Earle. *1 Corinthians: A Commentary*. Edinburgh: T. & T. Clark, 2021.

Engdahl, Hans. *African Church Fathers—Ancient and Modern: A Reading of Origen and John S. Mbiti*. Cape Town: UWC Press, 2020.

Epsen, Edward. "Eternity Is a Present, Time Is Its Unwrapping." *HJ* 51 (2010) 417–29.

Everitt, Nicholas. *The Non-existence of God*. London: Routledge, 2004.

Fair, Ian. *Conquering with Christ: A Commentary on the Book of Revelation*. Abilene, TX: Abilene Christian University Press, 2012.

Fee, Gordon. *The First Epistle to the Corinthians*. Rev. ed. Grand Rapids: Eerdmans, 2014.

———. *Revelation: A New Covenant Commentary*. Cambridge: Lutterworth, 2011.

Feldman, Fred. "Brueckner and Fischer on the Evil of Death." *PhS* 162 (2013) 309–17.

Finch, Jeffrey. "Athanasius on the Deifying Work of the Redeemer." In *Theosis: Deification in Christian Theology*, vol. 1, edited by Stephen Finlan and Vladimir Kharmalov, 104–21. Eugene, OR: Pickwick, 2006.

Finlan, Stephen. "Second Peter's Notion of Divine Participation." In *Theosis: Deification in Christian Theology*, vol. 1, edited by Stephen Finlan and Vladimir Kharmalov, 32–50. Eugene, OR: Pickwick, 2006.

Finlan, Stephen, and Vladimir Kharmalov, eds. *Theosis: Deification in Christian Theology*. Vol. 1. Eugene, OR: Pickwick, 2006.

Finnochiaro, Peter, and Meghan Sullivan. "Yet Another 'Epicurean' Argument." *PP* 30 (2016) 135–59.

Firestone, Robert. *Challenging the Fantasy Bond: A Search for Personal Identity and Freedom*. Washington, DC: American Psychological Association, 2022.

Fischer, John Martin. *God, Foreknowledge, and Freedom*. Stanford, CA: Stanford University Press, 1989.

Fischer, John Martin, and Neal Tognazzini. "Omniscience, Freedom, and Dependence." *PPR* 88 (2014) 346–67.

Fischer, John Martin, and Patrick Todd. "The Truth about Freedom: A Reply to Merricks." *PR* 120 (2011) 97–115.

Fitzmyer, Joseph. *First Corinthians*. New Haven, CT: Yale University Press, 2008.

Flint, Thomas. *Divine Providence: The Molinist Account*. Ithaca, NY: Cornell University Press, 1988.

———. "Should Concretists Part with Mereological Models of the Incarnation?" In *Metaphysics of the Incarnation*, edited by Anna Marmodoro and Jonathan Hill, 67–87. Oxford: Oxford University Press, 2011.

Forbes, Helen Foxhall. "The Theology of the Afterlife in the Early Middle Ages, c. 400–c. 1100." In *Imagining the Medieval Afterlife*, edited by Richard Matthew Pollard, 153–75. Cambridge: Cambridge University Press, 2020.

Freddoso, Alfred. "Logic, Ontology, and Ockham's Christology." *NS* 57 (1983) 293–30.

Frey, Jörg. "Second Peter in New Perspective." In *2 Peter and the Apocalypse of Peter: Towards a New Perspective*, edited by Jörg Frey, Matthijs den Dulk, and Jan van der Watt, 7–74. Leiden: Brill, 2019.

Furnish, Victor Paul. *2 Corinthians*. Garden City, NY: Doubleday, 1984.

Garber, Daniel. *Leibniz: Body, Substance, Monad*. Oxford: Oxford University Press, 2009.

Garrett, Aaron. "'This Tablet, Which Itself Will Quickly Perish.'" In *If I Should Die*, edited by Leroy Rouner, 140–54. Notre Dame, IN: University of Notre Dame Press, 2001.

Gavrilyuk, Paul. "How Deification Was Rediscovered in Modern Orthodox Theology: The Contribution of Ivan Popov." *MT* 38 (2021) 100–27.

Gleason, Randall. "The Old Testament Background of Rest in Hebrews 3:7—4:11." *BS* (2000) 281–303.

Goetz, Stewart. "On the Nature of Human Persons and the Resurrection of the Body." *JAT* (2018) 300–312.

Golitzin, Alexander. "'The Demons Suggest an Illusion of God's Glory in a Form': Controversy over the Divine Body and Vision of Glory in Some Late Fourth, Early Fifth Century Monastic Literature." *SM* 44 (2002) 13–43.

———. "The Vision of God and the Form of Glory: More Reflections on the Anthropomorphite Controversy of AD 399." In *Abba: The Tradition of Orthodoxy in the West*, edited by John Behr, Andrew Louth, and Dimitri Conomos, 273–97. Crestwood, NY: St. Vladimir's Seminary Press, 2003.

Gordon, Scott. "The Economics of the Afterlife." *JPE* 88 (1980) 213–14.

Grant, Robert. "The Resurrection of the Body (continued)." *JR* 28 (1948) 188–208.

Grant, Sara. *Towards an Alternative Theology: Confessions of a Non-dualist Christian.* Notre Dame, IN: University of Notre Dame Press, 2002.

Graves, Shawn. "God and Moral Perfection." *Oxford Studies in the Philosophy of Religion*, vol. 5, edited by Jonathan Kvanvig, 122–46. Oxford: Oxford University Press, 2014.

Gregory of Nazianzus. *On God and Christ: The Five Theological Orations and Two Letters to Cledonius.* Edited by Frederick Williams and Lionel Wickham. Crestwood, NY: St. Vladimir's Seminary Press, 2002.

Greshake, Gisbert, and Jacob Kremer. *Resurrectio Mortuorum: zum Theologischen Verständnis der Leiblichen Auferstehung.* Darmstadt: Wissenschaftliche Buchgesellschaft, 1986.

Griffin, Carl, and David Paulsen. "Augustine and the Corporeality of God." *HTR* 95 (2002) 97–118.

Griffiths, Paul. *Decreation: The Last Things of All Creatures.* Waco, TX: Baylor University Press, 2014.

Grush, Rick. "Brain Time and Phenomenological Time." In *Cognition and the Brain: The Philosophy and Neuroscience Movement*, edited by Andrew Brook and Kathleen Akins, 160–207. Cambridge: Cambridge University Press, 2005.

Guillon, Jean-Baptiste. "Heaven before Resurrection: Soul, Body, and the Intermediate State." In *Heaven and Philosophy*, edited by Simon Cushing, 45–76. Lanham, MD: Rowman and Littlefield, 2017.

Gutenson, Charles. "Time, Eternity, and Personal Identity: The Implications of Trinitarian Theology." In *What about the Soul? Neuroscience and Christian Anthropology*, edited by Joel Green, 117–32. Nashville, TN: Abingdon, 2004.

Habets, Myk. *Theosis in the Theology of Thomas Torrance.* Aldershot, UK: Ashgate, 2009.

Hafemann, Scott. "'Divine Nature' in 2 Pet 1,4 within Its Eschatological Context." *Bib* 94 (2013) 80–99.

Halton, Charles. *A Human-Shaped God: Theology of an Embodied God.* Louisville, KY: Westminster John Knox, 2021.

Hamori, Esther. *"When Gods Were Men": The Embodied God in Biblical and Near Eastern Literature.* Berlin: de Gruyter, 2008.

Harding, E. M. "Origenist Crises." In *The Westminster Handbook to Origen*, edited by John McGuckin, 162–65. Louisville, KY: Westminster John Knox, 2004.

Harris, Murray. *Raised Immortal: The Relation between Resurrection and Immortality in New Testament Teaching.* London: Marshall, Morgan & Scott, 1983.

Hasker, William. *God, Time, and Knowledge.* Ithaca, NY: Cornell University Press 1989.

Heidegger, Martin. *Being and Time.* New York: Harper & Row, 1962.

Henninger, Mark. *Relations: Medieval Theories, 1250–1325.* Oxford: Clarendon, 1989.

Hernández, Juan, Jr. "The Relevance of Andrew of Caesarea for New Testament Textual Criticism." *JBL* 130 (2011) 183–96.

Hershenov, David. "Van Inwagen, Zimmerman, and the Materialist Conception of Resurrection." *RS* 38 (2002) 451–69.

Hewitt, Simon. Review of *Paradise Understood: New Philosophical Essays about Heaven*, by T. Ryan Byerly and Eric J. Silverman. *RS* (2018) 443–45.

Hick, John. *Death and Eternal Life*. New York: Harper & Row, 1976.

Higton, Mike. *Christian Doctrine*. London: SCM, 2008.

Hill, Jonathan. "Boredom and Divine Infinity." In *Philosophy and the Spiritual Life*, edited by Victoria Harrison and Tyler McNabb, 142–59. London: Routledge, 2023.

———. "Compositionalism, Nestorianism, and the Principle of No Co-member Parts." *RS* 59 (2023) 261–75.

———. "In Defence of Inactivity: Boredom, Serenity, and Rest in Heaven." *JAT* 8 (2018) 152–77.

———. "Incarnation, Timelessness, and Exaltation." *FP* 29 (2012) 3–29.

———. Introduction to *Metaphysics of the Incarnation*, edited by Anna Marmodoro and Jonathan Hill, 1–19. Oxford: Oxford University Press, 2011.

Hillman, T. Allan. "Substantial Simplicity in Leibniz: Form, Predication, and Truthmakers." *RM* 63 (2009) 91–138.

Hofweber, Thomas, and J. David Velleman. "How to Endure." *PQ* 61 (2011) 37–57.

Hooker, Morna. "On Becoming the Righteousness of God: Another Look at 2 Cor 5:21." *NT* 50 (2008) 358–75.

Hossfeld, Frank Lothar, and Erich Zenger. *Psalms 2: A Commentary on Psalms 51–100*. Minneapolis, MN: Fortress, 2005.

Houghton, John Wm. "Review of *Musical Scores and the Eternal Present: Theology, Time, and Tolkien* by Chiara Bertoglio." *ML* 40 (2022) 281–84.

Hudson, Hud. *The Fall and Hypertime*. Oxford: Oxford University Press, 2014.

———. *The Metaphysics of Hyperspace*. Oxford: Oxford University Press, 2005.

———. "The Resurrection and Hypertime." In *Paradise Understood: New Philosophical Essays about Heaven*, edited by T. Ryan Byerly and Eric Silverman, 263–74. Oxford: Oxford University Press, 2017.

Hudson, Nancy. *Becoming God: The Doctrine of Theosis in Nicholas of Cusa*. Washington, DC: Catholic University of America Press 2007.

Hume, David. *A Treatise of Human Nature*. Edited by David Fate Norton and Mary J. Norton. Oxford: Oxford University Press, 2000.

Idel, Moshe. "Enoch Is Metatron." *Imm* 24/25 (1990) 220–40.

Jackelén, Antje. *Time and Eternity*. Philadelphia: Templeton Foundation, 2005.

Jaworski, William. "Hylomorphism and Resurrection." *EJPR* 5 (2013) 351–58.

Jenkins, Willis. "After Lynn White: Religious Ethics and Environmental Problems." *JRE* 37 (2009) 283–309.

Jerome. *Dogmatic and Polemical Works*. Translated by John N. Hritzu. Washington, DC: Catholic University of America Press, 1965.

John of Damascus. *Writings*. Translated by Frederic H. Chase Jr. Washington, DC: Catholic University of America Press, 1958.

Johnson, David Kyle. "God, Fatalism, and Temporal Ontology." *RS* 45 (2009) 435–54.

Johnston, Mark. "The Personite Problem: Should Practical Reason Be Tabled?" *Noûs* 51 (2017) 617–44.

Jolley, Nicholas. *The Light of the Soul: Theories of Ideas in Leibniz, Malebranche, and Descartes*. Oxford: Oxford University Press, 1998.

Jollimore, Troy. *Love's Vision*. Princeton, NJ: Princeton University Press, 2011.

Jonas, Hans. *Mortality and Morality: A Search for the Good after Auschwitz*. Evanston, IL: Northwestern University Press, 1996.

Julian of Norwich. *The Writings*. Translated by Nicholas Watson and Jacqueline Jenkins. University Park: Pennsylvania State University Press, 2006.

Kagan, Shelly. *Death*. New Haven, CT: Yale University Press, 2012.

Kalumba, Kibujjo. "A New Analysis of Mbiti's 'The Concept of Time.'" *PA* 8 (2005) 11–19.

Kant, Immanuel. *Religion and Rational Theology*. Translated by Allen Wood and George de Giovanni. Cambridge: Cambridge University Press, 1996.

Käsemann, Ernst. *Essays on New Testament Themes*. London: SCM, 1964.

Kaufman, Frederik. "Late Birth, Early Death, and the Problem of Lucretian Symmetry." *STP* 37 (2011) 113–27.

Kazeem, Fayemi Ademola. "Time in Yoruba Culture." *AH* 36 (2016) 27–41.

Keating, James, and Thomas Joseph White. "Divine Impassibility in Contemporary Theology." In *Divine Impassibility and the Mystery of Human Suffering*, edited by James Keating and Thomas Joseph White, 1–26. Grand Rapids: Eerdmans, 2009.

Keene, Donald. *Essays in Idleness: The Tsurezuregusa of Kenkō*. New York: Columbia University Press, 1967.

Keene, Timothy. "A Missional Reading of 2 Corinthians 5:11—6:2; Especially 5:21." *Tran* 30 (2013) 169–81.

Keener, Craig. *The Gospel of John: A Commentary*. Peabody, MA: Hendrickson, 2003.

Kelly, J. N. D. *The Epistles of Peter and of Jude*. London: Black, 1969.

Kelly, Sean. "The Puzzle of Temporal Experience." In *Cognition and the Brain: The Philosophy and Neuroscience Movement*, edited by Andrew Brook and Kathleen Akins, 208–38. Cambridge: Cambridge University Press, 2005.

Kempis, Thomas à. *The Imitation of Christ*. Translated by Betty I. Knott. Glasgow: Collins, 1963.

Kenny, Anthony. *The God of the Philosophers*. Oxford: Clarendon, 1979.

Kharmalov, Vladimir, ed. *Theosis: Deification in Christian Theology*. Vol. 2. Eugene, OR: Pickwick, 2012.

Knafl, Anne. *Forming God: Divine Anthropomorphism in the Pentateuch*. Winona Lake, IN: Eisenbrauns, 2014.

Kneale, W. "Time and Eternity in Theology." *PAS* 61 (1960–61) 87–108.

Kripke, Saul. "Vacuous Names and Fictional Entities." In *Philosophical Troubles: Collected Papers*, 1:52–74. Oxford: Oxford University Press, 2011.

Laansma, Jon. *"I Will Give You Rest": The Rest Motif in the New Testament with Special Reference to Mt 11 and Heb 3–4*. Tübingen: Mohr, 1997.

Lakoff, George. "The Embodied Mind, and How to Live with One." In *The Nature and Limits of Human Understanding*, edited by Anthony Sanford, 47–108. London: T. & T. Clark, 2003.

Langford, Simon. "In Defence of Anti-Criterialism." *CJP* 47 (2017) 613–30.

Leftow, Brian. "A Latin Trinity." *FP* 21 (2004) 304–33.

———. *Time and Eternity*. Ithaca, NY: Cornell University Press, 1991.

———. "A Timeless God Incarnate." In *The Incarnation: An Interdisciplinary Symposium on the Incarnation of the Son of God*, edited by Stephen T. Davis, Daniel Kendall, and Gerald O'Collins, 273–99. Oxford: Oxford University Press, 2002.

Le Poidevin, Robin. *And Was Made Man: Mind, Metaphysics, and Incarnation*. Oxford: Oxford University Press, 2023.

———. "Identity and the Composite Christ: An Incarnational Dilemma." *RS* 45 (2009) 167–86.

———. "Multiple Incarnations and Distributed Persons." In *Metaphysics of the Incarnation*, edited by Anna Marmodoro and Jonathan Hill, 228–41. Oxford: Oxford University Press, 2011.

Levanon, Tamar. "Thomas Reid and the Evolution of the Idea of the Specious-Present." *HPQ* 33 (2016) 43–61.

Lewis, C. S. *The Problem of Pain*. London: Fontana, 1940.

Lewis, David. "Causation." *JP* 70 (1973) 556–67.

———. "Survival and Identity." In *Philosophical Papers*, 1:55–77. Oxford: Oxford University Press, 1983.

———. "Truth in Fiction." *APQ* 15 (1978) 37–46.

Lienhard, Joseph. *Contra Marcellum: Marcellus of Ancyra and Fourth-Century Theology*. Washington, DC: Catholic University of America Press, 1999.

Loader, William. *Jesus Left Loose Ends: Collected Essays*. Adelaide: ATF, 2021.

Lodge, David. *Paradise News: A Novel*. London: Penguin, 1991.

Loftin, R. Keith, and R. T. Mullins. "Physicalism, Divine Eternality, and Life Everlasting." In *Christian Physicalism? Philosophical Theological Criticisms*, edited by R. Keith Loftin and Joshua Farris, 99–116. Lanham, MD: Lexington, 2018.

Logan, Alastair. "Marcellus of Ancyra and the Councils of AD 325: Antioch, Ancyra, and Nicaea." *JTS* 43 (1992) 428–46.

Loke, Andrew. "Solving a Paradox against Concrete-Composite Christology: A Modified Hylomorphic Proposal." *RS* 47 (2011) 493–502.

Lombard, H. A. "Katapausis in the Letter to the Hebrews." *Neo* 5 (1971) 60–71.

Lombard, Peter. *The Sentences*. Book 4, *On the Doctrine of Signs*. Translated by Giulio Silano. Rome: Pontifical Institute of Mediaeval Studies, 2010.

Long, Steven. "Thomas Aquinas, the Analogy of Being, and the Analogy of Transferred Proportion." In *The Discovery of Being and Thomas Aquinas*, edited by Christopher Cullen and Franklin Harkins, 173–92. Washington, DC: Catholic University Press, 2019.

Lowe, Edward Jonathan. "Endurantism Versus Perdurantism and the Nature of Time." *RFNS* 98 (2006) 713–27.

Luckritz Marquis, Christine. *Death of the Desert: Monastic Memory and the Loss of Egypt's Golden Age*. Philadelphia: University of Pennsylvania Press, 2022.

Lucretius. *De Rerum Natura*. Edited by W. H. D. Rouse and Martin Ferguson Smith. Cambridge, MA: Harvard University Press, 1975.

Lumen Gentium. Dogmatic Constitution of the Church. Promulgated by Pope Paul VI. November 21, 1964. https://www.vatican.va/archive/hist_councils/ii_vatican_council/documents/vat-ii_const_19641121_lumen-gentium_en.html.

Lundhaug, Hugo. "The Body of God and the Corpus of Historiography: The Life of Aphou of Pemdje and the Anthropomorphite Controversy." In *Bodies, Borders, Believers: Ancient Texts and Present Conversations*, edited by Anne Hege Grung, Marianne Bjelland Kartzow, and Anna Rebecca Solevåg, 40–56. Cambridge: Lutterworth, 2016.

Luther, Martin. *Works*. Vol. 31, *Career of the Reformer*. Translated by Harold Grimm. Philadelphia: Fortress, 1957.

Malebranche, Nicolas. *Oeuvres Complètes*. Edited by André Robinet. Paris: Vrin, 1966.

———. *The Search after Truth*. Translated by Thomas Lennon and Paul Olscamp. Columbus: Ohio State University Press, 1980.

Mann, William. "Duns Scotus on Natural and Supernatural Knowledge of God." In *The Cambridge Companion to Duns Scotus*, edited by Thomas Williams, 238–62. Cambridge: Cambridge University Press, 2002.

Markman, A., and C. M. Brendl. "Constraining Theories of Embodied Cognition." *PsS* 16 (2005) 6–10.

Markschies, Christoph. *God's Body: Jewish, Christian, and Pagan Images of God*. Waco, TX: Baylor University Press, 2019.

Marmodoro, Anna. "On the Individuation of Powers." In *The Metaphysics of Powers: Their Grounding and Their Manifestations*, edited by Anna Marmodoro, 1–7. London: Routledge, 2010.

Marquardt, Kurt. "Luther and Theosis." *CTQ* 64 (2000) 182–205.

Matthews, Gareth. "On Being Immoral in a Dream." *Phil* 56 (1981) 47–54.

Maudlin, Tim. *Quantum Nonlocality and Relativity*. Oxford: Blackwell, 1994.

Mavrodes, George. "The Life Everlasting and the Bodily Criterion of Identity." *Noûs* 11 (1977) 27–39.

Mbiti, John. *African Religions and Philosophy*. London: Heinemann, 1969.

———. *New Testament Eschatology in an African Background*. Oxford: Oxford University Press, 1973.

Mbuvi, Andrew. *Jude and 2 Peter*. Cambridge: Lutterworth, 2015.

McArthur, Robert. "Timelessness and Theological Fatalism." *LA* 20 (1977) 475–90.

McClymond, Michael. "Salvation as Divinization: Jonathan Edwards, Gregory Palamas and the Theological Uses of Neoplatonism." In *Jonathan Edwards: Philosophical Theologian*, edited by Paul Helm and Oliver Crisp, 139–60. Aldershot, UK: Ashgate, 2003.

McDannell, Colleen, and Bernard Lang. *Heaven: A History*. New Haven, CT: Yale University Press, 1988.

McFarland, Ian. *The Word Made Flesh: A Theology of the Incarnation*. Louisville, KY: Westminster John Knox, 2019.

McInroy, Mark. "How Deification Became Eastern: German Idealism, Liberal Protestantism, and the Modern Misconstruction of the Doctrine." *MT* 37 (2021) 934–58.

McLaughlin, Ryan Patrick. *Preservation and Protest: Theological Foundations for an Eco-Eschatological Ethics*. Minneapolis, MN: Fortress, 2014.

McMahan, Jeff. "Death and the Value of Life." *Ethics* 99 (1988) 32–61.

McTaggart, John. "The Unreality of Time." *Mind* 17 (1908) 456–73.

Meconi, David Vincent. "The Consummation of the Christian Promise: Recent Studies on Deification." *NB* 87 (2006) 3–12.

———. *The One Christ: St. Augustine's Theology of Deification*. Washington, DC: Catholic University of America Press, 2013.

Meli, Mark. "Motoori Norinaga's Hermeneutic of Mono no aware: The Link between Ideal and Tradition." In *Japanese Hermeneutics: Current Debates on Aesthetics and Interpretation*, edited by Michael Marra, 60–75. Honolulu: University of Honolulu Press, 2002.

Merricks, Trenton. "Foreknowledge and Freedom." *PR* 120 (2011) 567–86

———. "How to Live Forever without Saving Your Soul: Physicalism and Immortality." In *Soul, Body, and Survival*, edited by Kevin Corcoran, 183–200. Ithaca, NY: Cornell University Press, 2001.

———. "Persistence, Parts, and Presentism." *Noûs* 33 (1999) 421–38.

————. "There Are No Criteria of Identity over Time." *Noûs* 32 (1998) 106–24.

————. "Truth and Freedom." *PR* 118 (2009) 29–57.

————. "The Word Made Flesh: Dualism, Physicalism, and the Incarnation." In *Persons: Human and Divine*, edited by Peter Van Inwagen and Dean Zimmerman, 281–300. Oxford: Clarendon, 2007.

Meyendorff, John. *Byzantine Theology: Historical Trends and Doctrinal Themes.* London: Mowbrays, 1975.

Miller, Kristie. "The Metaphysical Equivalence of Three- and Four-Dimensionalism." *Erk* 62 (2005) 91–117.

Mitsis, Phillip. "Epicurus on Death and the Duration of Life." In *Proceedings of the Boston Area Colloquium on Ancient Philosophy*, vol. 4, edited by John Cleary, 295–314. Lanham, MD: University Press of America, 1988.

Moltmann, Jürgen. *The Coming of God: Christian Eschatology.* London: SCM, 1996.

Mooney, Justin. "The Possibility of Resurrection by Reassembly." *IJPR* 84 (2018) 273–88.

Moore, Stephen. "Gigantic God: Yahweh's Body." *JSOT* 21 (1996) 87–115.

Morreall, John. "Perfect Happiness and the Resurrection of the Body." *RS* 16 (1980) 29–35.

Morris, Thomas. *The Logic of God Incarnate.* Ithaca, NY: Cornell University Press, 1986.

Mosser, Carl. "Orthodox-Reformed Dialogue and the Ecumenical Recovery of *Theosis*." *ER* 73 (2021) 131–51.

Mugg, Joshua. "Can I Survive without My Body? Undercutting the Modal Argument." *IJPR* 84 (2018) 71–92.

Mugg, Joshua, and James T. Turner Jr. (2017) "Why a *Bodily* Resurrection? The Bodily Resurrection and the Mind/Body Relation." *JAT* 5 (2017) 121–44.

Mullins, R. T. *The End of the Timeless God.* Oxford: Oxford University Press, 2016.

————. "Personal Identity over Time and Life after Death." In *Death, Immortality, and Eternal Life*, edited by T. Ryan Byerly, 99–111. London: Routledge, 2021.

Murphy, Francis. "The Patristic Origins of Orthodox Mysticism." *MQ* 10 (1984) 59–63.

Murphy, Nancey. *Bodies and Souls, or Spirited Bodies?* Cambridge: Cambridge University Press, 2006.

————. "Science and the Problem of Evil: Suffering as a By-Product of a Finely Tuned Cosmos." In *Physics and Cosmology: Scientific Perspectives on the Problem of Natural Evil*, edited by Nancey Murphy, Robert John Russell, and William Stoeger, 131–52. Berkeley, CA: Center for Theology and the Natural Sciences, 2007.

Nagasawa, Yujin. "Pro-Immortalism and Pro-Mortalism." In *Death, Immortality, and Eternal Life*, edited by T. Ryan Byerly, 115–33. London: Routledge, 2021.

Nagel, Thomas. *Mortal Questions.* Cambridge: Cambridge University Press, 1979.

Ndunjo, Moses Kirimi, and Dickson Nkonge Kagema. "An Assessment of John Mbiti's African Concept of Time and Its Implications for Christian Ministry." *IJHSS* 8 (2020) 140–49.

Neder, Adam. *Participation in Christ: An Entry into Karl Barth's Church Dogmatics.* Louisville, KY Westminster John Knox, 2009.

Nelson, Eric. *The Theology of Liberalism.* Cambridge: Harvard University Press, 2019.

Nelson, Herbert. "Time(s), Eternity, and Duration." *IJPR* 22 (1987) 3–19.

Nicolas, Jean-Hervé. *Catholic Dogmatic Theology: A Synthesis.* Book 1, *On The Trinitarian Mystery of God.* Washington, DC: Catholic University of America Press, 2022.

Noonan, Jeff. "The Life-Value of Death: Mortality, Finitude, and Meaningful Lives." *JPL* 3 (2013) 1–23.

Okè, Moses. "From an African Ontology to an African Epistemology: A Critique of J. S. Mbiti on the Conception of Time." *QAJP* 18 (2005) 25–26.

Olson, Eric. "Ethics and the Generous Ontology." *TMB* 31 (2010) 259–70.

———. "The Passage of Time." In *The Routledge Companion to Metaphysics*, edited by Robin Le Poidevin, 440–48. London: Routledge, 2009.

Onyeocha, Izu. "The Problematic of African Time." *Uche* 16 (2010) 1–38.

Origen. *On First Principles*. Translated by G. W. Butterworth. 1936. Reprint, Eugene, OR: Wipf and Stock, 2012.

Orlando, Eleonora. "Fictional Names and Literary Characters: A Defence of Abstractism." *Theoria* 31 (2016) 143–58.

Oropeza, B. J. *Exploring Second Corinthians: Death and Life, Hardship and Rivalry*. Atlanta: Society of Biblical Literature, 2016.

Ortiz, Jared, ed. *Deification in the Latin Patristic Tradition*. Washington, DC: Catholic University of America Press, 2019.

Pannenberg, Wolfhart. *Systematic Theology*. Vol. 3. Translated by W. Geoffrey Bromiley. Edinburgh: T. & T. Clark, 1998.

Parfit, Derek. *Reasons and Persons*. Oxford: Oxford University Press, 1986.

Park, Hyeong-Dong, and Olaf Blanke. "Coupling Inner and Outer Body for Self-Consciousness." *TCS* 23 (2019) 377–88.

Parsons, Terence. *Non-existent Objects*. New Haven, CT: Yale University Press, 1980.

Parvis, Sara. "Joseph Lienhard, Marcellus of Ancyra, and Marcellus's Rule of Faith." In *Tradition and the Rule of Faith in the Early Church*, edited by Ronnie Rombs and Alexander Y. Hwang, 89–108. Washington, DC: Catholic University of America Press, 2010.

Paulsen, David. "Early Christian Belief in a Corporeal Deity: Origen and Augustine as Reluctant Witnesses." *HTR* 83 (1990) 107–14.

Pawl, Timothy, and Kevin Timpe. "Incompatibilism, Sin, and Free Will in Heaven." *FP* 26 (2009) 398–419.

———. "Paradise and Growing in Virtue." In *Paradise Understood: New Philosophical Essays about Heaven*, edited by T. Ryan Byerly and Eric Silverman, 97–108. Oxford: Oxford University Press, 2017.

Paz, Yakir. "Metatron Is Not Enoch." *JSJPHR* 50 (2019) 52–100.

Peacocke, Arthur. *Creation and the World of Science: The Re-shaping of Belief*. Oxford: Oxford University Press, 1979.

Pelser, Adam. "Temptation, Virtue, and the Character of Christ." *FP* 36 (2019) 81–101.

Philo. *On the Creation: Allegorical Interpretation of Genesis 2 and 3*. Translated by F. H. Colson and G. H. Whitaker. Cambridge: Harvard University Press, 1981.

Pigden, Charles. "Ought-Implies-Can: Erasmus, Luther and R. M. Hare." *Sophia* 29 (1990) 2–30.

Pini, Giorgio. "Before Univocity: Duns Scotus's Rejection of Analogy." In *Interpreting Duns Scotus*, edited by Giorgio Pini, 204–22. Cambridge: Cambridge University Press, 2021.

Plantinga, Alvin. "On Ockham's Way Out." *FP* 3 (1986) 235–69.

Plato. *Complete Works*. Edited by John M. Cooper. Indianapolis, IN: Hackett, 1997.

Playoust, M. R. "Oscar Cullmann and Salvation History." *HJ* 12 (1971) 29–43.

Plotinus. *The Enneads*. Translated by Lloyd Gerson. Cambridge: Cambridge University Press, 2017.

Power, Sean Enda. "The Metaphysics of the 'Specious' Present." *Erk* 77 (2012) 121–32.

Price, Richard, ed. *The Acts of the Council of Constantinople of 553: With Related Texts on the Three Chapters Controversy*. Liverpool: Liverpool University Press, 2012.

Pseudo-Dionysius. *The Complete Works*. Edited by Paul Rorem. New York: Paulist, 1988.

Putt, Sharon. "Letting Go of Detachment: Eckhart's *Gelassenheit* and the Immanence of the Spirit." In *The Spirit, the Affections, and the Christian Tradition*, edited by Dale M. Coulter and Amos Yong, 161–79. South Bend, IL: University of Notre Dame Press, 2016.

Rabbinowitz, J., and I. Epstein, eds. *Hebrew-English Edition of the Babylonian Talmud: Ta'anith*. London: Soncino, 1984.

Rahner, Karl. "Experience of a Catholic Theologian." In *The Cambridge Companion to Karl Rahner*, edited by Declan Marmion and Mary E. Hines, 313–26. Cambridge: Cambridge University Press, 2005.

———. *Theological Investigations II*. Baltimore: Helicon, 1963.

———. *Theological Investigations XVII*. London: Dartman, Longman & Todd, 1981.

Rasmussen, Joshua. "Presentists May Say Goodbye to A-Properties." *Ana* 72 (2012) 270–76.

Ratzinger, Joseph. *Eschatology: Death and Eternal Life*. Washington, DC: Catholic University of America Press, 1988.

Rea, Michael. Introduction to *Analytic Theology: New Essays in the Philosophy of Theology*, edited by Oliver Crisp and Michael Rea, 1–30. Oxford: Oxford University Press, 2009.

Rees, B. R. *Pelagius: Life and Letters*. Woodbridge, UK: Boydell, 1998.

Reichardt, Ulfried. "Time and the African-American Experience: The Problem of Chronocentrism." *AAS* 45 (2000) 465–84.

Robinson, Michael. *Eternity and Freedom: A Critical Analysis of Divine Timelessness as a Solution to the Foreknowledge/Free Will Debate*. Lanham, MD: University Press of America, 1995.

Rocca, Gregory. *Speaking the Incomprehensible: Thomas Aquinas on the Interplay of Positive and Negative Theology*. Washington, DC: Catholic University of America Press, 2004.

Rogers, Katherin A. "Anselmian Meditations on Heaven." In *Paradise Understood: New Philosophical Essays about Heaven*, edited by T. Ryan Byerly and Eric Silverman, 30–48. Oxford: Oxford University Press, 2017.

———. "The Incarnation as Action Composite." *FP* 30 (2013) 251–70.

———. *Perfect Being Theology*. Edinburgh: Edinburgh University Press, 2000.

Rosenbaum, Stephen. "The Symmetry Argument: Lucretius against the Fear of Death." *PPR* 50 (1988) 353–73.

Rowlands, Mark. *The Nature of Consciousness*. Cambridge: Cambridge University Press, 2001.

Russell, Bertrand. *Mysticism and Logic*. New York: Anchor, 1957.

Russell, Norman. *Cyril of Alexandria*. London: Routledge, 2000.

———. *The Doctrine of Deification in the Greek Patristic Tradition*. Oxford: Oxford University Press, 2004.

Schacter, Daniel. "Adaptive Constructive Processes and the Future of Memory." *APs* 67 (2012) 603–13.

Schäfer, Peter. *The Jewish Jesus: How Judaism and Christianity Shaped Each Other.* Princeton, NJ: Princeton University Press, 2012.

Schlesinger, George. "How Time Flies." *Mind* 91 (1982) 501–23.

Schmaltz, Tad. "Malebranche on Ideas and the Vision in God." In *The Cambridge Companion to Malebranche*, edited by Steven Nadler, 59–86. Cambridge: Cambridge University Press, 2000.

Schüle, Andreas. "'Soul' and 'Spirit' in the Anthropological Discourse of the Hebrew Bible." In *The Depth of the Human Person: A Multidisciplinary Approach*, edited by Michael Welker, 147–65. Grand Rapids: Eerdmans, 2014.

Scott, Robert. *Miracle Cures: Saints, Pilgrimage, and the Healing Powers of Belief.* Berkeley: University of California Press, 2010.

Senor, Thomas. "The Compositional Account of the Incarnation." *FP* 24 (2007) 52–71.

Shakespeare, William. *Complete Works.* Edited by Richard Proudfoot, Ann Thompson, and David Scott Kastan. Walton-on-Thames, UK: Nelson, 1998.

Shapiro, Lawrence. *Embodied Cognition.* London: Routledge, 2011.

Shaw, George Bernard. *Collected Plays with Their Prefaces.* Vol. 2. Edited by Dan H. Laurence. London: Reinhardt, 1971.

Sherwin, Michael. *By Knowledge and By Love: Charity and Knowledge in the Moral Theology of St. Thomas Aquinas.* Washington, DC: Catholic University of America Press, 2005.

Sider, Theodore. *Four-Dimensionalism: An Ontology of Persistence and Time.* Oxford: Clarendon, 2001.

Silverman, Eric. "Conceiving Heaven as a Dynamic Rather Than Static Existence." In *Paradise Understood: New Philosophical Essays about Heaven*, edited by T. Ryan Byerly and Eric Silverman, 13–28. Oxford: Oxford University Press, 2017.

Sinclair, Robert, Curt Hoffman, Melvin Mark, Leonard Martin, and Tracie Pickering. "Construct Accessibility and the Misattribution of Arousal: Schachter and Singer Revisited." *PsS* 5 (1994) 15–19.

Singer, Irving. *The Nature of Love.* Vol. 3, *The Modern World.* Chicago: University of Chicago Press, 1989.

Skow, Brad. "Why Does Time Pass?" *Noûs* (2012) 223–42.

Skrzypek, Jeremy. "Causal Time Loops and the Immaculate Conception." *JAT* 8 (2020) 321–43.

Smith, Garrett. "Analogy after Duns Scotus: The Role of the *Analogia Entis* in the Scotist Metaphysics at Barcelona, 1320–1330." In *Interpreting Duns Scotus*, edited by Giorgio Pini, 223–45. Cambridge: Cambridge University Press, 2021.

Smith, John. "Philosophy and Religion: One Central Reflection." *IJPR* 38 (1995) 103–8.

Soars, Daniel. *The World and God Are Not-Two: A Hindu-Christian Conversation.* New York: Fordham University Press, 2023.

Sokolowski, Robert. *The God of Faith and Reason.* Notre Dame, IN: University of Notre Dame Press, 1982.

Solomon, Sheldon, Jeff Greenberg, and Tom Pyszczynski. "Pride and Prejudice: Fear of Death and Social Behavior." *CDPS* 9 (2000) 200–204.

Sommer, Benjamin. *The Bodies of God and the World of Ancient Israel.* Cambridge: Cambridge University Press, 2009.

Sonderegger, Katherine. *Systematic Theology: The Doctrine of God*. Vol. 1. Minneapolis, MN: Augsburg Fortress, 2015.

Southgate, Christopher. *The Groaning of Creation: God, Evolution, and the Problem of Evil*. Louisville, KY: Westminster John Knox, 2008.

Starr, James. *Sharers in Divine Nature: 2 Peter 1:4 in Its Hellenistic Context*. Stockholm: Almqvist, 2000.

Stavrakopoulou, Francesca. *God: An Anatomy*. London: Picador, 2021.

Stead, G. C. "Divine Substance in Tertullian." *JTS* 14 (1963) 46–66.

Strack, Fritz, Leonard Martin, and Sabine Stepper. "Inhibiting and Facilitating Conditions of the Human Smile: A Non-obtrusive Test of the Facial Feedback Hypothesis." *JPSP* 54 (1988) 768–77.

Strickland, Lloyd. "The Doctrine of the 'Resurrection of the Same Body' in Early Modern Thought." *RS* 46 (2010) 163–83.

Strobel, Kyle. *Jonathan Edwards's Theology: A Reinterpretation*. London: T. & T. Clark, 2013.

Stump, Eleonore. *Aquinas*. London: Routledge, 2003.

———. "Aquinas' Metaphysics of the Incarnation." In *The Incarnation: An Interdisciplinary Symposium on the Incarnation of the Son of God*, edited by Stephen T. Davis, Daniel Kendall, and Gerald O'Collins, 197–218. Oxford: Oxford University Press, 2002.

———. *The Image of God: The Problem of Evil and the Problem of Mourning*. Oxford: Oxford University Press, 2022.

———. *Wandering in Darkness: Narrative and the Problem of Suffering*. Oxford: Oxford University Press, 2010.

Stump, Eleonore, and Norman Kretzmann. "Eternity." *JP* 79 (1981) 429–58.

Sullivan, Clayton. *Rethinking Realized Eschatology*. Macon, GA: Mercer University Press, 1988.

Swift, Jonathan. *Gulliver's Travels*. Edited by David Womersley. Cambridge: Cambridge University Press, 2012.

Swinburne, Richard. *The Christian God*. Oxford: Clarendon, 1994.

———. "The Irreducibility of Causation." *Dia* 51 (1997) 79–92.

———. "Why the Life of Heaven Is Supremely Worth Living." In *Paradise Understood: New Philosophical Essays about Heaven*, edited by T. Ryan Byerly and Eric Silverman, 350–60. Oxford: Oxford University Press, 2017.

Tanner, Kathryn. "Eschatology without a Future." In *The End of the World and the Ends of God: Science and Theology on Eschatology*, edited by John Polkinghorne and Michael Welker, 222–37. Harrisburg, PA: Trinity, 2000.

Tanner, Norman, ed. *Decrees of the Ecumenical Councils*. Washington, DC: Georgetown University Press, 1990.

Tatian. *Oratio ad Graecos and Fragments*. Translated by Molly Whittaker. Oxford: Clarendon, 1982.

Taylor, Jeremy. *Holy Living and Holy Dying*. Vol. 2, *Holy Dying*. Edited by P. G. Stanwood. Oxford: Oxford University Press, 1989.

Tennyson, Alfred Lord. *A Selected Edition*. Edited by Christopher Ricks. London: Routledge, 2007.

Tertullian. *Against Praxeas*. Translated by Ernest Evans. London: SPCK, 1948.

———. *Tertullian's Treatise on the Resurrection*. Translated by Ernest Evans. London: SPCK, 1960.

Teske, Roland. "'Vocans Temporales, Faciens Aeternos': St. Augustine on Liberation from Time." *Trad* 41 (1985) 29–47.

Thrall, Margaret. *2 Corinthians 1–7: A Critical and Exegetical Commentary*. Edinburgh: T. & T. Clark, 2000.

Tolkien, J. R. R. *The Letters of J. R. R. Tolkien*. Boston: Houghton/Mifflin, 1981.

———. *The Silmarillion*. London: Allen & Unwin, 1977.

Tomkinson, J. L. "Sempiternity and Atemporality." *RS* 18 (1982) 177–89.

Tooley, Michael. *Time, Tense and Causation*. Oxford: Oxford University Press, 1997.

Townsend, Luke Davis. "Deification in Aquinas: A Supplementum to the Ground of Union." *JTS* 66 (2015) 204–34.

Trabbic, Joseph. "The Human Body and Human Happiness in Aquinas's 'Summa Theologiae.'" *NB* 92 (2011) 552–64.

Trisel, Brooke Alan. "Does Death Give Meaning to Life?" *JPL* 5 (2015) 62–81.

Trottmann, Christian. "Benedict XII and the Beatific Vision." In *Pope Benedict XII (1334–1342): Guardian of Orthodoxy*, edited by Irene Bueno, 81–106. Amsterdam: Amsterdam University Press, 2018.

———. *La Vision Béatifique des Disputes Scolastiques à sa Définition par Benoît XII*. Rome: École Française de Rome, 1995.

Turner, James T., Jr. *On the Resurrection of the Dead*. London: Routledge, 2018.

Urmson, J. O. *Aristotle's Ethics*. Oxford: Blackwell, 1988.

Vander Laan, David. "The Paradox of the End without End." *FP* 35 (2018) 157–72.

Van Dyke, Christina. "Aquinas's Shiny Happy People: Perfect Happiness and the Limits of Human Nature." *Oxford Studies in the Philosophy of Religion*, vol. 6, edited by Jonathan Kvanvig, 269–91. Oxford: Oxford University Press, 2014.

Van Ee, Joshua. "Wolf and Lamb as Hyperbolic Blessing: Reassessing Creational Connections in Isaiah 11:6–8." *JBL* 137 (2018) 319–37.

Vaninskaya, Anna. *Fantasies of Time and Death: Dunsany, Eddison, and Tolkien*. London: Palgrave MacMillan, 2020.

Van Inwagen, Peter. "And Yet They Are Not Three Gods but One God." In *Philosophy and the Christian Faith*, edited by Thomas Morris, 241–78. Notre Dame, IN: University of Notre Dame Press, 1988.

———. "Creatures of Fiction." *APQ* 14 (1977) 299–308.

———. "Not by Confusion of Substance, but by Unity of Person." *Reason and the Christian Religion: Essays in Honour of Richard Swinburne*, edited by Alan Padgett, 201–26. Oxford: Clarendon, 1994.

———. "The Possibility of Resurrection." *IJPR* 9 (1978) 114–21.

Varela, Francisco, Evan Thompson, and Eleanor Rosch. *The Embodied Mind: Cognitive Science and Human Experience*. Cambridge: MIT Press, 1991.

Vaughan, John. *Life Everlasting*. New York: Kenedy, 1922.

Velleman, J. David. "Beyond Price." *Ethics* 118 (2008) 191–212.

Viazovski, Yaroslav. *Image and Hope: John Calvin and Karl Barth on Body, Soul, and Life Everlasting*. Cambridge: Lutterworth, 2015.

Vishnevskaya, Elena. "Divinization and Spiritual Progress in Maximus the Confessor." In *Theosis: Deification in Christian Theology*, vol. 1, edited by Stephen Finlan and Vladimir Kharmalov, 134–45. Eugene, OR: Pickwick, 2006.

Volf, Miroslav. "Enter into Joy! Sin, Death, and the Life of the World to Come." In *The End of the World and the Ends of God: Science and Theology on Eschatology*, edited by John Polkinghorne and Michael Welker, 256–57. Harrisburg, PA: Trinity, 2000.

Wagner, Andreas. *God's Body: The Anthropomorphic God in the Old Testament.* London: T. & T. Clark, 2018.

Wagoner, Brady. *The Constructive Mind: Bartlett's Psychology in Reconstruction.* Cambridge: Cambridge University Press, 2017.

Wahlberg, Mats. "Was Evolution the Only Possible Way for God to Make Autonomous Creatures? Examination of an Argument in Evolutionary Theodicy." *IJPR* 77 (2015) 37–51.

Wainwright, William. "God's Body." *JAAR* 42 (1974) 470–81.

Ward, Keith. *Religion and Human Nature.* Oxford: Oxford University Press, 1998.

Ware, James. "Paul's Understanding of the Resurrection in 1 Corinthians 15:26–54." *JBL* 133 (2014) 809–35.

Warfield, Ted. "Divine Foreknowledge and Human Freedom are Compatible." *Noûs* 31 (1997) 80–86.

Warren, James. "Lucretius, Symmetry Arguments, and Fearing Death." *Phron* 46 (2001) 466–91.

Wessling, Jordan. *Love Divine: A Systematic Account of God's Love for Humanity.* Oxford: Oxford University Press, 2020.

White, Lynn. "The Historic Roots of Our Ecologic Crisis." *Science* 155 (1967) 1203–7.

White, Thomas Joseph. *The Trinity: On the Nature and Mystery of the One God.* Washington, DC: Catholic University of America Press, 2022.

Wilkinson, David. *Christian Eschatology and the Physical Universe.* London: T. & T. Clark, 2010.

Williams, A. N. *The Ground of Union: Deification in Aquinas and Palamas.* Oxford: Oxford University Press, 1999.

Williams, Bernard. "The Makropulos Case: Reflections on the Tedium of Immortality." In *Problems of the Self,* 82–100. Cambridge: Cambridge University Press, 1973.

Wilson, Brittany. *The Embodied God: Seeing the Divine in Luke-Acts and the Early Church.* Oxford: Oxford University Press, 2021.

Witherington, Ben, III. *Isaiah Old and New: Exegesis, Intertextuality, and Hermeneutics.* Minneapolis, MN: Fortress, 2017.

Wolters, Albert. "'Partners of the Deity': A Covenantal Reading of 2 Peter 1:4." *CTJ* 25 (1990) 28–44.

Wood, William. "Analytic Theology as a Way of Life." *JAT* 2 (2014) 43–60.

Woodward, James. "Interventionism and the Missing Metaphysics: A Dialogue." In *Metaphysics and the Philosophy of Science: New Essays,* edited by Matthew Slater and Zanja Yudell, 193–228. Oxford: Oxford University Press, 2017.

———. *Making Things Happen: A Theory of Causal Explanation.* Oxford: Oxford University Press, 2004.

Wray, Judith Hoch. *Rest as a Theological Metaphor in the Epistle to the Hebrews and the Gospel of Truth.* Atlanta: Scholars, 1998.

Wright, N. T. "The Meanings of History: Event and Interpretation in the Bible and Theology." *JAT* 6 (2018) 1–28.

———. *Paul and the Faithfulness of God.* London: SPCK, 2013.

———. *Surprised by Hope: Rethinking Heaven, the Resurrection, and the Mission of the Church.* New York: HarperOne, 2008.

Yang, Eric, and Stephen T. Davis. "Composition and the Will of God: Reconsidering Resurrection by Reassembly." In *Paradise Understood: New Philosophical Essays about Heaven*, edited by T. Ryan Byerly and Eric Silverman, 213–27. Oxford: Oxford University Press, 2017.

Yates, John. *The Timelessness of God*. Lanham, MD: University Press of America, 1990.

Yoda, Tomiko. "Fractured Dialogues: Mono no aware and Poetic Communication in The Tale of Genji." *HJAS* 59 (1999) 523–57.

Young, Frances, and David Ford. *Meaning and Truth in 2 Corinthians*. 1987. Reprint, Eugene, OR: Wipf & Stock, 2008.

Zagzebski, Linda. *The Dilemma of Freedom and Foreknowledge*. Oxford: Oxford University Press, 1991.

———. "Omnisubjectivity." In *Oxford Studies in the Philosophy of Religion*, vol. 1, edited by Jonathan Kvanvig, 231–47. Oxford: Oxford University Press, 2008.

Zimmerman, Dean. "The Compatibility of Materialism and Survival: The 'Falling Elevator' Model." *FP* 16 (1999) 194–212.

———. "Material People." In *The Oxford Handbook of Metaphysics*, edited by Michael Loux and Dean Zimmerman, 491–526. Oxford: Oxford University Press, 2003.

Zwiep, Arie W. *The Ascension of the Messiah in Lukan Christology*. Leiden: Brill, 1997.

Subject and Name Index

Scripture Index

9781666791112